# Constitution Café

# Constitution Café

## JEFFERSON'S BREW FOR A TRUE REVOLUTION

### Christopher Phillips

W. W. NORTON & COMPANY
New York • London

Disclaimer: To guard participants' privacy, names have been changed; occupations and other biographical information, and the locales at which dialogues took place, have at times been changed. Sometimes participants portrayed in this book are composites of those who took part in actual dialogues, and some dialogues are composites.

For information about permission to reproduce selections from this book, write to Permissions, W. W. Norton & Company, Inc., 500 Fifth Avenue, New York, NY 10110

For information about special discounts for bulk purchases, please contact W. W. Norton Special Sales at specialsales@wwnorton.com or 800-233-4830

Manufacturing by Courier Westford
Book design by Chris Welch Design
Production manager: Julia Druskin

Library of Congress Cataloging-in-Publication Data

Phillips, Christopher, 1959 July 15–
Constitution cafe : Jefferson's brew for a true revolution / Christopher Phillips. — 1st ed.
p. cm.
Includes bibliographical references.
ISBN 978-0-393-06480-3 (hardcover)
1. Constitutional history—United States. 2. Democracy—United States.
3. Democracy—Philosophy. 4. Jefferson, Thomas, 1743-1826—Political and social views.
I. Title.
JK31.P45 2011
320.973—dc23

2011018129

W. W. Norton & Company, Inc.
500 Fifth Avenue, New York, N.Y. 10110
www.wwnorton.com

W. W. Norton & Company Ltd.
Castle House, 75/76 Wells Street, London W1T 3QT

1 2 3 4 5 6 7 8 9 0

For my loves, Ceci and Cali

# CONTENTS

A little rebellion now and then is a good thing.

— *Thomas Jefferson, 1787*

# Constitution Café

# I

# Constitution Café

For over fifteen years, I have been facilitating weekly philosophical dialogues called Socrates Café, hoping to revive a form of inquiry made famous by the ancient Greek philosopher. A hallmark of a vibrant democracy is that citizens willingly consider a wide range of objections and alternatives to their own way of seeing things. Socrates Café is meant to be a space for friends and foes, intimates and strangers alike, to explore—thoughtfully and reasonably—timely and timeless existential problems, an exploration that itself makes people feel more bound to one another.

Over time, my project gained wide notice; I began traveling extensively to inaugurate new groups—not just in places like cafés, libraries, and senior centers, but in prisons, nursing homes, institutions for the mentally ill, schools, and universities. At last count, there are well over 500 Socrates Café groups that gather regularly around the globe, with many more in cyberspace, bringing together people of different backgrounds and experiences who thrive on impassioned yet thoughtful discourse.

But do they make any real difference in the grander scheme of things? I often receive letters that attest to their worth, such as one from a community activist in California. "Nothing is sadder to me than seeing someone who isn't confident or privileged enough to . . .

fulfill her own dreams, whatever they may be," she wrote. "I believe the work you do does that. [Socrates Café] gives people the opportunity to connect not only to a deeper part of their own psyche, but to connect that deeper part of themselves to ideas that affect us all. In a society as egocentric as the one we live in today, that is essential."

But nagging questions persist: Is Socrates Café at best a tiny oasis? Isn't there more intolerance and dogmatism than ever? Can it be that "the system" itself poses roadblocks to direct, much less meaningful, participation by everyday citizens concerned about our nation? Is our democracy on life support?

As a government major at the College of William & Mary, I immersed myself in studies of my other "hero," Thomas Jefferson, himself a devotee of Socrates. As he wrote to his personal secretary William Short, "the superlative wisdom of Socrates is testified by all antiquity, and placed on ground not to be questioned." Socrates couldn't have said it better himself when Jefferson exhorted his nephew Peter Carr to "fix Reason firmly in her seat, and call to her tribunal every fact, every opinion. Question with boldness . . . Do not be frightened from this inquiry by any fear of its consequences."

To Jefferson, no topic was out of bounds when it came to subjecting it to bold questioning—not even, in his view, the existence of God, and certainly not the worth of our Constitution, though many continue to believe it is the product of divine inspiration. Jefferson, for one, derided those who looked at constitutions "like the ark of the covenant, too sacred to be touched." He believed that such people "ascribe to the men of the preceding age a wisdom more than human." To him, "We might as well require a man to wear still the coat which fitted him when a boy as civilized society to remain ever under the regimen of their barbarous ancestors."

Yet Americans venerate the Constitution, even if many of us don't actually seem to know what's in it. It's over our heads, out of our reach. It's considered untouchable, beyond reproach by us mere mortals, and this intimidating ideal only serves to make us feel like the system it begets can never be changed, no matter how much it contributes to record levels of political apathy and anger. Sure, we argue over the way elected officials and judges interpret the Constitution, but few of us have qualms about the Constitution itself. Meanwhile, our politicians outdo one another in declaring themselves more true to the Constitution than their opponents. From the president on down, they give their solemn oath to preserve, protect, and defend it.

As dysfunctional as people of most political persuasions believe our government is, they are just as convinced that the Constitution still works. But does it?

I decided to shake things up a bit with a little experiment.

# II

# In the Beginning

## Best and Worst Democracy

It is an unseasonably warm evening, and those taking part with me in a Socrates Café philosophical dialogue have opted to abandon the coffeehouse where we usually gather and instead meander along macadam Duke of Gloucester Street. The pedestrian walkway bisects the heart of Colonial Williamsburg, the historic district of Williamsburg, Virginia, which was the capital of "old Virginia," the first established colony, chartered by the British monarchy in 1606.

The dozen people with me are debating the question "What is the best democracy?"

"Even with all our country's defects, we already have the best democracy," says Stuart, who proposed the question after reading, and taking umbrage with, a passage in *The Audacity of Hope* in which Barack Obama makes the jarring confession that it's "hard to shake the feeling these days that our democracy has gone seriously awry," its best days behind us.

"We have a free market system that's the envy of the world, and constitutionally guaranteed freedoms and rights that people in most other countries can only dream about."

We had chosen a week earlier the topic to be discussed today, and Stuart, like many others present, has come bearing a book or two from which to draw citations to support his perspective.

He pulls from his leather satchel *Democracy in America,* by Alexis de Tocqueville, the French aristocrat and political thinker. "After journeying here in the early nineteenth century to observe our new democratic system," he says, "Tocqueville concluded that Americans have the ideal government, because 'the people name those who make the law and those who execute it,' and they 'form the jury that punishes infractions of the law.'"

"But since our nation's beginnings, the people themselves have never had the right or opportunity to make the law," Sara, his political opposite, says. Sara recently graduated from a "nearly Ivy League college," where she served as student body president. Now armed with a degree in cultural anthropology and burdened with a mountain of debt from student loans, she is again living with her parents, unable to find work.

Sara says next, "The representative system was imposed on us by the Framers. It wasn't one chosen by the people. If our Constitution's Framers felt that most of their fellow Americans lacked the ability to decide for themselves the form of government they believed would best serve their hopes, needs, dreams, how can that be the 'best democracy'?"

Stuart is silent for a spell. Then he says, "When I served on jury duty, I felt I was part of democracy at its best. Maybe we didn't make the law, but we put aside our personal views and fulfilled our sworn oath to uphold the laws on the books. We weighed and debated on its merits the evidence presented to us, and reached a unanimous verdict.

"I admit I tried to wriggle out of jury duty. What a dressing down the judge gave me. I'm grateful he made me serve my turn. Because it made me appreciate like never before this great system our Framers devised."

"Well, if we can be entrusted as jurors to decide a citizen's fate, we should be given more constitutional clout in determining our

democracy's fate," says Alejandra, who gave up a lucrative career in
the world of high finance to become regional director of a nonprofit
dedicated to helping our nation's less fortunate youth. "By that I
mean that the Constitution itself should have stated that the people
themselves are the ultimate deciders."

"Originally, to live in a democratic society meant that everyone
had equal access to power," Frank then says. A classical scholar
who was denied tenure, Frank turned to his other passion, gourmet
cooking; he has a thriving catering business in spite of the economic
downturn."

"The Greek terms *demos* and *kratos* translate as 'rule by the people,' or even 'people power,'" he goes on. "In the ancient Greek city-
states, elections were the least of it. All citizens took part in the
popular assemblies. Any of them could propose laws. So all were
deciders. That smacks of 'best democracy' to me."

What he says gives Helen, a vivacious octogenarian, pause. "You
know, when we were victorious in the civil rights movement, I
thought we'd reached the pinnacle," she says. "But really, it was during the struggle itself that those of us involved were part of democracy at its best." Looking at Frank, she says, "We had faith and trust
in one another to make decisions together, as equals. We had our
main movers and shakers, sure, but truth be told, all of us were leaders. It was when we were on the outside looking in that we activists
enjoyed among ourselves the best democracy. Once we had access to
the established political system, it turned out that it was still out of
reach—because the system itself was tilted way in favor of powerful
interests and against us everyday folks."

"The local government of my childhood neighborhood, where I
still have plenty of family, invoked eminent domain to tear down a
historic black neighborhood, most of whose owners are descendants
of slaves, the properties passed along from generation to generation,"
Helen goes on. "They wanted to build a highway bypass, so there'd

be quick access to a new shopping development. That neighborhood is a living museum. I joined the community in protesting full force, and the project has been canceled. But any time the government wants, it can revive it and destroy homes, communities, history. The Supreme Court ruled that it has the ironclad constitutional right to do that, without our advice and consent. A democracy isn't really possible if a constitution allows a small group of public officials to wield so much power."

We pass by a sidewalk gift shop peddling colonial era paraphernalia. Beside it is a life-size bronze sculpture of Thomas Jefferson seated on a bench, watching the world go by. At the stand, I buy a replica of the U.S. Constitution. It occurs to me, after Helen's remark, that it might serve as a handy reference as our dialogue continues.

Contemplating the replica, Marjorie says, "The small clique of Framers who authorized themselves to construct that document left us with a constitutional republic, not a democracy."

Marjorie and I were fellow government majors during our undergraduate days at the College of William & Mary, the alma mater of Thomas Jefferson, who was often a principle topic of our conversations. A self-described recovering politician, Marjorie abandoned life as an elected public servant after just one term. She had found herself quickly marginalized because of her uncompromising stances, particularly on green issues.

"Most of those who constructed our Constitution were surely glad that Thomas Jefferson was at a safe distance from the proceedings," she says. "The Framers didn't truck with his notions of making the Constitution a reflection of the democratic ideals in the Declaration of Independence."

Leafing through a book on Thomas Jefferson until she finds a particular passage, she says next, "To him, the best democracy was one with 'every citizen an acting member of the government.' Only this would 'attach him by his strongest feelings to the independence of his country.'

Jefferson believed that if most citizens were deliberately sidelined, they'd 'become inattentive to the public affairs.' Once that happened, he warned, the professional politicians 'shall all become wolves'—doing as they will because of an apathetic citizenry, bringing out the worst rather than the best in our politics.'"

Sara, a dictionary in hand, says, "Merriam-Webster defines 'democratic' as 'of or relating to one of the two major political parties in the United States.' By this definition, it's perfectly 'democratic' that we sign off our support to political candidates from one of the principle parties, and then tune out, expecting the work to get done for us.

"That sounds to me like the definition for 'the worst democracy.' It's describing a system that permits politicians to be wolves. For the best democracy to be happening, we'd have to engage in outright revolt against the current system and replace it with one in which every citizen is an acting member of government."

"It seems like a lifetime ago, but the Obama campaign was itself a sign of rebellion," says Frank. "Those of us who volunteered felt like we were part of an insurgency for making our form of government 'the best'—more participatory and inclusive. Obama may have left all his followers adrift when he became president, but the energy that was evoked from that movement is still out there, demanding to be harnessed. You can't put the genie back in the bottle. Like Jefferson said, 'A little rebellion now and then is a good thing.'"

Our walk takes us to the steps of the Raleigh Tavern. The Raleigh, as it is known, opened its doors in 1717, and is named after Sir Walter Raleigh, the English writer and explorer who in 1584 spearheaded the first, albeit unsuccessful, attempt to establish an English colony in the New World. Situated at a well-traveled crossroads, it was once the most popular gathering place in the Virginia Colony. We enter and make our way to the tavern's Apollo Room. The elegant space has served many uses, from the site for debutante balls to the nerve center for plotting the American Revolution.

Born and raised in the area, I've visited the tavern countless times. To this day, I never fail to feel a thrill upon entering, since to me the Raleigh is the place where the American Revolution was launched.

As a child, I was regaled by my mother, a genealogy and colonial era history buff, with stories of her Pegram forebears (my mother's maiden name is Pegram) who'd migrated from England in the 1660s and settled in the heart of what is now known as Colonial Williamsburg. George Pegram, a surveyor, was the first to arrive. One of his descendents, Daniel Pegram, lived near the Governor's Palace, a stone's throw from the Raleigh. He was prominent enough to have dealings with one of our founding fathers, Peyton Randolph, president of both the First and Second Continental congresses. Daniel Pegram[1] was also a member of Bruton Parish Church—the oldest Episcopal Church in the United States, founded in 1607—at the same time that its rolls included Patrick Henry, George Washington, and Thomas Jefferson. Daniel's nephew George Pegram, a founder of one of the earliest Masonic lodges, organized and led a troop during the Revolutionary War. He eventually was promoted from captain to major general for distinguished service, and served in the House of Delegates starting in 1786, when Thomas Jefferson also was a Virginia legislator. Pegram may well have voted on Jefferson's proposed reforms to the comprehensive set of statutes, or legal codes, encted by the legislature since the state constitution had gone into effect. Among other things, it called for radical land reform, universal public education, a reformed criminal code, and the creation of a form of governance in which those at the bottom rung of the political hierarchy would have the most clout. If passed, it would have made Virginia a laboratory for democracy.

1. The tombstone of Daniel Pegram's wife, Sarah, is on the grounds of Bruton Parish in Colonial Williamsburg.

But what about at the federal level? Didn't Jefferson help make it a testing ground for democracy as well?

It is widely assumed that, as one of our most influential founders, Jefferson was personally involved in the crafting of our federal Constitution, but in fact he was overseas serving as U.S. minister to France at the time of the Constitutional Convention. Dissatisfied with many facets of the Constitution concocted by our Framers, Jefferson not only proposed his own ideas for ensuring that the Constitution's governing blueprint perpetuated the democratic experiment, but he proposed in all seriousness that every generation of Americans have a chance to create society anew by rewriting the Constitution from scratch, formulating new foundational laws that "suit the change in circumstances as well as men." He was convinced that only if such a democratic rite of passage, involving all Americans, was held periodically—he recommended twenty-year intervals—would the revolutionary spirit of his time be kept alive for generations to come.

Jefferson's antidote for societal stasis, as he told the historian Samuel Kercheval, was to take periodically "as a tally, every provision of our constitution, and see if it hangs directly on the will of the people." Those provisions that turn out not to reflect the people's will, he believed, should be entirely redone. "Let us then go on perfecting [the Constitution]," he urged, by supplanting "those powers which time and trial show are still wanting."

It occurs to me now: what if his radical proposal was put to the test in some way today? To be sure, he had in mind that this constitutional makeover would be undertaken every twenty years, and over two hundred years have passed since he first proposed it. But better late than never. I consider the replica of the United States Constitution in my hand. I rip it to bits.

"Let's tap into that rebellious energy that's out there across the political spectrum. Let's go back to square one and write a brand new

Constitution, one that might overthrow the status quo and create the 'true democracy' that Jefferson envisioned," I say to my fellows.

"If we were the Framers, what would our Constitution look like? If we made as if we had the authority to rewrite it, what articles would we propose? What freedoms and rights and responsibilities would we give ourselves? What form of government would we create?"

Helen looks dubious. "How does make-believe 'constitution creation' bring us any closer to real salvation? How will this solve the vast income inequalities in this nation, the unemployment crisis, the foreign policy disasters that have caused us to lose our stature around the world?"

"Real or otherwise, a Constitution in itself can't solve our problems," says Sara. "It can't make those who govern accountable, can't ensure human rights and justice for all. But it *can* be a statement of our vision for the 'American way' of governing. It can be a declaration of our values, and a guidepost for bringing our nation's promise and practice into greater alignment."

Stuart looks at me and says, "This idea of yours should be opened up to all Americans. I bet most are like me, and have never looked all that closely at the Constitution. Taking part in the drafting of a new one will give people a great chance to put the existing Constitution under the microscope and come to appreciate its powers for achieving—or preventing—the creation of the best democracy."

And so I decided to embark on a journey across America to take the constitutional pulse of the nation. At Constitution Café, a space dedicated to the Jeffersonian idea of freedom, a broad cross-section of actual and aspiring Americans grapple with how they would sculpt the United States Constitution if they could start from scratch. The constitutional articles that participants construct often address perceived flaws, loopholes, and omissions in the Constitution. At times, this leads to significant revisions of existing articles or the creation of altogether new ones.

In the course of their exchanges, Constitution Café–goers often arrive at insights about whether our current Constitution, and the institutions it props up (and that in turn prop it up), are impediments to, or facilitators of, our higher democratic hopes and dreams. This in turn can prompt thoughtful exchanges on whether our Constitution—as Barack Obama, former professor of constitutional law, maintains—has "proved a sufficient defense against tyranny," or whether we need "to heed Jefferson's advice to engage in a revolution every two or three generations."

In making their case for new and improved articles, those taking part reason, persuade, argue, and bend over backward to ensure that everyone has the opportunity to introduce and convince others to support his or her big constitutional ideas (usually a two-thirds majority approves the final language for any given article crafted by the group). For as Thomas Jefferson had it, one "cannot have his way in all things" when engaged in such democratic deliberations, but must "acquiesce on seeing that of others preponderate at other times." Indeed, "without this mutual disposition," Jefferson asserted shortly after he became president—at a time when deep political rifts already were developing among Americans—"we are disjointed individuals, but not a society." The new Constitution that has been crafted so far is by no means exhaustive. Not only do gaps remain to be filled, but even the articles that have been constructed are not meant to be the last word, just a starting point for deeper debate.

It may seem less than auspicious that an imaginative yet earnest effort to renew American democracy should be launched in a Virginia tavern. But if such a space was good enough for the likes of Thomas Jefferson, it's good enough for us.

Jefferson first happened upon the Raleigh when he was a law

student at William & Mary. The tavern's Apollo Room became his favorite haunt. After Jefferson was elected in 1774 to Virginia's House of Burgesses, he regularly held court there with fellow patriots. As he wrote in his memoirs, he and his colleagues gathered to consider "the state of things" in the colony in particular and in the New World as a whole, at a time when a perfect political storm was brewing—one the fractured colonists were woefully unprepared for. These confabs prompted Jefferson and those with him to take political action—from boycotting British goods after Parliament passed new taxes on staples without their consent, to holding a day of "fasting, prayer and humiliation" to show their full support of Boston after the Tea Party—galvanizing the colonists to act in concert against the crown. Largely unheralded to this day, Jefferson and his fellow burgesses were arguably far more decisive in sparking the American Revolution than the instigators of the Boston Tea Party, whose actions would have ended with a whimper if not for Jefferson and his fellows at the Raleigh Tavern.

In the Apollo Room, Jefferson surely admired the gilt-framed painting hanging on the wall with the inscription *Hilaritas Sapientiae et Bonae Vitae Proles*—Joy Springs from Wisdom and Good Living. Like the Greeks of Athens in the Western world's first democracy, Jefferson believed that good living in a democracy came not from relying on the mythic high-mindedness of iconic statesmen; rather, it hinged on cultivating the inherent virtues of its ordinary citizens and bringing them to the decision-making table. He held that only if all the country's citizens were full "participators" and "sharers" in governance could America achieve the type of all-around excellence—what the Greeks called *arete*—that culminated in greater *eudaimonia*, the exalted state of well-being and satisfaction brought about in large measure by direct participation in the political arena.

President John F. Kennedy characterized a reunion of Nobel

Prize winners as "the most extraordinary collection of talent, of human knowledge, that has ever been gathered together at the White House, with the possible exception of when Thomas Jefferson dined alone." Kennedy noted that Jefferson, by age 32, "could calculate an eclipse, survey an estate, tie an artery, plan an edifice, try a cause, break a horse, and dance a minuet." He might have added that by that age, Jefferson had already tried to establish a revolutionary code for governance that would require each generation to try anew the cause of democracy. Constitution Café aims to revive his effort.

As the Constitution Café adventure unfolded, I came to wonder even more about the principal inspiration behind this project: What set Thomas Jefferson on course to become not just an unlikely patriot, but a foremost instigator of the American Revolution? How did Jefferson, a person of patrician standing, wind up becoming known as "man of the people"? How did someone locked into such intractably backward notions of African-Americans and women become our foremost advocate for creating a society founded on the belief that we are all created equal?

And why are many of Jefferson's most exemplary ideas unsung or underemphasized, when they might hold keys to resuscitating democracy today?

## Declare This

*Original Preamble to the Constitution:* **"We the People of the United States, in Order to form a more perfect Union, establish Justice, insure domestic Tranquility, provide for the common defence, promote the General Welfare, and secure the Blessings of Liberty to ourselves and our Posterity, do ordain and establish this Constitution of the United States of America."**

"We've been studying the Constitution in class today," William says. "I didn't realize that the Constitution wasn't ratified by the states until two years after it was signed by the Framers."

At a high school situated in a county in the heart of Appalachia, I'm exploring with students the prospect of rewriting the Preamble to the Constitution. My mother was born in a coal-mining camp not that far away. The hauntingly beautiful mountainscape encompasses one of the most perennially economically depressed regions in the nation.

Today is Constitution Day—the anniversary of the day the delegates of the Constitutional Convention signed the Constitution on September 17, 1787. In 2004, the late Robert Byrd, the longest-serving U.S. senator in history, introduced a bill subsequently passed by Congress that requires all schools that receive federal funding to devote this day to educational programs on the Constitution.

"Last week, we studied the Declaration of Independence," William says next. "That was pretty exciting. Thomas Jefferson really told off the king. He basically said, 'Because you just don't get that we're all born free and equal, because you treat your loyal subjects in the New World as if we're in servitude to you, we're forced to declare our independence from you, and good riddance.'"

"I enjoyed studying the Declaration, but the Constitution is *so* boring," says Jeanne. "It's mostly about how the spoils of power are divided. It hardly says anything about freedom and equality and rights—not until way near the end, like an afterthought, in the Bill of Rights that was added to it two years after the Constitution was ratified. I don't think whoever wrote the Constitution even read the Declaration."

This prompts Margaret to say, "Why isn't the Declaration part of the Constitution? Everyone in the United States celebrates Independence Day, the day the Declaration was, well, declared. If Constitution Day is such a big deal, why aren't there any fireworks to celebrate it too?"

Then she says, "We should insert the Declaration at the beginning of the Constitution, make it the Preamble. The Declaration should be *law*, the law to end all laws. The rights it gives—to life, liberty, and the pursuit of happiness—are nowhere mentioned outright in the Constitution. Yet all those patriots battling in the Revolutionary War did so because they were fired up by the rights and freedoms the Declaration promised them. There would've never *been* a Constitution if they hadn't fought and sacrificed and won against the odds.

"In those toughest times, in places like Valley Forge, when the troops under George Washington were freezing, when they didn't have blankets or soles on their boots, and they were running out of bullets, the words in the Declaration kept hope alive in their hearts and inspired all their heroics. It not only kept their eyes on the prize, it *was* the prize. Yet somehow, it was left out of the Constitution. It's time to fix that. The Declaration's rights need to be put right up front in the preamble, as Law Number One."

"If it's the Preamble, would the Declaration be a law?" I ask. "Or are the only actual laws the constitutional articles that follow the Preamble?"

"It would be a law," she says without hesitation. "Anything within the Constitution itself can be considered law."

"Well, the Preamble, as the introduction, is supposed to kind of map out what the rest of the Constitution will accomplish," says Jeanne. "So with the Declaration as the Preamble, all the laws that follow it would be aimed at making the inalienable rights in the Declaration come true."

"Not all of the Declaration should be inserted," William says now. "We're not declaring our independence from the king of England anymore. All the stuff in the Declaration that dresses down King George is outdated.

"Really, just a small part of the Declaration, the most important part, should lead off the Constitution: 'We hold these truths to be self-evident, that all men are created equal, that they are endowed by their Creator with certain unalienable rights, that among these are life, liberty, and the pursuit of happiness.'"

"It's this section that President Obama said his grandmother used to read to him, and that inspired him to be a politician and help people," Bobby says. "It's this section that Dr. Martin Luther King, Jr., said motivated him to start the civil rights movement. A lot of others who've tried to move mountains when it comes to making people in America more free were also inspired by this section in the Declaration. It's like they believed that these rights in the Declaration already were part of the Constitution."

"Well, we should update a little bit that part William quotes, so it says 'all men and women'—all humans, in other words—'are created equal,'" says Dottie.

"This is great," says Margaret, animated. "With this updated Declaration part of the Constitution, we'll *have* to start treating one another equally. Because, as I've said, it would be the Law with a capital *L*."

"But we're not all created equal," says Jeanne. "Some are born into riches, some into desperation. Some have all kinds of talents, some hardly any. Some are able to make the most of however much or little talent they have, because their parents and the schools they go to have the resources that allow them to. But others aren't in a situation in life even to know they have talents, much less figure out how to make the most of them."

"All the more reason to be treated equally," says Margaret. "The Declaration says that all 'are endowed by their Creator with certain unalienable rights.' In other words, no matter how unequal the circumstances we're born into, no matter how unequal our talents, we're *still* equal before the eyes of our Creator. So we Americans should see one another as equally important, with *equally* unalienable rights, to life, liberty, and the pursuit of happiness. And *that* means that whether we have a little talent or a lot, whether we have a little money or a lot, we're equally deserving when it comes to figuring out what our talents are, and having the opportunity to do something with them."

I now ask, "Are these rights—to life, liberty, and the pursuit of happiness—equally important?"

William says: "Let me put it this way: Without the right to life and liberty, you can't pursue happiness. And without the right to pursue happiness, life and liberty don't mean much. The pursuit *is* life, it *is* liberty."

"How so?" I ask.

"The pursuit is all about making something of yourself, like Margaret sort of said."

"No," says Jeanne flatly, "it's about having the right to *try* to make something of yourself. It's the trying that makes you happy, that makes you feel alive. I may never become the Olympic track star I want to be, but I'm free to try. Just having the freedom to try gives me a feeling that's . . . beyond happy. Sometimes while I'm training after school, running all up and down these mountains, I can sort of see beyond them and imagine the life I'm going to make for myself when I graduate from high school and college. I can see myself in medical school at Harvard University, and then coming back here to open a doctor's clinic so no one in these parts ever again suffers in silence." Then she says, "And I'll tell you what, I can run a lot faster and farther than I could a couple years ago, because of all this trying."

"You may never make your dreams come true all the way, or your dreams may change over time," says Margaret. "But in a way, as long as you have the freedom to pursue them, whatever they may be at any moment, and as long as you have not only the inspiration, but also some of the basic means to do so, that in itself is a big part of making dreams come true."

"My parents weren't able to go to school when they were my age," she then says. "My granddaddy was injured and disabled in a coal-mining accident. So my daddy, just fourteen years old, had to quit school and start working in the mines. My daddy is out of steady work right now. My momma, she left us a while back, in the dead of night. If anyone has a right to be miserable, it's my daddy. But he doesn't complain. He does all sorts of odd jobs to make sure I can stay in school. He's making sure my life is a lot more about the right to life, liberty, and the pursuit of happiness than his ever could be."

Desiree, listening intently, now says, "We need the rights to life and liberty, I agree. But the guaranteed right to the pursuit of happiness? Who cares about happy. My mom, I've never seen her crack a smile. But she's fulfilled in her way. Like just about everyone's parents in this class, she works whenever and wherever, so my life isn't as tough as hers. And you can tell it makes her fulfilled. I've offered to help out. She won't hear of it. She says I can help out best by staying in school and then going on to college and making something of myself."

Then Dottie says, "Does happy even matter? Can't you be free to be miserable, frustrated? Shouldn't we have the right to be happy or not happy? Many people I admire aren't very happy, some of them not happy at all, but they sure have made big differences in the world, as doctors, teachers, moms. They've sure made it possible for other people to be happy if they want to, by giving them more opportunities than ever to pursue happiness."

This inspires Bobby to say, "People with lots of money who I'm familiar with on TV don't seem very happy. But people I know around these parts with no money think they'll be happy if they have lots of money. There are things a lot more important than happiness—or at least, than having lots of money, as if that's what the road to happiness is paved with. The main thing is, happy or not, each person should have the right to lead a life she's proud of."

To which Margaret says, "Making the most powerful part of the

Declaration—with a few small changes—our new Preamble will be a reminder that whether you're up or down, you treat people a certain way, you treat *yourself* a certain way, with worth and dignity, because that is everyone's unalienable right."

> *Constitution Café Preamble:* Because we the people of the United States hold these truths to be self-evident—that all humans are created equal, that they are endowed by their Creator with certain unalienable rights, that among these are life, liberty, dignity, and the pursuit of happiness—we do ordain and establish this Constitution for the United States of America, in order to realize these truths and preserve and promote these unalienable rights.

## Dawn of the Declaration

Before the Declaration of Independence was even composed, the Virginia House of Burgesses,[2] the oldest governing body in the New World, already anticipating a full-fledged pancolonial movement for independence, began crafting a state constitution to replace its colonial charter. Jefferson was not on hand. "I was then at Philadelphia with Congress," he relates; he'd been appointed to attend the Second Continental Congress that had convened on May 10, 1775, with the purpose of directing the colonial war effort. Jefferson was nonplussed that his colleagues back in Virginia were writing a new constitution. He suggested they hold off on the project until such time as they received "a commission of greater latitude, and one more specific . . . by the people." But when it became clear that the

---

2. In 1621, in the dominion of "old Virginia," which comprised what is today Virginia and North Carolina, the first full-fledged legislature with its own elected assembly, known as the House of Burgesses, was established in the New World.

burgesses were moving forward despite his reservations, he turned his own energies to the task, albeit from afar: "knowing that the Convention of Virginia was engaged in forming a plan of government, I turned my mind to the same subject, and drew a sketch or outline of a Constitution, with a preamble."

Jefferson sent his completed draft directly to fellow patriot and legislator Edmund Pendleton, president of Virginia's constitutional convention, "on the mere possibility that it might suggest something worth incorporation into that before the Convention." To Jefferson's disappointment, it didn't arrive in time to be considered. Pendleton, it turns out, received it "on the day on which the committee of the whole had reported to the House the plan they had agreed to." The constitution for Virginia that was set to be approved, Jefferson relates, "had been so long in hand, so disputed inch by inch, and the subject of so much alteration and debate; that they were worried with the contentions it had produced, and could not . . . have been induced to open the instrument again." As a consequence, it looked like his own proposed constitutional draft—which he'd titled "A Bill for new-modelling the form of Government and for establishing the Fundamental principles thereof in future"—was destined for the trash bin. However, Jefferson proudly recounts, the Virginia legislators were so impressed by the preamble he'd composed that it was "tacked" to the beginning of their document and became part of the commonwealth's new law of the land. The text of Jefferson's constitutional preamble is almost precisely the same as what he later drafted for the Declaration of Independence. "The fact is," Jefferson later explained, "that the preamble was prior in composition to the Declaration; and both having the same object, of justifying our separation from Great Britain, they used necessarily the same materials, and hence their similitude."

While Jefferson was pleased that the Virginia assembly had included his preamble, he nonetheless found the commonwealth's new constitution wanting as a whole. "This constitution was formed when we were new and unexperienced in the science of government," he later said, and so those who crafted it were ignorant of the "very capital defects in it."

Less than a year and a half after the Commonwealth of Virginia's constitution was ratified, Jefferson was given the opportunity to remedy its defects, or so he was led to believe at the time. While the state constitution itself remained intact, soon after the Declaration of Independence was issued, the Virginia legislature asked Jefferson to head a committee responsible for proposing reforms to the statutes that they'd enacted. From the latter part of 1776 until 1779, Jefferson relates that he was "occupied in the reformation of the laws to the new organisation and principles of our government." He and his fellow Revisors, as they were called, were given the unprecedented opportunity "to take up the whole body of statutes and Virginia laws, to leave out everything obsolete or improper, insert what was wanting, and reduce the whole within as moderate a compass as it would bear, and to the plain language of common sense."

But the new set of statutes painstakingly produced by the five-man committee proved in nearly all cases to be far more progressive than what their fellow assemblymen cared for, even if the new statutes were truer to the letter and spirit of the organization and principles of government set forth by Virginia's constitution. Though Jefferson's committee had a few signal successes, most elements in the reform package were summarily rejected by the assembly, which was dominated by the landed gentry.

While this discouraging experience further cemented the political status quo in Virginia, Jefferson, never-say-die, continued to sculpt a draft constitution for the commonwealth. While his project was tailored for Virginia, it was also meant to serve as a blueprint for promoting democratic governance on a national scale. Indeed, the framework for his drafts sometimes parallels that of the U.S.

Constitution, though the specific articles that comprise his version often diverge in remarkable ways. This thought experiment "reveals Jefferson as a founder of political institutions as well as a scribe for revolutionary sentiment."[3]

Jefferson spent much of the remainder of his life pondering and attempting to lay the groundwork for a genuinely revolutionary framework for governance. He didn't undertake this endeavor by pontificating in a vacuum. Rather, as with all his intellectual achievements, they were grounded in direct experience, from his stint as head of the committee to reform Virginia's statutes, to his conversations with colonists from a variety of experiences, to his observations of Native American societies. Most of all, his project was driven and informed by his immersion in the revolutionary cause. In lauding Jefferson as our nation's "first great democrat," the social philosopher John Dewey characterizes him as that "rare person in politics, an idealist whose native faith was developed, checked, and confirmed by extremely extensive and varied practical experience." He got his hands dirty in the political trenches, with the insights gained from these experiences serving as grist for his notions on human rights, happiness, and freedom, which in turn drove his ideas for ideal democratic governance. As Jefferson scholar Lloyd Kramer asserts, Jefferson is unique among political thinkers of his time for his "frequent participation in the struggle for political power."

## Fundamental Act of Union

John Hancock—president of the Continental Congress and the Declaration's first signer—characterized the Declaration as "the foundation of a future government." Jefferson himself considered the

3. Jeremy Bailey, *Thomas Jefferson and Executive Power* (Cambridge University Press, 2010).

Declaration "the fundamental act of union of these states." To political scientist Dennis J. Mahoney, Jefferson in effect was claiming that it is not the Constitution, but rather "the Declaration that constitutes the American nation."

> The Constitution of the United States is sometimes pronounced, by scholars or politicians, to be neutral with respect to political principles. But the Constitution was not framed in a vacuum. It was devised as the Constitution of the nation founded by the Declaration of Independence. The Declaration prescribes the ends and limits of government, and proclaims the illegitimacy of any government that fails to serve those ends or observe those limits. The Constitution is thus ruled by the Declaration. The Constitution provides for the government of the regime created by the Declaration: the regime of equality and liberty.

After the Revolutionary generation had passed, political luminaries continued to take it as a given that the Declaration was the Constitution's reason for being, and as such, was itself part of our foundational law. For instance, John Quincy Adams, the sixth president of the United States, asserted that the Declaration contained nothing less than "the fundamental elements and principles of American constitutional law." In his view, the Declaration and Constitution "are parts of one consistent whole, founded upon one and the same theory of government."

Even Abraham Lincoln, in his Gettysburg Address in 1863, asserted that the United States was founded "four score and seven years ago"—in 1776, when the Declaration was issued, rather than in 1789, when the Constitution was ratified. Such evidence supports the view of intellectual historian James A. Colaiaco, who, like

Mahoney, argues that "the Constitution is ruled by the Declaration, which may be considered its real preamble."

Charles L. Black, the acclaimed scholar of constitutional law, argues in *A New Birth of Freedom* that the Declaration is without doubt part of the Constitution. Black contends that the "the Declaration as a whole was an act of 'constitution,'" and so the rights and freedoms it sets forth not only have the "force of law" but are in fact "an act of *law*." To Black, this means that it's our federal lawmakers' obligation to enact laws that give people the inalienable rights enumerated in the Declaration, thus bringing the disenfranchised into the fold as relative equals. Black believes that the "general diffusion of material welfare" must be seen as "an indispensable part in the general diffusion of the right to the pursuit of happiness."

To Jefferson, however, the general diffusion of *political* welfare, with all Americans governing as equals, was even more important, and is what would lead to an overall sense of societal well-being.

# III

# Constitution Making and Remaking

The Framers of our Constitution were radicals, if only in one sense: they wouldn't settle for simply reforming our original governing document, the Articles of Confederation and Perpetual Union. They decided that no amount of revising would salvage the Articles, and so "the United States needed to be constituted anew—not merely with greater power, but also in a way that resolved the underlying uncertainties that had been generated by the Articles of Confederation."[1]

The Articles of Confederation had become operative on March 1, 1781, after they were ratified by all thirteen original states. They created a highly decentralized form of government. The states had insisted on creating a confederation that allowed them to remain sovereign over most of their affairs, since their inhabitants, as the erudite constitutional historian Clinton Rossiter put it, "were in no mood to give a faraway, central regime in the United States what they were busy denying to a faraway, central regime in Britain."[2] Under the Articles, there was no president or federal judiciary. And because the Confederation Congress couldn't levy taxes or regulate

1. Philip Hamburger, *Law and Judicial Duty* (Harvard University Press, 2008).
2. Clinton Rossiter, *1787: The Grand Convention* (W. W. Norton, 1966).

commerce, it was hamstrung when it came to raising money to pay foreign and domestic debts and building a militia to defend itself from insurrections from within or an army to waylay threats from without. The result was that the United States proved "incapable of providing the security, diplomacy, and open commerce upon which the nation relied."[3]

Clinton Rossiter concedes that "it is conceivable that a stable, effective pattern of government for the Union could have emerged prescriptively out of the Confederation Congress."

> The first government of the United States fought a successful war, made a viable peace, laid the foundations for a new order of diplomacy, established enough credit at home and abroad to pay its most pressing expenses, conducted a kind of political and social academy for the continental elite, created a functioning bureaucracy, and above all maintained itself as a symbol of American unity.

Even so, our nation's first constitution lurched "from crisis to crisis . . . because it made the exercise of the limited authority it granted almost exclusively dependent on the good will of each of thirteen states, not one of which had any overpowering reason . . . to trust any or all of the other states."

This "fatal flaw" in the Articles alarmed the likes of prominent Virginia assemblyman James Madison, who was among those who "had begun to wonder out loud whether a government without power to tax, to regulate trade, and to pass laws that individuals were bound to obey was a government at all."[4] At Madison's

3. Keith Dougherty, *Collective Action Under the Articles of Confederation* (Cambridge University Press, 2001).

4. Rossiter, *1787: The Grand Convention.*

urging, in January 1786 the Virginia legislature invited all the states to send delegates to a convention in Annapolis, Maryland, to discuss ways to remedy the Articles' defects. But only five of the states sent delegates to the gathering. Without a quorum, no concrete decisions could be made. However, Madison and Alexander Hamilton—at the time an assemblyman in New York's legislature—managed to persuade the rest on hand to approve a motion to hold a full-fledged convention in May 1787 in Philadelphia, where participants would be charged with taking specific measures to revise the Articles.

However, the Articles of Confederation contained the hard and fast stipulation that any changes made to it had to be "agreed to in a Congress of the United States, and be afterwards confirmed by the legislatures of every State." Yet only twelve states were represented at the gathering that got underway at the Pennsylvania State House (now Independence Hall) in Philadelphia. Plus, the representatives' only official charge at this summit was to consider revising specific provisions of the existing Articles. So when a majority of the 55 delegates from the twelve states determined that the Articles could not be saved and made the decision to supplant them with an entirely new Constitution, they had no real legal sanction.

Even so, when Jefferson learned of their plan from his post as U.S. minister in France, he claimed to "like much" in principle "the general idea of framing a government which should go on of itself peaceably, without needing [as the Articles did] continual recurrence to state legislatures." Fellow Virginia patriot Patrick Henry, on the other hand, "smelt a rat in Philadelphia, tending toward the monarchy." Leery of the intentions of the convention's organizers, whom he believed wanted to create "a consolidated government," he turned down an invitation to serve as one of the delegates. Rhode

Island, sharing Henry's suspicions, declined to send any delegates. The seeds of future deadlock were sown.[5]

Even if those taking part had been authorized to carry out the task of creating a new Constitution, they were not representative of most Americans. Though a few, like Benjamin Franklin, had humble beginnings, the typical delegate to the Constitutional Convention was nonetheless "a privileged member of the upper class in what was still a hierarchical society" and did not "represent directly, in any reasonable way, American society as a whole." Rather, most of the 55 Framers represented faithfully the "white, adult, male, affluent or near-affluent segment of the population."[6]

But couldn't the same thing be said about our Founding Fathers? After all, those 56 patriots who signed the Declaration of Independence were also unrepresentative of Americans as a whole. One telling difference, though, was that they signed a galvanizing and unifying document—befitting of Jefferson's characterization of it as "an expression of the American mind"—that set the colonists free. The Constitution, on the other hand, was meant by those who crafted it to rein them in a good bit.

Only eight of our Declaration's signers also attended the Constitutional Convention and served as Framers. But even with the absence of the likes of Jefferson and most other Founding Fathers at the Constitutional Convention, political scientist Robert Dahl of Yale contends that "among the Framers were many men of exceptional talent and public virtue." For instance, James

---

5. Henry himself would later lead the effort in Virginia against ratifying the new Constitution, and he nearly succeeded; the Constitution was ratified by an 89-to-79 vote.

6. Joseph C. Morton, *Shapers of the Great Debate at the Constitutional Convention of 1787* (Greenwood Press, 2005).

Madison might not have been a signer of the Declaration, but he was—and still is, in Dahl's estimation—"our greatest political scientist." Yet even the incomparable Madison "could not foresee the future of the American republic, nor could he draw on knowledge that might be gained from later experiences with democracy in America and elsewhere." While the knowledge of Madison and his fellow Framers "may well have been the best available in 1787," the fact was that "reliable knowledge about constitutions appropriate to a large representative republic was, at best, meager." And so they were "limited by, so to speak, their inevitable ignorance." Nonetheless, the Framers felt certain that "the high value they placed on republicanism was overwhelmingly shared by citizens of all the states."

But the Framers never asked their fellow Americans what they wanted, and so never gave them a chance to weigh in on what specific type of republican system they preferred. Rather, with Madison—who would come to be known as the "Father of the Constitution"—steering the proceedings, the delegates agreed to keep their discussions private, supposedly so they could speak freely. As a consequence, there was no public record of the proceedings. Jefferson, dismayed by this news, wrote to John Adams, "I am sorry [the delegates to the federal convention] began their deliberations by so abominable a precedent as that of tying up the tongues of their members." In his estimation, "Nothing can justify this example but the . . . ignorance of the value of public discussions." On September 17, 1787, the new Constitution was approved—but by only 39 of the 55 delegates.

More than two hundred years after the fact, Robert Dahl asks some unsettling questions: "Have we Americans ever had an opportunity to express our considered will on our constitutional system? For example, how many . . . have ever participated in a referendum that asked them whether they wished to continue to be governed under the existing constitution? The answer, of course, is: none."

We're not alone, however. Not even in ancient Athens, the cradle of Western democracy, did "the people" generally have a voice. In recent years, new national constitutions have supplanted outmoded ones in emerging democracies throughout the world, from Kenya to Ecuador to Serbia. In nearly all cases, referenda were held so the people themselves could vote on the new constitutions. However, in no instance were they invited to the table and asked to participate themselves in the framing of their governing document.

Winston Churchill famously said that "democracy is the worst form of government except all the others that have been tried." But has democracy ever been fully tried? Perhaps, paraphrasing G. K. Chesterton on Christianity, we might conclude that "democracy has not been tried and found wanting; it has been found difficult and not tried."

## Of, By, and for the People?

**Article VII of the U.S. Constitution. "The Ratification of the Conventions of nine States shall be sufficient for the Establishment of this Constitution between the States so ratifying the Same."**

"I'd always assumed that the Constitution says somewhere that ours is a government 'of the people, by the people, and for the people,'" says Jennie.

I'm at the Green Dragon Tavern in the North End of Boston. The original version of this watering hole is where Sam Adams and his fellow Sons of Liberty plotted the Boston Tea Party. To this day, it is one of the most popular bars in the city. Jennie and most of the others with me are members of an organic produce cooperative located some hours away. I'd been in close touch with them ever since I'd helped them inaugurate a Socrates Café several years ago. Today is one of their delivery days in the city, and when I told them of my project, they suggested we meet at this pub, perhaps to put us in a more revolutionary spirit.

Jennie, the co-op's associate director, says next, "It turns out that the phrase I'd thought was the soul of the Constitution was actually in Lincoln's Gettysburg address. He told the 15,000 people who came out to hear him speak at the Union victory ceremony that the Civil War hadn't been fought just to preserve the Union, but to launch a 'new birth of freedom.' Lincoln claimed that with the Civil War won, a 'government of the people, by the people, for the people' would at last be created and 'shall not perish from the earth.'"

She looks at us. "But there's never been such a government in the United States. And there will never be unless the Framers of the Constitution themselves are democratically elected. It's not enough for the very first words of the preamble to be 'we the people.' Because this doesn't gloss over the fact that our Constitution was created by 55 well-off white males who met behind closed doors. They even created an article for how this Constitution of theirs would be ratified that virtually guaranteed it would become the law of the land. Article VII required the approval of just nine of the original thirteen colonies. And guess what: exactly nine states voted to ratify it—not by direct vote of the entire population, but via conventions mostly attended by well-off property holders."

This prompts Sylvia to say to me, "If this Constitution project of yours is to feature a government of, by, and for the people, it has to include an article detailing a democratic process for ratification. But even more importantly, there needs to be, in this or a separate article, a spelled-out process for how Framers for drafting the Constitution are chosen. Our existing Constitution doesn't have an article addressing this because its authors simply appointed themselves."

"To me," she goes on, "it's not just the form of government created that determines whether it's of, by, and for the people, but the process by which the form of government is decided upon. And this requires a totally open process for choosing Framers."

I ask what kind of specific process they'd recommend.

Faith is the first to respond. "We could create an article that deals both with how to choose Framers and how to ratify the Constitution they construct. It might say, 'Each state shall name, by democratic voting procedures, X number of delegates to take part in a constitutional convention. Upon construction of a Constitution by the convention delegates, its final ratification will require the approval by a majority of voters in each state. Only then shall the Constitution be deemed established between the States.'"

"It would be better if delegates to be Framers at a constitutional convention are chosen randomly," says Jennie, "just as people are picked to sit on juries. That way, the Framers would be representative of the populace as a whole."

Looking at Faith, she says, "By a 'democratic voting process' for delegates, I assume you mean a conventional election with traditional campaigning, followed by a vote in which people choose from among a list of candidates. If that's so, that would mean that those with the most money to campaign and to get their message out would most likely be elected as delegates. *That* would mean that those elected to be Framers would *not* be those who are most representative of Americans. The advantage of a random selection process for gathering delegates—as long as the random sample is large enough—is that it assures that there'll be a true cross-section of Americans serving as Framers."

Then Sylvia says, "I was a member of the Students for a Democratic

Society in the 1960s." She is referring to the New Left student activist movement founded in 1960, which spearheaded broad-scale student protests against U.S. policy in Vietnam. The SDS flourished until 1969, when it unraveled over differences in the tactics supported by various factions.

She has with her a copy of the original SDS constitution. "Its preamble, approved at our convention in 1962, states that ours was 'an association of young people on the left' that 'seeks to create a sustained community of educational and political concern' and that 'maintains a vision of a democratic society, where at all levels the people have control of the decisions which affect them and the resources on which they are dependent.'"

"The SDS constitution claimed that its mission was to create a society with government of, by, and for the people," she continues, "even though it makes clear its belief that just a subset of Americans"—she again refers to the SDS constitution—"'liberals and radicals, activists and scholars, students and faculty' are those most adept at realizing 'a democratic society, where at all levels the people have control of the decisions which affect them and the resources on which they are dependent.'

"But I've often since wondered, can one small segment, no matter how well-intentioned—whether the Framers of our original Constitution, or of the SDS constitution—ever really create a government of, by, and for the people, if most of the people are left out of the process of creating the constitution itself?"

This brings Rafael to say, "I'm not sure that a constitution has to include the participation of potentially everyone, or of even a random sample, in order to create a government of, by, and for the people. Maybe what matters most is that the final product—whether devised by two people or two hundred million—details how to make such a government come true."

"The constitution of the nonprofit social justice group I worked for was created by just two people," he goes on. "But it described itself as an organization in which all involved in our group in any way made decisions as equals. It claimed to be of, by, and for all those both working for the organization and those being served by it. And in the policy-making and program implementation process, everyone's vote counted equally. But only staff members got to take part in these votes.

"I proposed at a staff meeting that we change our policy for how we decide policy. I suggested that if our group is really going to be what its constitution claims, then the people we serve must play an equal part in the decision-making process. That'd be real empowerment, really democratic. I was accused of being too idealistic, as if that somehow is an affliction. Those opposed to my view argued that the people we served were too down and out to take part in making decisions on their own behalf. My opinion was: 'You want to make them less down and out? Let them decide with us, as equals.' They thought I was nuts. I left the organization soon afterwards."

Then he says, "Now I'm thinking that maybe Sylvia's suggestion is right on target, that a constitution—whether for a nonprofit, a gated community, a radical movement, or a country—has to be created by all those who are impacted, or at least by a genuinely representative and random sample of all those who will have to live by its rules. That way, it will really be a product of 'we the people.'"

To which Faith says, "I'm starting to come around to this viewpoint too. If the constitution created by a randomly selected group of Framers calls for a type of government in which all those involved will make decisions as equals, there'll be a greater likelihood that that'll actually become a reality."

*Constitution Café Article:* Each State shall appoint to a Constitutional Convention delegates authorized to construct a federal Constitution. The delegates in each State shall be chosen randomly. In order to have a viable random sample, the number of delegates chosen per respective State to be Framers shall be fifty times the total number of that State's members of Congress. When said Constitution is completed by the Framers, it will require the Ratification of a majority of voters in each of the States, and only then shall it be sufficient for the Establishment of this Constitution between the States so ratifying the Same.

## Not So Grand Convention

As the Constitution-making process unfolded, Jefferson was regularly apprised of its goings-on by James Madison. Jefferson grew increasingly at odds with his fellow correspondent. Joseph Ellis, acclaimed historian of the American Revolutionary period, relates that "Jefferson was writing Madison from France with expressions of great doubt about the powers granted to the federal government over domestic affairs, powers that Madison had championed more effectively than anyone else at the Constitutional Convention." By the time the Constitution was crafted, Jefferson had come to the conclusion, as he told John Adams, that "all the good of this new constitution might have been couched in three or four new articles to be added to the good, old and venerable fabrick" of the Articles of Confederation.

Many delegates shared Jefferson's views, and so they did not consider their convention so grand. When the new Constitution was presented for the Framers' final stamp of approval before proceeding to ratification by the states, several refused to sign it. Many other delegates, who from the outset had been strongly opposed to the idea of writing a new Constitution instead of revising the Articles, as had originally been planned, had long since left.

Political scientist John Vile contends that these delegates didn't so much "attribute the problems [in the Articles] to the existing governmental structure as to the consequences of emerging from under colonial denomination." They were confident that in due time, as Americans became more seasoned in self-rule, any challenges emerging from the decentralized form of governance set forth by the Articles would be surmounted. Furthermore, Vile notes, they were as wary as Jefferson of "drastically entrusting the national government with significantly increased powers that might be abused."

## We the People?

Those who stayed on to frame the Constitution chose the words "we the people" to lead off the Preamble in a deliberate attempt to create the appearance that the document was "an act of law by the people of the United States for their entire land."[7]

On September 17, 1787, the U.S. Constitution, after being ratified by just nine of thirteen states in so-called popularly elected ratifying conventions, was adopted. On March 4, 1789, it officially went into operation as the new law of the land, replacing the Articles of Confederation. While his overriding concern at the time was to push through its approval, James Madison himself later confessed that the ratification protocol set forth by the Framers in Article VII of the Constitution was wanting: "It is admitted that the convention have departed from the tenor of their commission. Instead of reporting a plan requiring the confirmation of *all the states*, [the Framers] have reported a plan which is to be carried into effect *by nine states only*."

Even "the Father of the Constitution" appeared to concede that a

7. Hamburger, *Law and Judicial Duty*.

process of ratification that required such meager support diminished the Constitution's integrity as a binding document.

## Ordinary Framers

Only one state at our nation's founding devised a democratic plan for choosing the Framers of its state constitution.

By the early summer of 1776, most legislatures were preparing, as historian Gary B. Nash puts it in *The Unknown American Revolution*, to have their state constitutions "up and running before July 4," when the Declaration of Independence would be issued. But in constructing their constitutions, many state legislatures took shortcuts, amending their English charters "simply by deleting all reference to the English Crown. Letting it go at that, they continued to govern themselves as before. By itself, the decision *not* to change was a slap in the face of those who wanted to write afresh on a clean slate."

Pennsylvania was the exception, making the emphatic decision *to* change by allowing any male, including those who did not own property or pay taxes, not only to vote for the candidates vying to serve as Framers of the new state constitution, but to be candidates themselves. Predictably, Pennsylvania's elites waged a forceful campaign to dissuade anyone from actually voting for a common person to serve as a Framer. But common people—farmers, shop owners, artisans—had a strong advocate in James Cannon, a militia leader and math tutor. "Honesty, common sense, and a plain understanding, when unbiased by sinister motives," are the best criteria for choosing constitutional delegates, Cannon asserted. He further maintained that not only are regular people "fully equal to the task" of framing a constitution, but in fact are "the most likely to frame us a good Constitution."

But the elite interests, according to Nash, made the case that only people like them—wealthy, well educated, and familiar with political proceedings—could craft a constitution that perpetuated the traditional virtues of "decency, and respect, and venerations introduced for persons in authority." Cannon, however, exhorted Pennsylvanians "to reject the upper-class view that in order to write a constitution, men needed 'great learning, knowledge in our manners, trade, constitution and policy of all nations.'" His Jeffersonian perspective was that common people would best serve "the common interests of mankind." On the other hand, Cannon contended, "Great and over-grown rich men will be improper to be trusted. . . . They will be too apt to framing distinctions in society, because they will reap the benefits of all such distinctions."

Cannon's arguments proved persuasive: the great majority of Pennsylvania delegates chosen to serve as constitutional Framers hailed from humble origins. So it was that in the summer of 1776, while the Second Continental Congress was convening at the State House in Philadelphia and preparing to break all ties with Britain, just down the corridor was taking place what historian Sean Wilentz calls a "now-obscure State Convention that drafted and approved the most egalitarian constitution produced anywhere in Revolutionary America."[8]

The Pennsylvania constitution called for a government that was more of, by, and for the people than any other constitution crafted on the federal or state level. It declared that government's only purpose is to further the "common benefit, protection, and security of the people, nation, or community," and so is expressly "not for the particular emolument or advantage of any single man, family, or set of men who are only part of that community." Though it excluded women and slaves from participating, it nevertheless was remarkably

---

8. The state convention included one very uncommon person, Benjamin Franklin, who managed to traverse the corridor and serve both as a delegate to the Continental Congress and a framer of Pennsylvania's constitution. Indeed, Franklin was unanimously chosen to be the titular president of the state convention.

progressive for its time. It established a blueprint for governance that allowed ordinary Pennsylvania males to have unprecedented say in political affairs. Among other things, Pennsylvania's constitution contained a pioneering provision that stipulated that no bill passed by the General Assembly could become law until it had been printed and distributed to all male Pennsylvanians for their consideration. As Gary Nash points out, "This allowed time for public discussion of each law before the next annual election of representatives." Only if the male populace as a whole approved of the legislation did it then become official law.

The government that Pennsylvania's Framers brought into being, Nash notes, was "a heavy blow to wealthy merchants, large property owners, and assorted conservatives." From the moment the constitution was enacted, these anticonstitution forces plotted its demise, and in 1790, they prevailed. In Sean Wilentz's words, "Time would prove unkind to the Pennsylvania Constitution of 1776.

> Alarmed moderate and conservative notables from around the state, seeing democracy boiling over, quickly regrouped as the Republican faction, and they capitalized on some overbearing miscalculations by the radicals. . . . The Pennsylvania radicals failed to seek approval of the new constitution through a popular referendum. . . . The decision ensured their constitution went into effect, but at the cost of alienating a considerable portion of the moderate citizenry. . . .

When push came to shove, the Framers of the original state constitution failed to have enough faith in their fellow Pennsylvanians to allow them to vote on whether to approve the document they crafted, though they themselves had been elected by popular vote. Their decision ensured that their constitution went into effect but also ensured its demise. In September 1790, fourteen years after the radical constitution was enacted, "the Republicans won ratification of a new state constitution that eradicated most of the democratic provisions of its predecessor." This successful effort overturned a constitution that might over time have paved the way, in Pennsylvania and perhaps elsewhere, for realizing the Jeffersonian ideal of universal participation in governance.

## Making Amends

*Article V of the Constitution:* **"The Congress, whenever two-thirds of both Houses shall deem it necessary, shall propose Amendments to this Constitution, or, on the Application of the Legislatures of two-thirds of the several States, shall call a Convention for proposing Amendments, which, in either Case, shall be valid to all Intents and Purposes, as part of this Constitution, when ratified by the Legislatures of three-fourths of the several States, or by Conventions in three-fourths thereof, as the one or the other Mode of Ratification may be proposed by the Congress. . . ."**

"If Congress hadn't tampered with Article V, which describes how an amendment to the Constitution can be ratified, I feel sure we'd have eventually passed the Equal Rights Amendment," says Karina, referring to the proposed amendment, known as the ERA, that stipulated that equal rights under any federal, state, or local law could not be denied on account of a person's gender. It was approved by Congress for possible ratification in 1972.[9]

9. The first version of this amendment seeking to abolish legal sex discrimination was introduced in 1923 as a result of the effort of Alice Stokes Paul, the suffragist leader who had spearheaded the successful campaign for passage of the

"A revised Article V of the Constitution can make sure that the injustice done to us activists who'd labored for over ten years for its ratification won't be repeated," she says.

I'm in Lafayette Square in New Orleans. I had contacted about 50 people who had given me their email addresses when I was last in the city for a book event, just before Hurricane Katrina struck, and came to find that most had moved away. Still, a smattering of folks are on hand for my gathering in this revitalized city (shortly after our dialogue, the BP oil disaster occurred). We are seated in a circle in the square that was founded in 1788 and named after the French aristocrat Marquis de Lafayette.

"Before my involvement in the effort to have ratified the Equal Rights Amendment," Karina says now, "I'd thought Article V was cut and dried."

Article V establishes the process for ratifying a proposed amendment to the Constitution. In order for a proposed amendment to have a chance of being ratified, either two-thirds of the members of both chambers of Congress first have to approve it, or two-thirds of the legislatures of all the states (34 all told) must call for a national convention at which it would have to pass muster. Then, in order for the proposed amendment to become part of the Constitution, it either must be ratified by legislatures of three-fourths of the states (38 in all), or ratified by state conventions in three-fourths of the states.

Karina goes on to say now, "In the case of the ERA, Congress added another hoop to ratification that was never envisioned by the Framers. It established a seven-year deadline, from the time it

---

Nineteenth Amendment guaranteeing women the right to vote. A version of this amendment was subsequently introduced, and rejected, in every session of Congress, until the ERA was finally approved in revised form in 1972.

approved the ERA for possible ratification in 1972, for it actually to be ratified."

After successfully making its way through both chambers of Congress, the ERA briskly advanced toward ratification. In the first year alone, 22 states approved it for ratification. But then the amendment stalled as conservatives launched a well-orchestrated opposition drive. In the following years, 13 more states approved it, but that still left it three votes short of the total number needed. When it became evident to the amendment's principal proponents, such as the League of Women Voters, that the ERA would not be ratified by the 1979 deadline, they appealed to Congress to extend the deadline indefinitely. Congress did extend the deadline by three more years, to 1982; but it refused to completely eradicate the deadline. By then, the Reagan era was in full swing, and with the likes of the conservative political activist Phyllis Schlafly bending the president's ear, the ERA was removed from the Republican Party platform. Consequently, the ERA was never ratified.

"My gripe isn't so much with the Republicans of that time as it is with the actions of Congress in 1972 when it gave the ERA its blessing but with an arbitrarily imposed deadline for its ratification," says Karina. "We should have been able to wait out the conservative era, and then we'd have gotten the three additional states needed for ratification.

"So a new and improved article on the amendment process should establish that there is absolutely no deadline for seeking ratification of a proposed amendment that has been approved for possible ratification."

"If anything, I'd have this article we're making impose an across-the-board deadline for *all* proposed amendments," says Hal, who sells bootleg DVDs when he isn't studying to be a paralegal at a local community college. "I'd put the deadline at a decade, the total length of time that Congress gave ERA proponents. If you can't ratify a proposed amendment in ten years, then it's obvious that the people in most states do not want to be part of the Constitution."

Carl, who sometimes uses Lafayette Square as a base to sell his art, shakes his head in disagreement. "The Twenty-Seventh Amendment, the latest to be ratified,[10] was approved by Congress for possible ratification in 1789. It was finally ratified in 1992—over two hundred and two years later! It just goes to show that you never know when the time has finally come for a proposed amendment to be ratified. So it's best by far for the article on making amendments to state that Congress can't impose a ratification deadline."

Then he says, "I'd still like to see ten more states ratify the Child Labor Amendment, which would give Congress sole authority to determine child labor laws, taking this out of the purview of the states, where child labor protections vary a great deal. It was approved by Congress in 1924 and has since been approved by twenty-eight states. And for this proposed amendment Congress didn't impose any sort of deadline for ratification. Surely ten more states eventually will see the wisdom of having it as part of our Constitution, and it will be ratified. And just as surely, if Congress hadn't arbitrarily imposed a deadline, I bet that three more states would have eventually seen the wisdom of approving the ERA. The beauty of the open-ended time frame that the Framers conceived of—and which this revised article will etch in stone—is that it gives all the time in the world for our collective wisdom to reach the point where progressive amendments are ratified."

"I agree that there shouldn't be a deadline on constitutional amendments that are approved for possible ratification," says Janet, an emergency room nurse. "But that's not the same thing as saying

10. The Twenty-Seventh Amendment prohibits any law that increases or decreases the salary of members of the Congress from taking effect until the start of the next set of terms of office for representatives.

I agree that they should have an endless opportunity to become part of the Constitution. What this article we're crafting should make clear is that once a proposed amendment is approved for possible ratification, then each state has one—and only one—opportunity to vote on it, up or down. With the ERA, its proponents sought again and again to get state legislatures to change their minds after they had voted to reject it for ratification. Meanwhile, several states tried to have their yes votes changed to a no.

"But because the existing Article V isn't clear on the subject, Congress decided that states that voted to reject the ERA could take a revote and possibly approve it. Yet it also ruled that states that had approved it but then, over the passing years, decided they wanted to rescind their vote, couldn't do so. Talk about arbitrary. So this article should say that once a state has voted for or against a proposed constitutional amendment it doesn't have the option of later changing its vote. If, after all states have taken a vote, and the amendment has not been approved for ratification, then you have to start from square one and try, try again."

"I wish we could start all over again with the ERA," says Karina. "This amendment has been reintroduced in Congress every single year since the ratification deadline passed in 1982. But it has never again been put to another vote in those chambers. We can't start all over again if we can't even get it put to another vote by Congress."

"I have to say I agree with you on that point," Hal says to her, "even though we are political opposites in every other respect."

"The Federal Marriage Amendment was introduced as a joint resolution by several members of Congress in May 2003," he goes on.[11] "This resolution has never been debated by the House. Yet the

11. The Federal Marriage Amendment reads, "Marriage in the United States shall consist only of the union of a man and a woman. Neither this Constitution or

millions of Americans who like me believe marriage should only be allowed between a man and a woman are stuck with their cowardice.

"An amended amendment process should require Congress to debate any proposed amendment that is introduced by one or more of their members. Obviously this wouldn't guarantee that most proposed amendments would be approved by the two chambers, much less go on to be ratified. But at least they would be formally considered by Congress, rather than tabled indefinitely, which is the same thing as killing them."

Karina thinks about this. "As much as I detest this particular amendment Hal wants to have passed, I do agree that Congress should have to debate it and vote on it, as well as the perennially reintroduced ERA."

"You're both overlooking that there's already another way to have an amendment introduced," says Janet. "Article V of the Constitution says that 'on the application of the legislatures of two-thirds of the several States,' Congress is obligated to 'call a Convention for proposing Amendments.' This means that the states can go around Congress and initiate the amendment process themselves. This route was meant by the Framers to prevent Congress from bottling up constitutional amendments they didn't care to consider. Yet it's never once been used in our nation's history."

But it was almost used. In the early twentieth century, the various state legislators asked the U.S. Senate to approve a proposed amendment calling for the direct election of senators. If ratified, this would have replaced the constitutional provision stipulating that senators must be appointed by the state legislatures. When the Senate refused to approve this proposed amendment, the state

---

the constitution of any state, nor state or federal law, shall be construed to require that marital status or the legal incidents thereof be conferred upon unmarried couples or groups."

legislators began the process of initiating a convention to ratify it themselves. This prompted the Senate to quickly give in; it voted to have the amendment forwarded to the states, where it was put to a vote according to the traditional amendment route, and ratified. The Seventeenth Amendment to the Constitution was adopted on April 8, 1913, and obviated the need for the states to follow through with plans to hold a convention to amend the Constitution. There has never been another attempt by the states to organize an amendment convention. The Senate capitulated in this one instance because if a convention of the states had been held, not only would this particular amendment have been debated, but many other amendments likely also would have been proposed and considered, possibly further diluting the power of the legislative branch—because once a convention to propose amendments is convened by the states, as the members of the Senate well knew, those attending can propose as many amendments as they care to.

After a considerable pause, Karina says, "I like how, when the Twenty-First Amendment was ratified, it repealed the Eighteenth Amendment that had enacted Prohibition. For a brief time, the amendment process was used by Americans as a way of engaging in a debate over their core values. If we'd continued to use it for that purpose, we'd have many other amendments by now.

"For instance, there might be any number of amendments on marriage ratified and repealed and ratified over the years. While I hope that same-sex marriages would be allowed, it might be, heaven forbid, that this Federal Marriage Amendment might be the first one approved. But this might in turn be the impetus for generating a strong movement to repeal it in favor of one allowing same-sex marriage."

Then Carl says, "Since the Twenty-Seventh Amendment was approved in 1992, after a two-hundred-plus-year wait, no additional amendments have been ratified. I know some people think that's a sign of how near perfect our Constitution is. But to me it only goes to show how intimidating the current amendment process is, and what a need there is for it to be changed."

> *Constitution Café Article:* The Congress shall debate any pro-
> posed amendment to this Constitution that is sponsored
> by at least five percent of members of either Chamber. Pro-
> posed amendments shall advance to the ratification process
> whenever two-thirds of both Houses approve proposed
> Amendments to this Constitution. Alternatively the Legis-
> latures of two-thirds of the several States have authority to
> call a Convention for proposing Amendments. In either case,
> such Amendments shall be valid to all Intents and Purposes,
> as part of this Constitution, when ratified by the Legislatures
> of three-fourths of the several States, or by Conventions in
> three-fourths thereof. There shall be no deadline for ratifying
> Amendments that have been approved either by two-thirds
> of both Houses or by Legislatures of two-thirds of the sev-
> eral States.

## All People to the Power

Jefferson believed, as he told the Greek intellectual Adamantios Coray, that the amendment system the Framers put in place was "too difficult for remedying the imperfections which experience develops from time to time."

But is Article V of the Constitution the last word when it comes to amending the Constitution?

Constitutional scholar Bruce Ackerman maintains in *We the People* that though they've never exercised it, Americans can ratify amendments to the Constitution without having to go through the labyrinthine process detailed in Article V. To make his case, he points out that a principal Framer stressed, during Constitution ratification debates at his own state convention, that Article V was by no means the only avenue for amending the document. During a ratification debate in Pennsylvania, James Wilson insisted that "the people may change the constitutions whenever and however they please." Wilson further commented, "As our constitutions are superior to our legislatures, so the people are superior to our constitutions," and so they not only "have the power, if they think proper, to repeal and annul" the Constitution but have "direct authority" for "amending and improving" it.

Given that he was a leading Framer of the Federal Constitution, Wilson's words carried great weight. His statements were widely noted and quoted, and went a long way toward pacifying anti-Federalists' concerns about the proposed Constitution, paving the way for its passage.

Jefferson told Adamantios Coray that "a greater facility of amendment" should be provided in the Constitution so that it could be revised periodically. An easier amendment process, he believed, would "maintain [the Constitution] in a course of action accommodated to the times and changes through which we are ever passing." But James Madison was opposed to any process that might bring about frequent changes to the Constitution, since this to him "would, in a great measure, deprive the government of that veneration . . . without which perhaps the wisest and freest governments would not possess the requisite stability."

Because this Madisonian perspective has prevailed over Jefferson's, the tendency today is to believe that the longer-lived and more unchanging our Constitution, the better. Constitutional scholar Albert Blaustein offers an encomium to our Framers: in devising a "constitutionally limited republic," they engineered the creation of an ideal "regime that balanced order and liberty." Further, to Blaustein, the fact that our Constitution "has withstood the test of time," and rarely been amended since the addition of the Bill of Rights, is proof that it is immutable. But what if its longevity and relative stasis have impeded the type of inventiveness that might better enable a democratic society to evolve? Or, might we at least challenge Blaustein's argument that the Constitution has served us well? Robert Dahl, for one, wonders, "How well does our constitutional system meet *democratic* standards of the present day?"

"We have not yet so far perfected our constitutions as to venture to make them unchangeable," Jefferson held. He lamented how "some look at constitutions with sanctimonious reverence, and deem them like the arc of the covenant, too sacred to be touched. They ascribe to the men of the preceding age a wisdom more than human, and suppose what they did to be beyond amendment. I knew that age well; I belonged to and labored with it."

The men of Jefferson's age had no monopoly on wisdom, not even for their own time, and he believed that, by attaching a transcendent sanctity to a Constitution created by a small group of his contemporaries, later generations would do the Framers themselves, and democracy, a grave disservice.

# IV

## Commons and Goods

Thomas Jefferson was not exactly a "unifier," then or now. He was certainly not a consensus choice for president—his election was bitterly contested.[1] Jefferson had agreed to come out of retirement and serve as leader of the Democratic-Republicans after party leaders convinced him that he stood the best chance of defeating incumbent John Adams, whose party platform—which tried to reconcile the various factions within the Federalist camp—promoted a heavy-handed, paternalist approach to governance that threatened to even further encroach on individual liberties. The Federalists had already wrested power from the people with the passage of the Alien and Sedition Acts in 1798, which extended the amount of time it took for immigrants to become citizens and gave the president the power to deport any alien "dangerous to the peace and safety of the United States," to deport aliens whose home countries were at war with the U.S., and to fine or imprison (or both) those whose

---

1. Though they later reconciled, Jefferson's decision to throw his hat in the ring in a rematch against Adams (he lost the 1796 presidential election by just three electoral votes) led to a protracted estrangement from his longtime friend; both of them, notes Joseph Ellis, "when forced to choose, had opted for party over friendship."

writing was considered "false, scandalous, and malicious" against the government. The election ended in a tie—between Jefferson and Aaron Burr[2] (Adams finished third). According to the Constitution, it would now be up to Congress to choose the next president. It took 36 ballots over six days before Jefferson was elected, with Burr ultimately serving as vice president.

Nearly twenty years later, Jefferson called the pivotal election "as real a revolution in the principles of our government as that of 1776 was in its form; not affected indeed by the sword, but by the rational and peaceable instrument of reform, the suffrage of the people." But even if, in this "revolution of 1800," Jefferson did "restore the democratic impulse of the American Revolution after its betrayal by the Federalists," as Joseph Ellis contends, the election itself was just barely peaceable, and rationality was often missing in action.

> Both parties engaged in . . . negative campaigning, an assault on their adversary's program rather than an emphasis on their own platform. The Federalists, for instance, left no stone unturned in their attempts to link the Republicans with the bloody excesses of the French Revolution. Jefferson and his adherents, they charged, were "artful and ambitious demagogues" who led "discontented hotheads."[3]

The Republicans were no slouches either when it came to attacks. They "drew on early political writings by Adams to tag him as a

---

2. Because the Framers had failed to distinguish in the Constitution between electoral votes for a president or vice president, Jefferson and his running mate Burr wound up in an electoral tie for the presidency. The Constitution was subsequently amended to make sure this never happened again.

3. John Ferling, *Adams vs. Jefferson* (Oxford University Press, 2005).

monarchist."[4] As Sean Wilentz notes, the "attacks and counter-attacks," coupled with "the harsh ideological as well as personal tone," served to harden partisan loyalties.

In the aftermath of this contentious election, the electorate remained deeply divided, their divergent principles apparently unbridgeable. In his inaugural address, Jefferson exhorted Americans to come together and "unite in common efforts for the common good." It appears to be the only time in his voluminous writings and speeches that he specifically used the term "common good," though he did use the phrase "public good" on occasion, a term that doesn't necessarily take into account a citizen's private welfare. While many or most common goods might be public ones, some—such as the right to life, liberty, and the pursuit of happiness—clearly have both public and private implications. Perhaps Jefferson didn't make more mention of the "common good" because he took it for granted that all citizens valued it as he did. After all, his native Virginia is a commonwealth rather than a state, and "commonwealth" translates as "for the common good." To have a common "weal" is to have a share in government, and as a result, to be mutually responsible for cultivating the well-being of fellow citizens.

But how does society go about putting this into practice? How do its members look out for one another? Is the government responsible for spreading the wealth and seeing to it that each citizen has a share of certain basics that he or she needs in order to be a full contributor to society?

During Jefferson's eight years in office, he did away with Federalist hegemony and "enabled the nation to move piecemeal from

4. From Pulitzer Prize–winning historian Edward J. Larson's *A Magnificent Catastrophe: The Tumultuous Election of 1800, America's First Presidential Campaign* (Free Press, 2007).

the habits of 1800, laced as they yet were with restrictive customs from colonial days, toward egalitarianism and democratization." His primary legacy was that, because of his implemented policies, "despite wide inequities in the distribution of wealth, most free citizens believed they enjoyed the same rights and opportunities as all other free men."[5]

In a national poll conducted by the nonpartisan Center for the Constitution, headquartered in the lifelong residence of James Madison in Montpelier, Virginia, a broad cross-section of Americans was asked whether the Constitution charges the federal government with realizing the common good. Less than half responded in the affirmative. The director of the Center was himself disappointed in the results: "Sadly, almost half the population does not feel that the government was designed with this goal."

Yet the Constitution makes no explicit mention of the common good. It does, though, authorize Congress to provide for "the general welfare." Are the common good and the general welfare one and the same?

## Common Goods, Bads, and the General Welfare

*From Article I, Section 8, Clause 1 of the Constitution:* "**The Congress shall have Power To . . . provide for the . . . general welfare of the United States. . . .**"

"The Preamble says that a big part of the Constitution's purpose is 'to *promote* the general welfare,'" says Harry, a 45-year-old information technology specialist. "Then, when it gets down to listing Congress's powers, it says its job is to '*provide for* the . . . general welfare of the United States.' I prefer 'promote' rather than

5. Ferling, *Adams vs. Jefferson.*

'provide' for the general welfare. Because you don't provide for the general welfare, you promote it, or contribute to it, by *providing* for the common good. Otherwise, there's no general welfare to promote. So a new article that deals with this subject should decree that Congress promotes the general welfare by providing for the common good."

I'm with about a dozen others in the expansive food court at the Mall of America. Literally the goods capital of North America, the nation's largest mall is situated in the Twin Cities suburb of Bloomington, Minnesota. We strain to hear one another over the peals of glee and fright coming from riders on the nearby indoor roller coaster. A security guard has been hovering around us, eyeing my constitution café sign. He decides that if I'm an oddity, I'm of the harmless variety, and moves on.

"Aren't those two terms interchangeable?" asks Audrey, the owner of a Wisconsin-based travel agency who with her teenage son makes a bimonthly trip to the mall.

Harry retrieves a dictionary from his shoulder bag. "Welfare, as defined by Merriam-Webster, concerns the 'state of doing well especially in respect to good fortune, happiness, well-being, or prosperity.' So I take the 'general welfare' to mean that state of doing well in which society as a whole is happily prospering. That can only happen if essential common goods are provided to everyone, in order to promote this state of doing well, since common goods are the building blocks of the general welfare."

"I'm not sure that providing for the common good is how you go about promoting the general welfare," says Nadine, who works at a nearby kiosk that sells an eclectic mix of new and used CDs, and who has joined us on her break. "Common goods are like open bins that all Americans can grab stuff from. You're giving up something—like, you're relinquishing a percentage of your income—so that tax dollars can be put towards acquiring certain goods to be put into a public bin, because Congress has said you have to for the sake of society's prosperity. But if contributing to the common good takes away from my personal prosperity and happiness—like, if I'd prefer to keep that income for myself so I can buy private goods that I consider more important to my personal well-being—then it detracts from the general welfare, which is the sum of all individual welfares."

"You make common goods sound like common bads. But a true common good is something that's as good for each individual as it is for society as a whole, the best investments we can make in one another," Mildred, 85, says to her. Mildred retired over two decades ago as an elementary-school teacher. "People only make sacrifices grudgingly if there's no sense of common cause or shared purpose. A true common good is as much for your benefit as it is mine and everyone else's, and as such, should improve both the individual and general welfare."

Then Mildred tells us, "My husband was in D-Day in World War II. Those of us here on the home front pitched in to help make sure all the troops had everything they needed to do their jobs well. Not only did we willingly give up luxuries, we deprived ourselves of essentials, in order to contribute to our common defense, which is a type of common good. We had a shared purpose, and understood that making such sacrifices was in all our best interests.

"We grew gardens in our front and back yards and in vacant lots so the produce at farms could be reserved for our soldiers. There were over twenty million 'Victory Gardens,' and over ten million tons of fruit and vegetables were harvested from them. We took part in drives to collect scrap metal, nylon, silk, anything that could be used for the war effort. Commodities from food to oil were rationed—in some cases voluntarily, in others by order of Congress—and hardly anyone complained. There was a surplus of goodwill. I became a more independent person by helping spearhead collection drives, and at the same time, I became more connected to and concerned about the welfare of my community, really to that of America itself, since all these local projects contributed to its overall general welfare.

"After the war, I joined efforts that saw to it that even the poorest communities enjoyed essential 'public bin staples'—safe drinking water, cleaner air, public parks, a decent education. I eventually went back to school and earned my degree in education. I was a teacher for over thirty years in an underserved community. That's something I'd never have done if not for the 'sacrifices' I'd made during the war. I've discovered many times over that the more I give of myself, the more I get back in return."

"How would today's generation determine which common goods are needed in order to best promote the general welfare?" I ask.

"Just look at those goods our members of Congress provide themselves at taxpayer expense," says Harry. "They have the best taxpayer-subsidized health care plan on this planet. In fact, Congress exempted itself from the health care 'reform' legislation signed into law so it could continue to be guaranteed this 'public option' that it denied to the rest of us. All members of Congress also enjoy such 'uncommon goods' as exceptional child care plans, elder care, and guaranteed retirement income exponentially higher than what's provided to the rest of us by Social Security. They don't have to spend sleepless nights worrying about how to pay their health care premiums or for day care for their children, or how they're going to live with dignity after they retire, because of the goods they authorize themselves from a private or exclusive bin— even though these goods are paid for by us. Yet as far as Congress is concerned, the rest of us should have no entitlement to these goods ourselves."

"So, this article needs to stipulate that members of Congress can't enjoy such goods if they're denied to their constituents," Audrey says now. "Congress is betraying its duty to promote the general welfare by providing only for themselves, on the public dole, goods that we all need in order to prosper."

"If that's promoting the general welfare, then it sounds too much like social welfare to me, and so a common bad," says Marvin. "Congress shouldn't be guaranteed these goods, and neither should any of the rest of us. Where do you draw the line with these basic 'must haves' we provide for one another? I can't have a house until everyone else has this good too?"

"You know what everyone else owes me?" he goes on. "Not a damn thing. My parents were as poor as church mice during the Great Depression, but they refused any part of Franklin Delano Roosevelt's make-work programs. The Supreme Court scandalously ruled that they were legal because they promoted the general welfare, but my parents, who ran a grocery, believed they just made people dependent on government. They weathered those tough times. By the time I was born, during the tail-end of the Depression, they were doing okay."

"When I got back from Vietnam," he goes on, "I went to school, got my degree in business, started a company with a few Marine buddies, and after years with a lot more downs than ups, I finally made it. My father would have been proud."

He holds out his two hands. "These are my insurance, when I use them with my head and heart. Anyone who uses them wisely in his professional pursuits will be able both to provide for himself and make the greatest contribution to society. People who live by their wits and don't look to be rescued by the government when times are tough are the greatest providers of our country's general welfare."

"Did you attend college with the GI bill?" I ask him. "I ask because that's what enabled my father to earn a college degree after his stint in the Army. He credits the GI bill in big part for his professional success."

"Yes, I did, and I'm grateful as hell for that," Marvin replies.

"Society believed it owed that 'good' to all of us who went to war on behalf of our country's common defense. I took advantage of that and other veterans' benefits. It definitely gave me a leg up in the world, and made it possible for me to do things with my life that my parents couldn't have dreamed of doing."

He looks at me. "So you're suggesting that I am obliged to the government to some degree for my own success, even if it was sort of quid pro quo."

"I don't compare my or anyone else's sacrifices to those of our soldiers," Mildred says to Marvin now. "But there's other people today who make sacrifices every day in their own way to keep this country strong. They work two and even three jobs without complaining, taking on work others turn up their noses at, to support their families. And they're still hurting, because they don't have what they need—basic goods like health care and day care—so they can do even better for themselves and, really, for the nation, to keep our economy going strong.

"We need to take a greater interest in their welfare, if for no other reason than that in doing so, we're helping our own welfare, and America's too. Isn't that what America is all about at its best—looking out for one another, taking an interest in one another's well-being, so we can all make the most of our lives? Making sure everyone is provided with certain basic common goods serves this objective."

Marvin looks straight at her, organizing his thoughts. "Just maybe there's a couple or few basic common goods that all folks should have so they can contribute better to the general welfare, as long as those on the receiving end are every bit as much on the producing end, giving far more to society than they expect to receive. I may be a conservative, but I agree with John F. Kennedy, who said, 'Ask not what your country can do for you, ask what you can do for your country.'

"I'll tell you what—my kids and grandkids should be the last in line for receiving any goods from the public goods bin. They contribute next to nothing, yet believe they're entitled to everything."

*Constitution Café Article:* The Congress shall have Power to provide for the common good in order to promote the general welfare of the United States. Congress shall not have Power to provide for itself any goods that it does not provide equally to all United States citizens.

## A Specific General Welfare

Jefferson certainly didn't believe that government had the latitude to provide whatever tangible common goods they or the electorate desired. Yet some members of Congress disagreed with him. He chastised the Framers for making such an ambiguous "general welfare clause"—the clause explored in this Constitution Café exchange—because it lent itself to so many conflicting interpretations. "Aided by a little sophistry on the words 'general welfare,'" Jefferson asserted, Congress could make the claim that "whatsoever they shall think or pretend will be for the general welfare" will in fact be good for society.

In a correspondence with Albert Gallatin, secretary of the treasury during his administration, Jefferson maintained that "Congress had not unlimited powers to provide for the general welfare, but were restrained to those specifically enumerated in the Constitution." He insisted that the general welfare clause "never meant that [Congress] should provide for that welfare but by the exercise of the enumerated powers"—those specific charges delegated to Congress in the Constitution—"so it could not have been meant that they should raise money for purposes which the enumeration did not place under their action."

By this reasoning, Congress could raise money for the common defense because the Constitution explicitly gave it this authority, but it could not raise money, say, for undertaking massive infrastructure projects such as the building of railroads, bridges, or ports, because, according to the Constitution, such projects were not under its specific purview. Jefferson claimed that the Framers clearly meant for this clause to be "a limitation of the purpose for which they may raise money" rather than an open-ended invitation for Congress to raise and spend money on whatever it saw fit.

Jefferson argued that specific constitutional amendments had to be ratified before Congress could allocate money for any project or initiative, no matter how well intentioned, that it was not specifically charged with carrying out, per the Constitution. Hence today, if Congress wanted to provide universal health care coverage, Jefferson would not be opposed to it in principle, but he would likely argue that a new constitutional amendment would first need to be ratified that charges Congress with providing this good to all Americans. And he would be livid that Congress has unconstitutionally created its own private bin with taxpayer dollars, providing itself with health care and many other goods that are out of reach for most Americans.

Jefferson's greatest concerns about Congress's excessively broad interpretation—in fact, what he viewed as its intentional misinterpretation—of the Constitution's general welfare clause stemmed from the passage of the Alien and Sedition Acts. The Federalist Congress that approved these acts made what to him was the specious claim that they had authority to do so under the general welfare clause, as they were acting in the interest of what today might be called "national security."

In 1798, after their enactment, Matthew Lyon, a congressman from Vermont who shared Jefferson's view that the Federalists had egregiously overstepped their bounds, wrote a letter to a newspaper accusing the Federalist Congress and the Adams administration of acting in such a way that "the public welfare [was] swallowed up in a continual grasp for power." Lyon was arrested and convicted under the very Alien and Sedition Acts that he was protesting. He was sentenced to four months in prison and fined for what at the time was the enormous sum of $1,000. While in prison, Lyon was reelected by his constituents, and in the election of 1800 that resulted in a tie between Thomas Jefferson and Aaron Burr, throwing the vote to the House of Representatives, it was Lyon who cast the deciding vote in Jefferson's favor.

## Mind Your Property

*From Article 1, Section 8, Clause 8 of the Constitution:* **"The Congress shall have power . . . To promote the Progress of Science and useful Arts, by securing for limited Times to Authors and Inventors the exclusive Right to their respective Writings and Discoveries."**

"The Framers put it in Congress's hands 'to promote the progress of science and useful arts, by securing for limited times to authors and inventors the exclusive right to their respective writings and discoveries,'" says Elisa, a software developer, reading from her copy of the Constitution. "At least in theory, Congress accomplishes this by dictating patent law."

I'm with Elisa and several others in a community center in Silicon Valley to explore the constitutional article that treats with intellectual property law. A patent grants exclusive rights to an inventor for a limited period of time.

Then Elisa says, "The case can be made that current patent law impedes the progress of science and useful arts. The language of this article needs to be changed so that Congress has clearer guidance on what it's supposed to be achieving."

Laura, a biophysicist and university professor, nods. "I would alter this article so it says that Congress's role is 'to promote the progress of science and useful arts *for the public good*.' These days, patent law mostly benefits the private good—individuals and corporations. Benefiting society is of secondary importance, if that.

"I'll give an example: Multinational seed corporations routinely gain patents on seeds for disease-resistant plants. While my own view is that such seeds destroy biodiversity, these corporations argue that they greatly benefit society, and that it costs a bundle to develop them, and so they deserve patents. But granting such patents gives a handful of companies a dangerous level of control over the food production chain. It's not just that it enables the patent holders to charge high prices to farmers who've become dependent on their product, but that they can even charge farmers who *don't* use their seeds.

"Here's the level of absurd control that patent law allows these corporations: If the wind blows a patented seed to another piece of farmland where this seed was never intended to be used, and if this crop inadvertently sprouts plants containing the patented seed, the patent holder can and often will sue that farmer."

As CBS News's website reports, the biotech giant Monsanto has sued small farmers whose fields have been "contaminated" with their genetically modified seeds for patent infringement. In one instance, a soybean farmer was subjected to a lawsuit filed by the corporation after it came onto his property to investigate whether any of his crop was grown with Monsanto seeds. The farmer is quoted as saying, "Pollination occurs, wind drift occurs. There's just no way to keep their products from landing in our fields." Yet, as CBS reports, any farmer, even if unknowingly, who has on his land patented pest- and weed-resistant seeds "must sign an iron-clad agreement not to re-plant the harvested seed, or face serious legal consequences—up to $3 million in damages."

Laura says now, "This points to a much bigger issue: Should

anyone be able to patent the things we need to sustain us? Can that ever be for the public good?"

"But even if we altered this article as you suggest," says Amanda, an artist, software designer, and autodidact, "if the rest of this article remained intact, it still would say that the way that Congress goes about promoting the progress of science and useful arts for the public good is 'by securing for limited times to authors and inventors the exclusive right to their respective writings and discoveries.' I have problems with this, because whenever exclusive rights are granted, even for a limited time, it's the same thing as granting a monopoly."

"If, through the hard work of some inventors and researchers," Amanda goes on, "they demonstrate that their discoveries can save lots of lives, such as through their use in new diagnostic tests or new drugs, they should be compensated generously—and their lawyers can haggle with the government over what 'fair compensation' amounts to. But they should never be allowed to patent such discoveries, or at least, not for more than the most extremely limited of times. They should *want* to put their findings into the public domain as quickly as possible—as soon as they've recovered their investment costs and made a decent profit—so other scientific minds can build on their work. Patent law should facilitate this."

"It should, but it doesn't," says Laura. "It's very much the exception rather than the rule when researchers collaborate to get all their findings speedily into the public domain. Scientists have been able to make remarkably rapid progress in early diagnosis of Alzheimer's because all the researchers in the U.S. agreed to share their findings immediately—and not just with one another, but with the public at large. For the very first time, all the scientists involved in such an initiative agreed beforehand that none of them 'owned' the data, and so none of them could try to procure patents.

"Researchers of Parkinson's disease are going to emulate this beautiful model of cooperation. But my point is, a constitutional article should make this model the rule. It's a virtuous model that puts human life ahead of profit. Yet just a tiny percentage of researchers are starting to use it. I believe that they should have to, that it shouldn't be a matter of choice whether they collaborate or whether they practice in isolation, which has been the prevalent model encouraged by existing patent law."

"Right now, patents are for twenty years, across the board, whether you've invented a video game or a lifesaving drug derived from someone's DNA, whether you've hit upon a speedier computer processing chip or come up with a piece of solar technology that can greatly decrease our use of nonrenewable energy resources," says Clint, an inventor and author who holds several patents.

"Congress may think it's being fair by allowing all inventions and discoveries to enjoy the same exclusive time period to have a monopoly, but it's not being fair to society. There needs to be some sort of sliding scale of exclusivity when it comes to granting patents. Though it may seem counterintuitive, the more valuable an invention or discovery is to society, the less time it should be granted exclusivity. So silly and mindless video games like the kind I develop for pure fun and profit might have a lengthy patent. But a patent on the discovery of a gene sequence that produces proteins that help alleviate diabetes might have the most limited of exclusive times. Because otherwise, anyone else who in the course of those two decades of exclusivity might have been able to tap into and apply this discovery in other medically beneficial ways is prevented from doing so."

"Thomas Jefferson, our nation's first administrator of the patent system, believed that patents should be granted sparingly," says Amanda. "If he were the chief patent officer today, scientists affiliated with big pharmaceuticals, biotech firms, and universities would never be granted patents on things like modified seeds, or on gene sequences that are part of everyone's DNA, or on medicines derived from plants used for centuries by indigenous groups. To him, the whole idea of inventions and discoveries in an open society is to share, not to horde."

"Most of all, he believed that patents were only meant to be granted for genuinely original inventions and discoveries," she continues. "So, for instance, the modified seed that Laura was talking about is still just a twist on an original seed. So it shouldn't be deserving of a patent. This article we're crafting can state that patents are only granted for genuinely original inventions. That in itself would resolve a lot of the problems with current patent law. I honestly don't so much blame inventors for their extreme greed as I do Congress, because the patent law it has enacted enables and encourages it."

"As most here know, I'd rather not have an article dealing with patents in the Constitution at all—or at least, I'd rather have an article that banishes them," says Elisa. "In an ideal democracy, patents wouldn't exist, because they're almost always obstacles to the progress of science and the useful arts in ways that benefit society. That's why those of us dedicated to the open-source movement shun the patent system."

She goes on, "Those who took part in the groundbreaking Alzheimer's research that Laura mentioned apparently practiced for the first and probably only time in their careers what 'open sourcers' dedicate their lives to. It's a pity that our Constitution doesn't prohibit patents altogether, so collaboration in research and development would be the rule, making our society truly open."

"I'm not completely agreeing with this," says Clint. "There's degrees of openness for an open society, and degrees of public benefit. In a totally open society, then yes, there'd be no patents. But there probably wouldn't be so many inventions, because few would be able to survive financially unless they're one of the fortunate few who have some other stable source of income.

"In the area of software, my specialty, any developer has a choice of whether to seek a certain amount of exclusivity for his product and make a buck, or to distribute his product for free with an open-source system. I recognize that an open-source operating system like Linux is every bit as top-of-the-line—in fact, has far fewer glitches and far fewer virus threats—than the operating systems of the world's biggest software developers. People assume that proprietary software is always better, when in fact open-source software, for anything from animation to visual effects to word processing, can often have more user-friendly and advanced applications.

"But it comes down to a matter of choice—and that's what democracy is about, choice. Without software patents, I wouldn't make money. Hundreds of thousands of other people involved in software research, development, and distribution would be without jobs. I wish I could be pure and be completely altruistic. I can't say my patented goods benefit society. They *do* at least occupy the time of people who might otherwise do something even more worthless. "

"The other issue," Clint continues, "is that the intellectual property rights protections ensured by the existing constitutional article in many instances help make our society even more open. Without these protections, anyone could reproduce and sell the works of writers and artists and musicians without paying them. Those artists wouldn't be able to subsist, wouldn't have the time to compose their works. That would be damaging to society because we'd miss out on so many great ideas. And here again, it boils down to a matter of choice. Lots of people offer up their creative works for free, especially when they're just getting started or trying to get a following. But they shouldn't *have* to go this route if they don't want to."

"Your point is well taken," says Amanda after a while. "We just have to make sure that these protections are only granted for truly original works, which to me are works that are only marginally reliant on anyone else's work or information. The patent-granting pendulum has swung way too far in the direction of private benefit. This new constitutional article can swing the pendulum back towards the middle."

> *Constitution Café Article:* The Congress shall have power to promote the progress of science and the useful arts for the public good by securing for limited times to authors and inventors the exclusive right to those Works deemed original, rather than mere modifications or improvements of existing Works. The limited time of exclusivity granted shall be determined by the perceived benefit of the Work to the public: the more timely the public value of the Work, the shorter the period of exclusivity that shall be granted.

## Patently Undemocratic

As noted in the dialogue, Jefferson was our nation's first administrator of the patent system; he was appointed to the post in 1790. Jefferson was keenly aware of the fact that a patent effectively gave the inventor a monopoly (the nation's first patent law granted up to fourteen-year exclusivity to patent holders, with another seven-year extension possible), and so he was stingy about granting patents. To the chagrin of many a patent seeker, he doled out patents only to those whose inventions he considered genuinely original. "Certainly an inventor ought to be allowed a right to the benefit of his invention for some certain time," he reasoned. However, not only did Jefferson refuse to grant patents to those seeking them for modifications or improvements of existing inventions, but he also drew the line when it came to discoveries or inventions that he believed any number of people might have come up with in due time:

for to embarrass society with monopolies for every utensil existing, and in all the details of life, would be more injurious to them than had the supposed inventors never existed; because the natural understanding of its members would have suggested the same things or others as good.

Jefferson himself was an avid inventor. With his son-in-law Thomas Mann Randolph, he devised a plow that could be used on hillsides, making it possible to grow crops on otherwise awkward stretches of arable terrain. He was thrilled that his discovery stood to benefit fellow farmers. Even though he was forever in financial trouble and might have become more solvent if he'd sought and received a patent, it wouldn't have occurred to him to do so. Jefferson was the first to acknowledge that while he may have developed a new application for the plow, the device itself had already been invented. It would have baffled him that modifications of existing works are routinely granted patents today. To him, this cheapens the notion of what constitutes an original work or discovery at the same time it makes our capitalist economy a more pervasively monopolistic one.

Jefferson believed that American inventors should have as their foremost goal the benefit of society, and so their motivations should be "based, not on profit, but on science, moderation and beauty." Indeed, he held that inventions and discoveries themselves are intrinsically he in nature, and as such, should be shared widely as a matter of course so others can pore over and plumb them, possibly expanding or enhancing their usefulness. By this conception, monopolies are counter to the nature and function of inventions and discoveries.

Jefferson asserted that the "peculiar character" of an original discovery or invention is such that "the moment it is divulged, it forces itself in to the possession of everyone, and the receiver cannot dispossess himself of it." To him, this is a beneficial transaction for all concerned. For no matter how widely an invention is dispersed, Jefferson contended, "no one possesses the less, because every other possesses the whole of it." Indeed, he argues, "he who receives an idea from me, receives instruction from himself without lessening mine; as he who lights his taper at mine receives light without darkening me." This not only points to the transformative potential of discoveries and inventions, but to what Jefferson saw as their implicit moral dimension, and how they light society's way to new, more liberating possibilities.

Jefferson maintained that democratizing newfound knowledge was particularly important when it came to scientific findings. As he told his friend Roger Weightman, "The general spread of the light of science has already laid open to every view the palpable truth that the mass of mankind has not been born with saddles on their backs nor a favored few booted and spurred." While the light of science did not remove Jefferson's blinders when it came to race matters or equality for women, it nonetheless has proven invaluable in enabling society over time to overcome irrationally held prejudices.

Jefferson would have been appalled that current patent law allows key areas of knowledge to be guarded by individuals and corporations for whom private gain is paramount. On the other hand, he would applaud today's open-source movement—not just for its promise of rapidly diffusing knowledge in ways that lead to new insights among the disciplines that might expand human horizons, but for the virtues possessed by open sourcers, who place altruism above financial profit in their efforts to share discoveries that can benefit society. As he maintained in a letter to Jeudy de l'Hommande, "Every discovery which multiplies the subsistence of men, must be a matter of joy to every friend of humanity."

For Jefferson, attempts to take credit for potentially transformative ideas, inventions, or discoveries are counterproductive. "The question who commenced the Revolution?" Jefferson wrote, "is as difficult as that of the first inventors of a thousand good things.

For example, who first discovered the principle of gravity? Not Newton; for Galileo, who died the year Newton was born, had measured its force in the descent of gravid bodies. . . . The fact is that one new idea leads to another, that to a third, and so on through a course of time until someone, with whom no one of these ideas was original, combines all together and produces what is justly called a new invention. I suppose it would be as difficult to trace our Revolution to its first embryo . . .

Whatever their origins, Jefferson believed that ideas must be spread expeditiously, so they can be combined and recombined in ways that further unleash human creativity and potential, and that might well have been unimaginable to the original inventor or discoverer, tinkerer, or thinker. Far more important than tracing ideas to their first embryo is facilitating ways for them to take root and then to promote their continual rebirth. Jefferson would argue that if the current patent process is not an enabler of this dissemination of knowledge, then it is in need of radical readjustment, since the whole purpose of ideas and inventions, as he told Isaac McPherson, is that they be "freely spread from one to another over the globe, for the moral and mutual instruction of man, and improvement of his condition."

## Standing (and Sitting) Army

*From several clauses in Article I, Section 8, of the Constitution:* **"The Congress shall have Power To . . . provide for the common Defence . . . ; To declare War, grant Letters of Marque and Reprisal, and make Rules concerning Captures on Land and Water; To raise and support Armies, but no Appropriation of Money to that Use shall be for a longer**

Term than two Years; To provide and maintain a Navy; To make Rules for the Government and Regulation of the land and naval Forces; To provide for calling forth the Militia to execute the Laws of the Union, suppress Insurrections and repel Invasions; To provide for organizing, arming, and disciplining, the Militia, and for governing such Part of them as may be employed in the Service of the United States, reserving to the States respectively, the Appointment of the Officers, and the Authority of training the Militia according to the discipline prescribed by Congress."

I am at People's Park in Berkeley, California, just a couple blocks south of the University of California campus. In 1969, the 2.8-acre plot of land owned by the university had largely been cleared, though it was not yet earmarked for a specific use. Tensions began when activists started converting the grounds into a community park without first consulting with and receiving the permission of the college administration. Radicals also had plans for the area to serve as a nerve center for organizing and conducting protests against the federal government's Vietnam policies.

Ronald Reagan, then governor of California, vowed to use whatever means necessary to end the takeover of the university property. On May 15, 1969—a day that became known as "bloody Thursday"— he called in several hundred police officers and sheriff's deputies, who ousted the 3,000 protesters from the park and its immediate surroundings. When word spread of what was transpiring, about 6,000 activists rallied to reclaim the park. Violence erupted. One student, James Rector, was shot to death, and over 100 were hospitalized. Reagan declared a state of emergency and deployed 2,700 National Guard troops to the area. Two weeks later, over 30,000 people marched past the now-barricaded park to protest its occupation. Though there were no more clashes at People's Park, tensions never altogether abated. The property is still owned by the university, which over the years has made occasional overtures to convert the land to uses other than a park, only to meet with stiff resistance. Today, People's Park is a popular gathering place well tended by local nonprofits in coordination with the university.

Most of today's Constitution Café participants were informed of the gathering by my postings on social networking sites. Among those who join me are a husband and wife. I see on the forearm of the husband a "dog tag tattoo." Also known as a "meat tag," these are popular tattoos among soldiers, who typically get them just before they're set to be deployed overseas. "You're a soldier?" I ask.

"We're 'full screws,' corporals," says Derrick. "My wife Vickie and I are in the Army. But her brother Josh here"—whom he proceeds to elbow gently—"is a civilian, and a crazy liberal one at that."

"My dad is retired military; he left as a full colonel. My parents live here in Berkeley, where I was born and raised," he then says. "Quite a few military bases were in the region until all the closings in the nineties. There are still a lot of military families living around here."

Then Vickie says, "We're getting ready to deploy to South Korea, and are here visiting Derrick's parents before we go. I get the sense that they're relieved we're not going to the hot spots in the Middle East. But who knows, with tensions flaring between North and South Korea, it may soon be the new hotspot."

"One reason there's so many hotspots is because our military presence makes them hot," says Ophelia, who sits down across from Derrick and those with him. "Our bases all over the world make it possible for us to insert ourselves into any conflict across the globe. We'd be better off without that ability. It weakens rather than strengthens our country when we try to be the policemen of the world."

"Congress could change the nature of our military from what it is now," she goes on. "It already has a constitutional way to do this, but lacks the backbone. Section 8 of the first article in the Constitution gives the legislative branch power to 'provide for the common defense,' 'to declare war,' and 'to raise and support armies.' It goes on to state that 'no appropriation of money to that use shall be for a longer term than two years.'

"With this power of the purse, Congress can cut off funding for any military incursion. If I were rewriting this article, I'd have it state that the military has to stand down in time of peace—and I would define time of peace as any time Congress has not officially declared war."

"I'd go a step further, and define peace as any time in which American soil is not under direct attack," says Amelia, a Berkeley student. "I'd have the article state that Congress can't declare war, and so the president can't wage a military conflict, unless American soil has been attacked.

"In such a case, Congress could have declared war after the terrorist attack of September 11, but it didn't. And since it chose not to, the president at the time shouldn't have been permitted to send troops to Iraq and Afghanistan."

"Even if Congress had declared war after the September 11 attacks, it shouldn't have been constitutionally permissible for it to then send troops to those two countries," says Josh. "There was no evidence Iraq was involved in harboring al-Qaeda terrorists, and in the case of Afghanistan, though terrorists did train there, they were citizens of other countries. Besides that, they also trained in 'friendly' nations like Pakistan. Should we have attacked those countries too?"

"We could argue back and forth about that forever," says Ophelia. "But if we at least can agree that it's up to Congress, not the president, to declare war—this is what in fact the Constitution already states plainly—then an improved article can further stipulate that no planned military offenses can receive a penny of federal money if

Congress hasn't declared war. This would place firm restrictions on how and when it can fund the military. We're in wars on multiple fronts abroad, one of them a preemptive war, yet Congress has never declared war. With this constitutional tightening-up of Congress's authority, it would have no choice but to cut off funding if it hasn't declared war."

She then says, "My grandfather gave his life for his country in the 'Korean Conflict.' It was never declared a war by Congress, no more than our incursions from Vietnam to Granada, Iraq to Kuwait, and many other places besides. In fact, there've only been five declared wars in our nation's entire history—the War of 1812, the Mexican-American War, the Spanish-American War, World War I, and World War II. All the many other incursions launched by presidents were unconstitutional. The president is only commander-in-chief; Congress is chief of declaring wars. Our country's military has turned into an unconstitutionally, not to mention unconscionably, militaristic invading force because Congress has allowed one president after another to commandeer their constitutionally designated authority and go to war whenever he wants."

"In preparation for this dialogue, I learned that James Madison related at the Constitutional Convention of 1787 that the original phrase in the article would have given Congress power to 'make war,'" Amelia says now. "But the wording was changed by the Framers to 'declare war.' This change gave the president authority to repel sudden and unexpected attacks on U.S. soil, but prevented him from launching a war unless Congress first formally voted for a declaration of war. So to prevent any future confusion on this issue, I agree that a revised constitutional article must state outright that U.S. troops shall not be sent abroad unless there is first a formal declaration of war by Congress."

"But the article we're re-creating should also state that troops must stand down at home, and U.S. military bases abroad, when there's no conflict," says Josh. "To our Founders, a standing army was just a step removed from a police state." He has a copy of the Declaration of Independence. "One of Jefferson's principle arguments for declaring independence from England was that the king 'has kept among us, in times of peace, standing armies.' Jefferson faulted King George for rendering 'the military independent of and superior to civil power.' He believed there needed to be a blanket prohibition of standing armies, because this was one of the 'fetters against doing evil which no honest government should decline.' If we want to follow through with his vision for preserving liberty at home, we have to do away with standing armies."

"In the existing Article I of the Constitution, Congress also is charged 'to provide for organizing, arming, and disciplining, the militia, and for governing such part of them as may be employed in the service of the United States,'" says Terence, who served in Vietnam. "The Framers intended for the civilian militia, not a professional standing army, to be our first line of defense, well trained and at the ready. By militia, the Framers were referring to what was the equivalent of our National Guard today—a reserve military force under state control though funded largely by the federal government, rather than a federally organized full-time professional force. Both enlistees in the National Guard and the U.S. armed forces today are made up of volunteers, but the difference between the two groups is that the men and women of the Guard aren't regular military.

"As this article also states, it's Congress's role 'to provide for calling forth the militia' and 'to execute the laws of the union, suppress insurrections and repel invasions.' But most of those duties now are ceded to a professional military that was never intended by the Framers to be permanent."

Then he says, "This article doesn't need to be changed all that much. Congress already has the ability, and responsibility, to stand down the army when it hasn't declared war. The Guard and Reserve would still be at the ready, funded and trained in peacetime, and they would simply resume their original and to my mind proper role as our primary defensive forces."

"Maybe we should've never allowed the military to become what it is," says Derrick. "But it is what it is and we need to deal with that. Even in a thought experiment like this, what's the use of proposing an article that doesn't reflect the reality of the nuclear era and the age of terrorism? I'm not saying this just because if the Army stood down, it'd put me out of a job, but because the world is too volatile a place now for us not to have a trained professional army."

Terence thinks about this, and then replies, "Much as I'd like to turn back the clock, I guess I agree: we can't defend ourselves today solely with Guard and Reserve troops. On the other hand, we shouldn't rely solely on a professional army of all-volunteer troops. All Americans have to be part of the shared risk and adversity of being at war to defend our nation.

"The best way for that to happen is if there were an additional constitutional clause that says that all able-bodied men and women age eighteen and over, without exception, are subject to being called on to serve. The existing article detailing Congress's authority on military matters doesn't say anything specific about conscription. What's needed is a clear-cut constitutional statement that all young Americans must take their turn in protecting our nation by serving in the military.

"A fair conscription process in time of declared war would mean that if you're eighteen, you have to be subject to the draft, no excuses, no exceptions. That way no one with connections can get out of serving when called on."

Terence then says, "During the Vietnam War, so many from well-connected families were able to secure continual deferments. They had lucrative careers waiting for them when they got out of college. Their parents pulled whatever strings necessary to get student deferrals or bogus health exemptions. So even with the draft back then, ours was mostly a poor person's army.

"War would never have been a first option in Vietnam if President Johnson's war strategists and members of Congress knew for certain that their own children—as well as members of Congress and government themselves who were of age to serve—were just as likely to be drafted as anyone else."

"It's true, you have to have shared adversity," says Vickie. "If only military families and soldiers feel the pain from the war, and get none of the gain, there's a huge disconnect. If the Constitution dictated that everyone, from extreme peace activists to extreme hawks, absolutely had to face the draft—in the Guard and Reserve in peacetime, and in our other armed services in time of declared war—maybe there'd be a bond among Americans that doesn't exist right now."

"If extreme doves like me had had to be part of the Guard," says her brother Josh, "and couldn't have gotten out of the draft no matter how well connected their families, it might have prevented what happened here at People's Park in the sixties, and the tragedy that followed at Kent State.[6] The doves in the Guard would've never opened fire on innocent civilians no matter what their orders were, no matter the consequences. And they would've tried to keep anyone else from doing so."

"You would agree to be drafted in the Guard or armed forces if it were constitutionally mandated?" I ask.

"I agree that I should have to face the draft if a constitutional article required all able-bodied young men and women to do so. I also believe I have the right to refuse to serve. I'm a pacifist. I object

---

6.  On May 4, 1970, an Ohio National Guard unit opened fire on students holding an antiwar protest on campus, killing four and wounding nine.

to the draft not on religious grounds, but moral ones. If I were ever drafted, I'd probably go to jail."

Then Josh says, "I do believe that some sort of national service should be constitutionally mandatory for conscientious objectors. But I understand that that's not the same type of shared adversity, of really putting oneself in harm's way."

"When Derrick and Vickie told me they were going to South Korea," he goes on, "I researched that country's conscription laws. All able-bodied males there serve for two years, with few exceptions, because of the endless conflict with North Korea, whose military has over 1.2 million soldiers. About 300,000 South Korean males are conscripted every year. Many try to get out of serving for health reasons or with student deferrals. But it's very rare that they succeed. Those who refuse to serve—about a thousand each year—are jailed."

Ophelia then says, "I can understand how some here think that if all Americans of a certain age were subject to a truly fair draft, it'd be the best way to see to it that everyone has a hand in defending our country. Maybe it would help see to it that the U.S. engaged in military conflict as a last resort.

"But even so, the military isn't the best way to protect our country. If we diverted the bulk of funding that Congress budgets for the military-industrial complex and used it instead to eliminate the most extreme forms of global poverty, our nation would come to be seen as the face of compassion instead of aggression. If we took the lead in winning the global wars against poverty, hunger, illiteracy, we'd rarely need to deploy our military, or defend our soil at home."

*Constitution Café Article:* Congress shall have the sole power to provide for the common defense, and to declare war. Congress shall raise and support Armies in time of invasion of

U.S. soil. No appropriation of money for the common defense shall be for a longer term than two years. Congress shall provide and maintain a Navy, and shall make Rules for the Government and Regulation of the land and naval Forces. There shall be no appropriations for U.S. military bases overseas in time of peace, which is tantamount to any time in which Congress has not issued a Declaration of War. When Congress issues such a Declaration, at least half of all military troops shall be drawn from conscription. Every able-bodied man and woman over age 18, without exception, shall be eligible for conscription. In time of peace, all who are conscription-eligible shall perform two years of public service.

## Citizen Soldiers

As a delegate to the Second Continental Congress, which convened after full-scale conflict broke out with Britain, Thomas Jefferson helped formulate the plan for conscripting troops to serve in the Revolutionary War. Jefferson called for a process that made sure that all eligible men would be equally likely to face the draft. He saw to it that the Continental Army was diverse in terms of class composition and so was not dominated by what he called "pauper hirelings." He shared with James Monroe—his fellow Virginian would become fifth president of the United States, following Madison—that it was "a subject of joy that we have so few of the desperate characters which compose modern regular armies" elsewhere. To Jefferson, this "proves more forcibly the necessity of obliging every citizen to be a soldier; this was the case with the Greeks and Romans, and must be that of every free state."

In peacetime, Jefferson was adamant that a standing army must stand down. "The Greeks and Romans had no standing armies," he told Monroe,

yet they defended themselves. The Greeks by their laws, and
the Romans by the spirit of their people, took care to put
into the hands of their rulers no such engine of oppression
as a standing army. Their system was to make every man a
soldier, and oblige him to repair to the standard of his country
whenever that was reared. This made them invincible; and
the same remedy will make us so.

As Jefferson expressed to James Madison in 1789, after the Constitution was ratified, "The following [addition to the Bill of Rights]
would have pleased me: . . . All troops of the United States shall
stand *ipso facto* disbanded at the expiration of the term for which
their pay and subsistence shall have been last voted by Congress."
He didn't want Congress to have any wiggle room when it came to
the possibility of maintaining a standing army in time of peace.

While Jefferson's proposed amendment was not added to the Bill
of Rights, the Framers of the Constitution nonetheless agreed with
his point of view. "What, sir, is the use of a militia?" asked Elbridge
Gerry, a Framer who, under James Madison, would become the fifth
vice president of the United States. "It is to prevent the establishment of a standing army, the bane of liberty." Luther Martin, another
Framer, asserted, "When a government wishes to deprive its citizens
of freedom, and reduce them to slavery, it generally makes use of a
standing army."

According to Richard H. Kohn, professor of history and peace at
the University of North Carolina at Chapel Hill, for Americans of
the founding era "the threat of a standing army was deeply rooted in
their political heritage."

The Boston Massacre in 1770, in which British soldiers killed
several Americans, and the Intolerable Acts of 1774, one of
which suspended civil government and put Massachusetts

under the rule of the local military commander, made hatred
of the army axiomatic in American politics.

Hence, "by the time of the Constitutional Convention, no American political leader could afford to ignore or even to question the
danger of standing armies in peacetime." At one point during the
Constitutional Convention, James Madison went so far as to propose that a clause be added to forbid standing armies in peacetime,
because "armies in time of peace are allowed in all hands to be an
evil." This clause was ultimately deemed unnecessary by the Framers, since to them it went without saying that Americans would
never accept a standing army in peacetime.

Yet our second president, John Adams, quickly expanded the
Army, the Federalist-dominated Congress authorizing his plan
to dispatch thousands of troops to deal with the undeclared war
between the United States and France. Despite the justification set
forth by Adams for the military buildup, much of the U.S. public
was alarmed, since a standing army of any magnitude could also
threaten liberties at home.

Political scholar Elizabeth J. Perry contends in *Patrolling the Revolution* that Jefferson's stance against a standing army proved pivotal
in his eking out a victory against Adams in the presidential election
of 1800. According to Perry, at that time there was "a widespread
preference among the electorate for a . . . citizen militia . . . over the
military professionalism advocated by the Federalists."

By the end of his second term as president, Jefferson had dramatically reduced the number of Army personnel. But with rising
tensions first with France and then with Britain, which would lead
respectively to the Quasi-War and the War of 1812, Jefferson's suc-
cessors arguably had little choice but to reverse this course and
establish a permanent and larger professional military.

Jefferson was no longer president when he acknowledged the

failure of the loosely organized, noncoercive form of conscription that was utilized at the start of the War of 1812. As he told Thomas Cooper in 1814:

> In the beginning of our government we were willing to introduce the least coercion possible on the will of the citizen. Hence a system of military duty was established too indulgent to his indolence. This [War of 1812] is the first opportunity we have had of trying it, and it has completely failed—an issue foreseen by many, and for which remedies have been proposed. That of classing the militia according to age and allotting each age to the particular kind of service to which it was competent was proposed to Congress in 1805 and subsequently; and on the last trial was lost, I believe, by a single vote. Had it prevailed, what has now happened would not have happened. Instead of burning our Capitol, we should have possessed theirs [that of the British Empire] in Montreal and Quebec. We must now adopt it, and all will be safe.

Our nation long since has adopted a professional military. Are we safer for it?

Our standing military has not stood down since the War of 1812. Today the United States has the world's largest defense budget. For fiscal year 2010, the base budget is $533.8 billion, with an additional $130 billion earmarked for the War on Terror. There are over 1.1 million active-duty military personnel, with over a quarter of a million stationed abroad.

In his farewell address, President Dwight D. Eisenhower, a five-star general who served as supreme commander of the Allied Forces in Europe during the Second World War, warned, "In the councils of government, we must guard against the acquisition of unwarranted influence, whether sought or unsought, by the military-industrial complex. The potential for the disastrous rise of misplaced power exists and will persist." By this perspective, our own military might have a greater potential to take down our democracy than an invading force might, bringing into question our nation's long-ago decision to continually build up and permanently maintain the professional armed forces.

## Million-Dollar Babies

"Dang," Michael, 13, says, drawing a frown from his teacher, after I tell him and his classmates that I want them to assume the mantle of our nation's Framers and take a stab at making a brand-new Constitution. I'm at a junior high school in the southwest U.S. Most of the students live in a resettlement shelter with their families, many of them evicted from homes in various stages of foreclosure.

After a protracted silence, Michael again speaks up. "I would want the Constitution to say that every baby born in the USA starts out with $250,000. The moment a baby enters the world, that money is put in a bank account in his name. The only hitch is, he can't touch it till he's eighteen. By then, he'll have decided what college he wants to go to, or whatever it is he's going to do with his life, and he'll have the money on hand to send him on his way."

He looks at us, animated. "Imagine: We'd all be making our way in the world with the same amount of cash. Whether we waste it on bling or make the most of it, what we do or don't make of ourselves, that's our call. But no one can complain he wasn't given a fair chance."

"Man, $250,000 won't be enough to do anything with by the time you're eighteen," says his friend Heath. "After inflation, that amount would hardly pay college tuition and board for four years. We'd all need at least a million bucks apiece."

"Okay, a million bucks gets my vote, too," agrees Michael. "The main thing is, we all get out of the starting gate with the exact same amount, so we'll have the same odds of succeeding."

He turns to me and says, "We've just been studying the Declaration of Independence, and it says we're all created equal. So the Constitution should put its money where the Declaration's mouth is, and make sure we're *treated* as equals. So that means we have to be pretty much financial equals. Like Heath says, a million-dollar payout on the day we reach voting age has a ring of 'equalness' about it."

Ahmad disagrees. "A million dollars doesn't get us all out of the starting gate as equals. If you're homeless, if your parents can't get work, and you can't touch a fraction of that money till you're eighteen, you'll have become desperate long before the time comes to collect the cash. In fact, knowing that money's there, untouchable, will make you *more* frustrated and desperate."

He looks at me. "There's kids a few miles from here who live in these fortresslike mansions. They might as well be a world away, their reality is so different. They couldn't care less if there's a million bucks waiting for them. They're already set for life. These trust-fund babies will get accepted in the best universities, get the best jobs, because they have all the advantages and connections those first eighteen years. Sure, we'd eventually get that million dollars, our own version of a trust fund—*if* we're not in jail by then, or worse, since our lives won't have been fair that first eighteen years."

Frannie isn't buying this. "You're telling me that knowing you've got a *constitutionally guaranteed* million-dollar pot of gold waiting for you when you're eighteen won't motivate you to work hard, stay in school, get a good education? Because you'll *know* the sky'll be the limit once you graduate. You'll *know* if you want to be a doctor, artist, athlete, whatever, you'll be able to support yourself."

Then she says, "As much as I may try to reach for the stars, and sometimes believe that I can just about touch them, the fact is that some of them are out of my reach without a certain amount of money at my fingertips. This article will make all the difference in my life."

"I wish, instead of one lump-sum payout, this constitutional article would let that money start trickling in right now," says Justine. "My parents scrape and claw, but still couldn't keep a roof over the heads of me and my sisters. They signed a loan for a home it turns out they couldn't afford, and everyone who convinced them to sign it knew it—and laughed all the way to the bank. My folks were working two, three jobs apiece and couldn't keep up with the payments. My dad was so ashamed when we were turned out on the street that I wouldn't go to sleep at night. I worried he might try to hurt himself. Then he got mad. Our home is one of thousands that are empty, no chance of anyone buying it. We're back there, 'squatting.' He says it's our right. I'm not so sure, but I'm glad he's mad instead of desperate.

"Mom and Dad have no credit, can't afford the steep rents, can't afford a car, health insurance, tasty meals. If I had that money, you *know* I'd pay for everything my family needs out of my own pocket. And I'd pay cash for a home of our own that no one *ever* could take from us."

Heath chimes back in. "I propose a clause to go along with Michael's article: that no kid inherits a dime, that the Constitution ban inheritances from here on out. That way, all of us will have that million waiting for us at age eighteen, and that's it. It'll make the playing field even more level. All that loot those rich kids would have inherited will go instead into the fund that'll pay for all of us to have million-dollar trust funds."

"That's got my vote," Frannie says. Then she frowns. "I'm wondering: should you have to do something to earn this money, or does it come to you automatically? I mean, shouldn't you have to show that you deserve to tap into that million-dollar ATM? If all you are your first eighteen years is a slouch or troublemaker, why should you get that money? Maybe it should be yours only if you're upright. Like, you should have to show you've been volunteering in your community, studying hard, helping out at home, things like that."

"I hear you, but to me, there should be no strings attached, so no one can make excuses for not succeeding," says Michael. "Sure, a few people will take advantage of their big payday and do nothing good with their lives if they don't have to. But I'm betting most will make the most of this opportunity."

Then he says, "We're offering up a *hopeful* article to the Constitution. It gives everyone the chance to do great things with their lives. For those who are dumb enough to do something bad before they turn eighteen, and wind up in jail, well, they can use their million dollars and atone for what they did—they can start 'scared straight' and drug prevention programs, things like that."

"Once this kicks in," says Michael, visibly proud that his proposed article to the Constitution is winning over his classmates, "only the hardest achievers, the most disciplined, will have the best things, because they've earned it. The only people those who haven't exerted themselves can blame for not succeeding are 'me, myself, and I.'"

Terence has been sitting still and silent until now, intently considering all the views proffered. He shakes his head, muttering, "I just don't know."

I ask him if he has something more he'd like to say. The students lean forward, intent on his every word. Clearly he is respected, and his views carry a lot of weight with them.

"My dad wouldn't agree with this million-dollar deal," he tells us. "He'd think it makes life too easy. My dad says life isn't meant to be fair. Like, he may be down and out right now, but he'd be the first to tell you, 'I've come back before and I'll come back again, because this great country provides everything I need to be a winner.'"

Then he says, "Though he's dog-tired from taking on menial work all day, and then looking for new work all afternoon and evening, my dad helps me with my homework, and with filling out college and scholarship applications. I'm going to be an astronaut. He tells me, 'A hundred colleges may reject you, but there'll be that one that says, "Welcome to our school, where we'll take you to the moon," and it will make those rejections just that much more sweet.'"

Then Terence asks us, "Did you see that movie *The Pursuit of Happyness*."

Just about all of us nod. "Will Smith, who plays Chris Gardner, a dad struggling to make ends meet, talks in that movie about Thomas Jefferson. He might just as well be my dad talking. Will's character says Jefferson was a wise man for giving us a country that doesn't guarantee us happiness, but guarantees us the freedom to pursue it.

"My dad doesn't want anything handed to him on a silver platter, just a shot at getting his hands on that platter through his own hard work. In the little free time he has, he reads civil engineering books. He's self-taught. If he'd had the chance to get a degree, he'd be king of the bridge-building world. You should see the bridges he's designed. He could build a bridge to the moon if he had the opportunity. I don't know how it is that my dad still has stars in his eyes, with his tough life. He raises me on his own. My mom died of cancer when I was little."

Looking at his classmates, he says, "I agree that all us Americans should have a head start, not just some. But I can't see being guaranteed a million-dollar payday at age eighteen. Right now, as my dad mentioned to me the other day, Congress is considering a bill to put $500 in an account for each newborn baby.[7] Even my dad is not

---

7. At the time of this dialogue, a bipartisan group in Congress was considering the possibility of reintroducing a piece of legislation, the America Saving for Personal Investment, Retirement, and Education Act, or ASPIRE, which would give every newborn a lifetime savings account, that would be opened when they are issued a Social Security card. If the bill ever passes, the federal government would make a one-time $500 contribution to the account.

opposed to that, because to him it's a way of showing that our government is making a no-strings-attached investment in each of us, without going overboard about it. Make that sum $50,000, and that sounds like a winner to me—and we can make that a constitutional right from here on out."

There is a pause. Finally Terence says, "I'll tell you what: if each of us *did* get a million dollars out of that starting gate, and I had that money in my hands when I turned eighteen, I'd open up a bridge-building company. With all the bridges crumbling in our country, it should do some good. I'd make my dad the chief executive and designer—great pay, benefits, the works. Not just because he's my dad, but because he's the hardest worker I know."

He turns even more serious. "But don't any of you tell him. If he knew it was sort of a gift, no matter how deserving and overdue, he wouldn't be so happy about it."

> *Constitution Café Article:* All U.S. citizens who have shown that they have "done some good," shall at age 18 receive an equal lump sum payment of at least $50,000.00. If, after receiving the payment, they "do bad," they shall have to return the money. No citizen shall inherit from his or her family so much as a red nickel.

## I.O.U.

Would Jefferson be of the mind that these students expect too much from their country, without demanding enough of themselves in return? Or do their proposals strike an ideal balance, giving our nation's youth an equal jump start in life without encouraging complacency?

The students' article to eliminate inheritance altogether is a more radical twist on one Jefferson himself crafted as part of his statute reform package for Virginia. The article, approved by the legislature in 1776, abolished the English holdover of primogeniture, in which firstborn males received all inheritance. It further eliminated English entails, enormous land grants to the privileged, which Jefferson characterized as remnants of "a system that perpetuated an artificial aristocracy of wealth," and of patrician "privilege and prerogative." As Jefferson wrote in his memoirs, "These laws, drawn by myself, laid the ax to the root of pseudo-aristocracy" in his home state. While Jefferson's bill still assumes some right of parents to provide for their families even after death, the students' constitutional article suggests that eliminating this right altogether is best for all Americans.

Jefferson had intended for the new inheritance laws to be just the first in a series of reforms that would have a leveling effect on society. He also proposed legislation that would make sure that each American had a sufficient amount of the most important currency of his day: land. Land promoted autonomy, liberty, and sociopolitical equality. Virginians could not vote if they didn't own land, much less take direct part in political decision-making; and the vast majority of males at the time were "nonfreeholders," meaning they did not own land.

In addition to the inheritance reform legislation, Jefferson introduced a bill calling for the allotment of a modest amount of land to all Virginia males "of full age neither owning nor having owned acres of land." He wanted to do away with the concentration of land in the hands of a few, lest Virginia become for all intents and purposes a Britain-like feudal system. Most importantly, distributing a modicum of arable land to nonfreeholders would provide them entrée to the political sphere.

To Jefferson, there were other tangible benefits to society as well: having a piece of land enabled people to be close to the earth, and in this way helped them become ideal democrats, since ties to land left them "tied to their country, and wedded to its liberty and interests, by the most lasting bonds." While he didn't think that everyone

should be a farmer, he did believe everyone had to appreciate the
practice of growing some of their own food on their own land,
since this nurtured such key agrarian-type values as self-sufficiency
and industry. Jefferson further contended that cultivating the soil
brought one into intimate contact with nature, and as a result nurtured the virtues of "honor, manliness, self-reliance, courage, moral
integrity, and hospitality." In his *Notes on Virginia*, Jefferson extols
farmers as the "cultivators of the earth," and as such "the most virtuous and independent citizens."

In proposing legislation calling for land redistribution to the
Virginia Assembly, Jefferson stressed that he was "conscious that
an equal division of property is impracticable." However, there
was abundant public land available in the commonwealth, and he
recommended that 50 acres be allotted to each landless male. He
maintained that it was by no means "too soon to provide by every
available means that as few as possible shall be without a little portion of land." Indeed, he contended, it was precisely when the nation
was just coming into being that legislators should complement the
revolution in the battlefield with revolutionary legislation that would
give all Americans a vital stake in the democratic experiment.

Jefferson's bill for distributing land was soundly defeated. Those
in the legislature with the bulk of power were the landed gentry, who
knew that meting out land to all males would dilute their political
clout. Moreover, while they were as ecstatic as the next person to be
rid of the British monarchy, they did not want to be rid of the privileged social and political distinctions that came with their wealth.

The Virginia legislators did, however, agree that most public land
in the commonwealth should be put into private hands. But they
differed with Jefferson over means and ends for doing so. Contrary
to Jefferson's hopes, the legislation that was passed paved the way
for most public lands to be sold to speculators, with the pretext that
the revenue was desperately needed for government coffers. Most of

the speculators proved to be the legislators themselves; they had the means to purchase huge public parcels, and so were able to augment their already significant holdings.

There would be other admirable efforts to distribute land to settlers in U.S. territories, particularly via the Homestead Act of 1862, by which Abraham Lincoln distributed unsettled land in the west to nonfreeholders.[8] But the more typical pattern was for state legislatures and members of Congress to sell public land to speculators (themselves foremost among them), and to railroad and cattle barons. The predictable outcome was that the landless poor drifted to cities, where they often lived in abject poverty. To Jefferson, democracy itself paid the highest price for this failure to provide citizens the basics needed to pursue happiness, because it ensured that political power remained in the hands of a few.

In modern times, land reform efforts in emerging democracies, though often paved with good intentions, have mixed track records. Where land reform has focused, as Jefferson himself proposed, on giving modest landholding titles to individuals, as occurred in Taiwan and South Korea soon after World War II, there have been some successes. But the far more typical outcome is that the promised land remains elusive, with vows by political leaders to enact sweeping reform policies rarely realized. In cases in which some land is redistributed, the process usually is slow and uneven, and often generates new conflicts, with those evicted or displaced when property is reallotted often left landless themselves.

8. Progressive Republicans tried to go much further than this in seeking to guarantee "forty acres and a mule" to free blacks at the end of the Civil War. But the majority in Congress rejected this effort, claiming that such land distribution verged on socialism; the consequence was it forced blacks into sharecropping and led to segregation.

In Brazil, where about 3.5 percent of landowners hold well over half of the nation's arable land, one of the most ambitious modern land reform efforts was launched during President Luiz Inácio Lula da Silva's two-term presidency.[9] Lula succeeded in reapportioning idle land to several hundred thousand of the nation's poor, who have since settled on small plots of farmland. But tens of thousands of landless families continue to live in camps, and violent disputes regularly break out between wealthy landowners and their privately hired militias and landless activists who seek to occupy typically idle parcels of their land.

An entire society suffers when some of its citizens don't have the necessary or instrumental means, such as a piece of land of their own, to fully pursue happiness—at least, if one subscribes to the Jeffersonian perspective that the common good and the individual good are entwined in a democracy.

9. Brazil's constitution states that use of all land must benefit society as a whole. Yet the most destitute own just 1 percent of the nation's land.

# V

# Character Counts

When Jefferson arrived in France in 1784 to begin his stint as U.S. minister, he was considered by freedom lovers in Europe a nearly transcendent figure, his works and deeds on behalf of the cause of liberty a continual source of inspiration. And on both sides of the Atlantic—from Corsica, Italy, where Pascal Paoli and his fellow sons of liberty were fighting long-time autocratic Genoese rule; to Ireland, where radicals were fighting for constitutional reforms; to London itself, where John Wilkes "had assumed Liberty's cause by opposing general warrants, which were issued at large and authorized the seizure of private papers"[1]— many people believed that no one could be "a sincere lover of liberty who was not in favor of communicating that blessing to all peoples." Few Americans more poignantly conveyed this blessing than Jefferson, who was certain that the "ball of liberty" sparked by America's successful struggle for independence "is now so well in motion that it will roll around the globe."

His liberty-loving admirers were able to overlook the fact that Jefferson was traveling with human cargo. Some no doubt did not

---

1. Pauline Meier, *Resistance to Revolution: Colonial Radicals and the Development of American Opposition to Britain* (W. W. Norton, 1992).

yet consider Africans "people," but others, perhaps, understood better than we do today that a leader or politician can be greater in public life than in his or her personal life. Along with his slaves James Hemings and James's sister Sally, with whom he would father at least one child, Jefferson was present in France when revolution at last broke out with the July 14, 1789, storming of the Bastille. Jefferson, who voiced his support for the French Revolution, was even invited to attend and offer counsel at meetings geared toward rewriting the French constitution.

As Annette Gordon-Reed has written, the Hemingses surely were aware that in Paris "the Société des Amis des Noir [The Society of Friends of Black People] was engaged in a very public . . . struggle to include free, tax-paying blacks in the deliberations of the newly constituted National Assembly." There is no question that Jefferson, who attended the assembly gatherings daily, was also privy to this development. One delegate to the assembly, Count Mirabeau, chided those who would not let blacks participate in the Assembly "with words that echoed the debate among the delegates to the American Constitution." Jefferson was likely on hand when Mirabeau delivered an impassioned speech to his fellow assemblymen:

> You claim representations proportionate to the number of inhabitants. The free blacks are proprietors and taxpayers, and yet they have not been allowed to vote. As for the slaves, either they are men or they are not; if the [white] colonists [in French territories who did not want to include blacks] consider them to be men, let them free them and make them electors and eligible for seats.

Mirabeau's powerful speech had its effect: just four years after Jefferson and the Hemingses returned to the United States, people of color in France "sat in the revolutionary National Convention, and the country abolished slavery in its colonies in 1794."

One might reasonably expect that the principal author of the Declaration of Independence, upon witnessing how French citizens (in large measure inspired by his own words) had abolished slavery, would make every effort to replicate their success. Jefferson might not only have taken the lead in calling for the end of slavery in the United States, but argued à la Mirabeau for giving blacks the right to be full participants in all dimensions of American society. While he did not come close to striving to achieve such a progressive objective in the United States, he did take some initiative in attempting to resolve the issue.

Long before he left for France, Jefferson demonstrated both his acute awareness of the fact that slavery had to be abolished, and his own unwillingness to risk much of his political capital to bring this about.

Paul Finkelman, a specialist in American legal history, race, and the law, argues that while Jefferson, as chair of the committee to revise Virginia's legislative statutes, was in an ideal position to address the issue of manumission, or formal emancipation, he "failed to take the lead." So when his fellow assemblymen, soon after the Declaration of Independence was issued, "approached Jefferson with draft legislation that would have brought gradual emancipation to Virginia, he declined to add it to the proposed revisions." For blacks of his time, then, his Declaration amounted to hollow words.

In his *Notes on Virginia*, Jefferson defends himself, contending that in fact he'd proposed an amendment that would have both educated and granted manumission to the children of slaves. Jefferson claims his amendment was never seriously considered because "the public mind would not yet bear the proposition." He would have us believe that while he was far ahead of the public mind on the matter, his fellow Americans simply were not ready to end slavery. But the evidence suggests a murkier conclusion. Jefferson himself acknowledges in his memoirs that if this amendment had been enacted, the freed slaves would have been "colonized" elsewhere, rather than allowed to stay on in Virginia as free and equal citizens.

Peter Onuf, the Thomas Jefferson Memorial Foundation Professor at the University of Virginia, asserts that Jefferson missed an unparalleled chance to tap into the progressive public mind and bring about emancipation:

> Before 1776 most Americans were not prepared to declare their independence. When Jefferson penned the Declaration, public argument needed to be shaped by argument and debate. The manumission movement faced similar obstacles. Many Revolutionary Virginians . . . were ready to consider some form of gradual emancipation. Jefferson might have helped shape the public mind on emancipation just as he had on independence. Even without Jefferson's lead, the legislature adopted a law allowing private manumission *without* expatriation. This suggests that the "public mind" on this issue may have been far in advance of Jefferson.[2]

Jefferson weighed in on the matter again, in 1784, the year before he assumed his post in France. As a member of Congress, Jefferson chaired the committee charged with administering the federal territories and detailing the process by which they could eventually achieve statehood. He drafted a provision that would have made slavery illegal in all existing western territories and all other new territories acquired by the United States after 1800. This provision

2. Onuf further asserts that that there is no evidence that this amendment Jefferson claims to have prepared ever in fact existed.

was rejected by one vote. Remarking later on its defeat, Jefferson said that "the fate of millions unborn [was] hanging on the tongue of one man, and Heaven was silent in that awful moment." This was the one and only time in Jefferson's long political career that he made a fairly audacious attempt to prevent the further expansion of slavery in the United States; but even if it had passed, his provision would have left slavery intact in the original thirteen states. And Jefferson certainly did nothing to set a personal example; he retained throughout his life all of his own slaves at Monticello, rather than granting them their freedom.

Jefferson did make one other attempt to stem slavery: in a draft of his "thought experiment" constitution for Virginia, he composed a clause that proposed gradually bringing slavery to an end. The draft article, which was never submitted to any legislative body much less implemented, reads in part: "The General assembly . . . shall not permit the introduction of any more slaves to reside in this state, or the continuance of slavery beyond the generation which shall be living on the 31st day of December 1800; all persons born after that day hereby being declared free." Finkelman believes this "slavery clause suggests that, in the deepest recesses of his heart and mind, Jefferson *knew* that something had to be done about slavery." If so, Jefferson did not act on this knowledge, but kept it trapped in his notebook.

Perhaps, though, it is not so much this "slavery clause" but the Declaration of Independence that most clearly indicates Jefferson's belief that slavery had to be done away with, and his willingness in this instance to take a vocal public stand. Jefferson's original draft of the Declaration, before it was subjected to editorial revision by the Continental Congress, included a caustic denunciation of the slave trade as "a cruel war against human nature itself," but it was stricken from the version approved by the Second Continental Congress. Still, the two words "created equal" would prove over time to carry the spark that would ignite change.[3] Frederick Douglass, the former slave who became a social reformer and one our nation's foremost abolitionists, held up the Declaration as "an abolitionist manifesto."[4]

This perhaps disproves the idea that actions always speak louder than words. In Jefferson's case, his words have had more resounding (and more positive) effects than the decisions he made in his personal life. Still, the chasm between Jefferson's ideals of liberty for all and his inability or unwillingness to champion the abolition of slavery leads us today to question his character.

An Associated Press–Ipsos poll found that a decided majority of Americans consider a presidential hopeful's character far more important than his or her political experience or specific stances on issues. But what on earth do we mean by character? And is good character a requirement only for our leaders? Or is it up to the rest of us too to conduct ourselves in a way that we can hold up as an example to our children, our fellow citizens, and to newcomers to the United States?

## Scout's Honor

*Article II, Section 1, Clause 5, of the Constitution:* **"No person except a natural born Citizen, or a Citizen of the United States, at the time of the Adoption of this Constitution, shall be eligible to the Office of President; neither shall any person be eligible to that Office who shall not have**

---

3. The original opening sentence of Jefferson's unedited draft of the Declaration is "We hold these truths to be sacred and undeniable; that all men are created equal and independent, that from that equal creation they derive rights inherent and unalienable, among which are the preservation of life, and liberty, and the pursuit of happiness."

4. James Colaiaco, *Frederick Douglass and the Fourth of July* (Palgrave Macmillan, 2006).

**attained to the Age of thirty-five Years, and been fourteen Years a Resident within the United States."**

After I finish describing my Constitution Café project, Francisco points to the Constitution I'm holding and says, "What does it say about the qualifications to be president? In case I decide to run someday, I'd like to go ahead and get started fulfilling them."

"It only says that the president has to be born on U.S. soil," I reply, "that he has to be thirty-five years old, and that he has to have resided in the U.S. at least fourteen years."

Francisco is incredulous. "That's it? You don't have to have done any good deeds? You don't have to take a test to show you know the Constitution? You don't have to be an upstanding citizen?"

I hand him the Constitution and let him and his fellow Boy Scouts examine the pertinent section. We're meeting in a park near the fringes of the Mission District of San Francisco, where I once lived and frequently held philosophical dialogues with elementary-school children (we called our gatherings a Philosophers' Club). Despite recent gentrification, gangs and drugs are still prevalent, and the area school dropout rate remains high.

"You can have been in a gang?" asks Arturo, still in disbelief. "You can have hurt someone and still try to become president of the United States?"

"You're not automatically barred from being president, or contending to be president, if you've done such things, though it may not help your chances of getting elected," I say. "According to the article you looked at, you can be removed from office after you've been elected if, as the Constitution says, you commit 'Treason, Bribery, or other high Crimes and Misdemeanors'[5] while in office. But

5. From Article II, Section 4, of the Constitution.

there's nothing that says you can't have committed a crime before you run for office."

This revelation gives the group pause. Francisco shakes his head and says, "That's not right."

Then Emilio, 15, says, "You want us to help you write a new article, so here it is: 'All presidential candidates should have to live by the Boy Scout's motto. They must promise to be trustworthy, loyal, helpful, friendly, courteous, kind, obedient, cheerful, thrifty, brave, clean, and reverent. Anyone who wants to be president of the United States should have to prove, by his actions, that he has these values before he can even think about running for the highest office. Because he's supposed to be the 'values leader' of all of us. He wants to be put on a pedestal, so he should have to be the American role model to end all role models."

Then he says, "As Scouts, there's more than one hundred merit badges you can earn, for everything from Civics, to Emergency Preparedness, to Citizenship in the World. Believe me, if you don't have these twelve Scout qualities, you'll never earn a single merit badge. Because you don't just master a project by accomplishing a task—because the tasks are designed so that you can only really master a subject if you also have mastered the Boy Scout qualities. A presidential candidate should have to show he's mastered these qualities too, if he's going to be worthy of the task of being president.

"Like, a presidential candidate might prove he's kind by giving a lot of his time and energy to helping out the poor. And, if he's already a politician, he can show he's thrifty by being even more careful with taxpayer money than with his own. And if he's never been a politician before, he can show that he's careful with his family's money, or with the finances of his business or the business of his boss. But when it comes to his own money, he should also show that instead of spending everything on himself or his family, that he also gives a lot to charities, so we'll know he's investing in the country's neediest people."

"And candidates for president can show they're 'clean' not just by being neat and tidy and organized, but by giving proof that they'd be an honest president instead of a dirty one," says Arturo, an imposing kid whose uniform is plastered with merit badges. "They can do this by making it known that they don't have a rap sheet that shows they've been arrested for things like accepting bribes. And they can have their wives give testimony that they've never cheated and never even hit on another woman."

"That's not the only way a candidate can show he's clean," says Nelson. "There's more positive ways. Like, all the people you've worked with over the years, as well as your friends, should come forward and tell about all the great things you've done, and how trustworthy and loyal you've been. You see, like we've been trying to explain to you, all these Scout values are connected. I've learned that you can't really practice one of them all the way unless you practice the rest of them all the way."

"I'm not sure presidents should have to practice the Scout value of always being cheerful," says Amado. "I mean, when the president is informed that one of the soldiers he's sent to war has been badly injured or killed, what's there to be cheerful about? Maybe he should have to rally the troops, keep them motivated, tell them right is on their side. But cheerful? You can put a brave face on things even as you cry, even be optimistic about how things are going to turn out over the long run, but not cheerful."

"How would a president demonstrate reverence?" I ask.

"Let me put it this way: whenever I give the Boy Scout oath, I pledge 'to do my best, to do my duty to God and my country,'" says Francisco. "When the candidate who's elected president gives his oath of office on Inauguration Day, he promises to obey the Constitution, 'So help me God.' That means that in obeying the United

States Constitution, he's honoring God, showing reverence for the higher power that inspired our patriots in the Revolution to fight and sometimes die for this great democracy."

"But a president isn't, or doesn't have to be, a Boy Scout," says Amado. "A president doesn't even have to believe in God, according to that article Chris showed us."

"Should this new article we're creating say he should have to?" I ask.

He mulls this over. "Reverence in a country like ours can mean being courteous and kind and helpful even to people who don't believe or think like you do. My dad says lots of people who claim they believe in God are all the time yelling and screaming at each other, and even trying to hurt others, just because they have different beliefs. So they're not being very reverent to the peaceful and loving God of Christianity. Our own Founding Fathers and Mothers came here to escape persecution just so they'd have a place to live in peace and harmony while they worshiped in their own way.

"A person who wants to be president must show by example that he's tolerant of people who don't look or think or believe like most other Americans do. A president would go out of his way to put his arm around these people and say, 'Let's be reverent to these people so we can all live in peace.'"

"I have a classmate at school who doesn't stand for the Pledge of Allegiance," says Arturo. "She believes in God. But it's against her religion to stand up and put her hand over her heart while we recite the Pledge to start the school day. I respect her. When other classmates tease or taunt her, I stand up for her, and they stand down. Any presidential candidate who allows people to be teased, or teases people himself, just because they don't look at things the way he does, or act like he would in every situation, should have to bow out of the presidential contest. He's not being reverent to the values of a country like America."

"A candidate for president should show he's always first to stand up for any kind of underdog," says Francisco. "This requires bravery and kindness on his part. I used to be a bully. I teased anyone who was weak or a sissy. Mr. Espinosa, our troop leader, straightened me out about that.

"My mom made me join the Scouts because I was hanging out with a gang. I didn't much like the Scouts at first. I acted up a lot, like I was too cool for the Scouts. But anytime I teased the other members of my Scout troop, Mr. Espinosa made me run laps, so I'd have some time and space, when I wasn't cramping for air, to think about whether I had what it took to be a Scout. After a while, he got through to me.

"See, according to our handbook, a Scout believes that being brave means having 'the courage to stand for what he thinks is right even if others laugh at or threaten him.' And I finally realized that I'd been leaning towards joining a gang not because I had courage, but because I didn't. A Scout learns bravery so he knows to go his own way when others tempt him to do bad things. If I can go my own way, the presidential candidates sure can too."

Emilio elbows him. "If you ever run for president, I'll testify that you were brave. You were the one who convinced me not to even think about joining a gang." Francisco smiles with pride.

Then Emilio says, "Scouting trains you to be the right kind of a leader, the do-gooder kind. See, you don't work to have the Scout qualities just for the sake of them, but so you always are strong in the right way, protecting the weakest and most helpless. It shouldn't be asking too much of people who want to be president to prepare to be that kind of leader."

"Really," he goes on, "we should make it a requirement, in a sep-arate constitutional article that we can work on later, that all the people who run for any office, like to be a senator or a congressman, have these Scout qualities. Because if the president's the only one who has them, and none of the people he has to work with to pass laws do, it'll be a constant battle between good and not-so-good."

"As long as at least the president has these qualities, we'll all be okay," says Arturo. "Because all the people running for other offices will know that voters want them to have these qualities—because these are the qualities that the voters themselves try to have and value the most. Besides that, all these other politicians usually have it in the back of their minds that one day they'll run for president, so they'll be sure to be on their toes and practice all the Scout qualities."

Then he says, "This article may be about the ideal qualities we want in a president, but most of all, if you read between the lines, it's really about the ideal qualities we want in ourselves."

Soon afterward, Nelson says, "There's another quality a candidate for president—and, like Emilio said, all the other candidates for high offices—should have besides the Boy Scouts' ones. He should be humble. Like, if I ever decide to run for president, I'm not going to go around everyplace bragging about all these Scout qualities I have. I'm not going to distribute a DVD about 'Nelson the All-Around Great Leader Boy Scout.' I'm going to let my actions speak for themselves. Like, I wouldn't ever run a negative campaign, smearing and slamming others candidates, no matter what they say about me. I'll just show quietly and humbly the person I try to be every day."

Everyone nods to this.

Amado seems to hesitate, then takes a deep breath and says, "My sister is a member of the Girl Scouts. Their motto is, 'Be prepared.' I think a president should have to follow that motto too."

He seems braced for teasing. But Arturo simply nods and says, "The best way to be prepared to be president is to know who the best people are to look to for advice, so that when unexpected troubles come along, you're ready to respond. The president is in charge of everything, but he can't know everything. So he has to show how prepared he is by surrounding himself with experts in different areas. That way, when the president needs advice on things like how to best respond if there's an oil disaster like the one in the Gulf of Mexico, or there's an outbreak of a new type of flu virus, he's got the right people on the spot to make sure matters don't just get worse and worse, but are handled in a way that the hurt and damage is kept to a minimum. President Obama was a Scout, so he has no excuse for not being prepared for what happened in the Gulf."

"My grandfather lost his retirement savings after putting in forty years on the docks," Emilio tells us. "He blames the 'rotten economic advisors' of at least the last two presidents for the fact that he's had to go to work at Wal-Mart as a greeter just to survive."

After a pause, Nelson says, "A candidate for president doesn't have to be a guy. She might be a Girl Scout. And if she practices this Girl Scout motto, she'll be a strong candidate. And she'll be an even stronger one if she practices that motto while also developing the Boy Scout values, since these are the values you need in order to be prepared for just about anything."

"Actually, Girl Scouts already have their own similar sorts of values," says Francisco. "I know, because my sister is also a Scout. Besides that motto that Amado mentioned, they also have a slogan: 'Do a good turn daily.' A president should wake up each morning with the thought, 'I'm going to do the American people a good turn today.' Like, he might wake up and say, 'You know what? I'm going to call someone everyday, someone I've read about in the newspaper who's having a hard time, and not just give her a pep talk, but offer all the help and support I can.' He'll also make sure his good turn stays out of the headlines. Because he's not doing it for publicity, but because he really wants to do his duty to God and country."

*Constitution Café Article:* No person except a natural-born citizen of the United States shall be eligible to the Office of President; neither shall any person be eligible to that Office who shall not have attained the age of thirty-five years, and been fourteen Years a Resident within the United States. Anyone eligible to be President must be trustworthy, loyal, helpful, friendly, courteous, kind, obedient, cheerful (when the occasion calls for it), brave, clean, humble, and reverent (respectful, and tolerant, especially of underdogs and people who think and believe differently). He or she shall be prepared, and shall do a good turn daily, and in so doing, shall further do their duty to God and country.

## Virtuous Politicians

The idea of constitutionally requiring elected officials to possess certain virtues isn't far-fetched, if constitutions of the Revolutionary era are our yardstick.

Pennsylvania's original constitution, for instance, stipulated that all prospective candidates demonstrate "virtue and wisdom." And to this day, New Hampshire's constitution states that "a constant adherence to justice, moderation, temperance, industry, frugality, and all the social virtues, are indispensably necessary to preserve the blessings of liberty and good government." Consequently, voters must "have a particular regard to all those principles in the choice of their officers and representatives," given that they have the "right to require of their lawgivers and magistrates, an exact and constant observation of them, in the formation and execution of the laws necessary for the good administration of government."

In *The Transformation of Virginia*, Rhys Isaac relates that Virginia's colonists looked at elections as opportunities to choose a candidate whose "virtue showed most clearly in their persons." They rejected "trials of strength between contending social classes and popular choice between rival programs," since they considered these "precisely the lines upon which . . . elections should *not* be conducted."

To this end, Isaac relates, a public announcement placed in Acco-mack County, Virginia, in 1771 seeking freeholders to vie for par-ticular offices made clear that prospective candidates must possess a range of virtues. For instance, the candidates must have "penetrating Judgment," so that they would be able "to scan each Proposal, to view it in every Light." They must further have the talent of "pierc-ing into Futurity," in order to "behold even how remote posterity may be thereby affected." What's more, the ideal officeholder, as the paragon of virtue, must be one "who regards *Measures*, not *Men*," and so, according to Isaac, "will follow his country's interest regardless of the effect of his course upon either his friends or his foes." Conse-quently, as the announcement stressed, candidates were expected to possess "that Fortitude, or Strength of Mind, which enables a Man, in a good Cause to bear up against all Opposition, and meets the Frowns of Power unmoved."

The virtues that Virginia's voters demanded in their elected rep-resentatives, according to Isaac, clearly "owed a great deal . . . to their own sense that they were engaged in a momentous struggle that would determine the destiny of mankind." In 1769, among all those vying to serve as Albemarle County's delegate in the Vir-ginia Assembly, Thomas Jefferson was deemed the person most reflective of voters' values, virtues, and aspirations in what would prove to be a pivotal moment. At age 26, Jefferson was elected to be his county's representative in the House of Burgesses. Upon arriv-ing in the stately chambers in Williamsburg, the political neophyte was struck by the fact that "our minds were circumscribed within narrow limits, by an habitual belief that it was our duty to be sub-ordinate to the mother country in all matters of government." This collective shortcoming, Jefferson surmised, was not due to any lack of "reflection and conviction" on the part of his brethren, but rather it resulted from "habit and despair."

Jefferson expressed his confidence that "they could bring their minds to rights on the first summons of their attention." And in fact, just ten days into his tenure as a burgess, the legislators' attention was summoned: Parliament had passed the Townshend Acts, placing levies on many of the colonists' common staples, such as glass, lead, paper, paints, and tea. In response, the burgesses passed a resolution establishing that they, not Parliament, were the only governing body that could legitimately impose taxes on the colonists. Their unusual feistiness prompted then-royal governor Lord Botetourt to dissolve the legislature. He was sure that this move would force the burgesses to capitulate, but it only heightened their resolve. Upon being evicted from their chambers, Jefferson relates that they repaired straight to the Raleigh Tavern, where they formed a "nonimportation association" aimed at rousing all colonists to boycott the newly taxed goods. This unexpectedly defiant act by the burgesses prompted England to do away with all the new taxes, except the pesky one placed on tea.

After the Townshend Act controversy was resolved, Virginia's royal governor called for new elections. Lord Botetourt was certain that the legislators' action had been out of step with their constituents' sentiments, and that the burgesses who'd opposed the Crown's will would be ousted from office. Just the opposite happened. Jefferson relates that all the burgesses "were re-elected without any other exception than of the very few who had declined assent to our proceedings." This was clear proof that the burgesses not only had dispensed with habit and despair, but now had taken up a cause—to put their colonists' interests above those of their mother country—that endowed them with the virtues most prized by their constituents.

## Men and Women Without a Country

*Article I, Section 8, Clause 4, of the Constitution:* "Congress shall have Power . . . To establish an uniform Rule of Naturalization. . . ."

The expressions on their faces range from excitement to incomprehension to disbelief.

"You want *us* to help you make a new Constitution for your country," says Enrique. His world-weary face is offset by wide-eyed wonder.

Enrique looks at his friend Ricardo for confirmation that he had not misunderstood my explanation in Spanish of what my project is about. Ricardo, who helped arrange this gathering in a mid-sized city in the South, once lived near my family and me in Mexico. He was a fixture at the Socrates Café I held in the historic plaza of San Cristobal de las Casas, nestled in the highlands of Chiapas. Though extremely industrious, the best job he could land back in Mexico was as a six-day-a-week handyman at a hotel that paid him the equivalent of $4 for a ten-hour workday. When Ricardo failed to show up for our dialogues, most felt sure the inordinately thoughtful father of three and local social justice activist had "gone north."

Nearly three years later, Ricardo called me in the United States. He said that he hadn't gotten in touch earlier because he was ashamed he hadn't shared his plans with me. But he said he wasn't sure at the time that he'd go through with it, and so he hadn't let anyone know outside his immediate family. He went on to tell me, with evident pride, that he had a well-paying job. But his voice broke when he confessed how much he missed his wife and three daughters.

Our joyful reunion was tempered by apprehension. Months earlier, federal officials had raided a local industrial plant employing undocumented workers. Friends and relatives of many of today's participants, including two of Ricardo's cousins, were taken into custody and likely will face deportation proceedings.

Those who join Ricardo and me at the diner where he works are mostly from Mexico, though at least one person is from Guatemala. All are in the United States illegally.

After I assure Enrique that I do indeed want the input of everyone on hand in helping create a new constitutional article, he says, "Your country's Constitution should say that the U.S. always puts out the welcome mat for refugees. The U.S. owes it to its unique history to have an article like that. It would reflect a core value that all Americans should share, of being welcoming to people who are unwelcome in their own homeland. After all, every American, even Native Americans, has ancestors who came here from somewhere else, and often because they were persecuted in some way."

"Right now, your Constitution gives Congress power 'to establish an uniform rule of naturalization,'" he instructs me. "But it doesn't say what that uniform rule should be. This new Constitution should have an article that says political asylum is automatically granted to all refugees."

"You can usually qualify for a green card only if you can prove that you're a political refugee, meaning your life would be in danger if you returned to your homeland," Ricardo now says. "Under those circumstances, I have no hope of becoming a legal citizen, much less bringing my family here so they can one day get citizenship.

"But the first Americans not only came here from someplace else, but came here because they were economic refugees, like we are. Keeping that in mind, this new Constitution should have an article that states, 'All refugees are to be welcomed.'"

"Our Constitution should place no limits of any kind on immigration?" I ask.

Guillermo, a cousin of Enrique's who entered the United States nearly a decade ago, replies: "Enrique and Ricardo only said there should be no limits on the number of *refugees* who immigrate. A refugee is someone who leaves his country to escape some kind of persecution. In our case, we were persecuted for trying to live like human beings, to put food on the table for our families, send our kids to decent schools. Anybody in his right mind would flee that situation to seek out a better life in another land."

"On the other hand," he goes on, "it should be impossible for the people in power who exploited Mexico and made our lives a nightmare to leave the country. They're not refugees. Yet they're welcomed in other countries with open arms."

Enrique nods. "Our former president Ernesto Zedillo is now a big shot at Yale.[6] While president, he called for peaceful dialogue to promote indigenous rights, all the while militarizing the areas around those indigenous communities that had leftist leanings. By the time he left Mexico for greener pastures, Mexico's indigenous inhabitants were in more desperate straits than ever. But he's a saint compared to our former president Carlos Salinas de Gortari,[7] whose corruptions and crimes are astonishing even by Mexican standards. On top of approving the scandalous NAFTA treaty and engaging in such a spending spree that the peso had to be devalued drastically, ruining the middle class and poor, he stole hundreds of millions from our treasury. Now he lives like a king in London."

"People like Salinas de Gortari cross borders—and usually in their own jets—whenever they want," says Guillermo. "There's a big difference between them and refugees like us, who may die crossing the desert to escape the persecutions of a Salinas de Gortari."

"We never had rights in Mexico, though our homeland's constitution says we all have equal rights," says Oscar. "Even when I was out in the open, I was invisible. I worked my fingers to the bone, and received less than nothing in return. Here, though I have no legal or constitutional rights, my employer treats me with respect. He pays me a good wage and has given me raises for my hard work. I stay

---

6. Zedillo, president of Mexico from 1994 to 2000, is director of Yale's Center for the Study of Globalization. He was the last president from Mexico's ruling Institutional Revolutionary Party, which had held power for seventy-one years, before Vicente Fox of the National Action Party was elected president.

7. Salinas de Gortari was Mexico's president from 1988 to 1994.

with my cousin's family, so I've been able to send most of my earnings back home. Now my children can eat nutritious meals, and they go to a good school instead of laboring in the fields with my wife."

"My brothers and several cousins were arrested by *la migra* [immigration enforcement officers], and are being deported," he then tells me. "They'll keep rounding us up until the economic crisis goes away. We're the convenient scapegoats. These days, I stay locked up in my apartment when my shift at work is over. None of us would even go to the May Day parade, because we were scared we might be nabbed."

He says next, "This community was dying before we got here. We were mostly made to feel welcome. We all met each other halfway: we overcame suspicions, because we knew we needed one another. Now, the locals and undocumented workers keep their distance."

"I know we're supposed to be helping you make a new article for the U.S. Constitution," says Enrique, "but I can't help thinking of my own country's. It is a beautiful document. Article 3 says it is the duty of Mexico's federal government to provide all children an education that will 'develop harmoniously all the faculties of the human being and shall foster in him at the same time a love of country and a consciousness of international solidarity, in independence and justice.'"

His smile is more sad than sardonic. "That is sheer poetry. But the reality is pure *mierda*. Millions of Mexican children have no hope of going to school. Millions more go to schools where the teachers are poorly paid and educated. But you're punished if you raise much of an outcry, if you insist to politicians that they do their job and enforce the constitution.

"In 2007, hundreds of teachers in Oaxaca, the poorest state in Mexico, were jailed for protesting the pitiful state of education. I was a teacher there. I earned under $200 a month. I couldn't support my family. So here I am, working in an industrial plant—or, I *was* working at one, until my boss's employment records were audited by immigration officials and he was forced to let go of all undocumented workers. Now I'm thinking about going back to Mexico. But if I do, I'll have to work like a slave for slave wages again. And there'll be no chance I can come back here, not with all the new security on the U.S. side of the border."

"Really, we have no country," says Oscar. "We aren't citizens of anyplace. I wish I could be a citizen here, wish I could vote, pay taxes, be even more active in the community. As hard as I work in the U.S. now, if I was a citizen, I would break my back to give thanks."

Then he says, "Americans who don't like our presence here call us 'wetback.' I know it's derogatory, even racist. But I take it as a compliment. Our backs are wet from working so hard." He grins. "Besides the 'wet-foot, dry-foot policy' the U.S. has for Cubans—if a Cuban arrives on dry land before he's apprehended, he's allowed to stay—your Constitution should establish a 'wet-back, dry-back' policy. Those whose backs are the wettest—who work the hardest, sweat the most, who give everything they have to make this great country even greater—should be the first in line to become citizens."

"We send back most of what we make to our families and relatives," Ricardo soon says. "The remittances we make are a top source of revenue for Mexico. That kind of contribution should earn us high honors and privileges as Mexican citizens. We don't do it for that reason, but it isn't right that the people who are honored in our country are the most dishonorable ones."

Susana breaks the silence following a lull. "My twin daughters were born here, so they automatically have the privilege of being citizens of the U.S." The soft-spoken Guatemalan is the only woman present.

"Do you believe they should be given automatic citizenship because they were born on U.S. soil, as our existing Constitution stipulates?" I ask.

She gives this a good deal of thought. "I'm glad it's that way, because of how things are. In an ideal world, I'd bring them back home to Guatemala, to a land of plenty. If I'm deported, they'll stay on here with relatives, though it would break my heart. It would be unfair for them to come with me to a country where they'd have no future. I've been reading how conservative legislators in some states, and some U.S. senators, want to change the Fourteenth Amendment so that children of economic refugees who are undocumented no longer can become U.S. citizens, but I think this would put us more in the shadows than ever."

"As long as there are economic refugees," she goes on, "a constitutional article like this one Enrique suggests is good and just. It puts the rest of the world on notice that if our home countries don't treat us well, we'll find a decent place for ourselves in the U.S. and work our hearts out to justify the privilege of being here.

"Exploitative countries like Mexico and Guatemala can't afford for *all* of us to leave. It's possible that the only way they'll ever enforce the rights in their constitutions is if they realize that they'll have an empty country if they don't."

Ramiro then says, "What I would give for such an article as the one we're talking about. It'd allow my family to come here and join me. No matter how much I might want to, I can't go back to Mexico. It would fill me with joy to be with my family again, but then would come the sadness for not being able to provide for them."

Then he says softly, "I just want the constitutional right to work at home and earn enough to live in dignity. I want the constitutional right to be with my children, the right to listen to my daughter breathe softly in her sleep." He falls silent for a moment. "I can see my Angelina in my mind, where she is still little. I see myself singing her to sleep while strumming my guitar. It's how I put myself to sleep at night. I haven't seen her in over four years."

Eventually, Ricardo says, "The constitutional article Enrique proposes would make sure Americans don't forget their 'founding identity,' no matter how hard some try.

"I hitchhiked once all the way to New York just to see the Statue of Liberty. At its base, there's a bronze plaque with a poem. I was so moved by it that I wrote it down, and I carry it with me." He pulls out of his pocket a folded piece of paper: "'Give me your tired, your poor, your huddled masses yearning to breathe free, the wretched refuse of your teeming shore. Send these, the homeless, tempest-tost to me, I lift my lamp beside the golden door.'"

He looks at me. "The narrator of the poem really is America itself, or Lady Liberty speaking on America's behalf. She's inviting all repressive countries to send their poor here, and she's promising us refugees that she'll not only leave the lamp on for us, but open the golden door and welcome us into this country. That's America at its most beautiful."

> *Constitution Café Article:* Congress shall have Power To establish an uniform rule that grants political asylum and facilitates the Naturalization of all Refugees. Congress shall prevent entry to the United States of corrupt world leaders.

## Room for One More

Jefferson generally extolled the virtues of maintaining an open-door policy when it came to immigration. In 1801, he delivered his first Annual Message (what is now the State of the Union) in the midst of a period of great influx of immigrants to the United States. Jefferson confronted the issue in his inimitable way, with questions: "Shall we refuse the unhappy fugitives from distress that hospitality which the savages of the wilderness extended to our fathers arriving in this land? Shall oppressed humanity find no asylum on this globe?"

He held that immigrants should not just be welcomed as guests, but expeditiously made U.S. citizens in order to ensure that they'd be "secured against like oppressions by a participation in the right of self-government." He feared that if immigrants did not promptly enjoy the constitutional rights of all Americans, they would continue to be exploited. Further, he stressed, he was guided in his sympathies toward immigrants by "the animating consideration that a single good government becomes thus a blessing to the whole earth, its welcome to the oppressed restraining within certain limits the measure of their oppressions."

Alexander Hamilton, himself originally an impoverished West Indian native, cited Jefferson's address in a published essay opposing immigration, ridiculing its "pathetic and plaintive exclamations." Hamilton referred to the new wave of immigrants as "truly the Grecian horse to a republic" and warned that the nation "cannot be too careful to exclude its influence." He'd argued at the Philadelphia Constitutional Convention that the only ones who should be welcomed to the United States in the future were Europeans "of moderate fortunes," who should be "placed on a level with first citizens."

Forgetting his own roots, Hamilton asserted that immigrants seeking U.S. citizenship must already share our cultural and ethnic backgrounds, since those who did not represented a threat to the "uniformity of principles and habits" necessary for "a common national sentiment." But to Jefferson, a shared background might mean a common love for and yearning to live in a democratic society with its promised freedoms to pursue and promote happiness. He believed that people of vastly different cultures and belief systems might nonetheless have a higher, shared allegiance to the principles of democracy itself.

Jefferson's predecessor as president, John Adams, and the Federalist majority in Congress, as part of the Alien and Sedition Acts, dramatically increased the length of time it took for an immigrant to become a U.S. citizen from five to fourteen years. While Adams and the Federalists in Congress claimed that it was vital to national security that immigrants reside in the United States for a significant amount of time before they could become citizens and obtain the right to vote, they may have had another motive; the fact was that immigrants tended to vote Republican. When Jefferson became president, the Immigration Act of 1802, which he endorsed, changed the residence requirement back to five years.

As he expressed in a correspondence with a Mrs. Church during the Revolutionary and Napoleonic wars in Europe, it was vital that the United States provide "a sanctuary for those whom the misrule of Europe may compel to seek happiness in other climes. This refuge once known will produce a reaction on the happiness even of those who remain there." Such a safe haven, he believed, would serve as fair warning to "their task-masters that when the evils of Egyptian oppression become heavier than those of the abandonment of country, another Canaan is open where the subjects will be received as brothers."

There is no reconciling Jefferson's hypocritical and inhumane stance when it came to supporting policies that allowed Africans to be brought against their will to the United States, where those who survived the harrowing journey were made slaves. But in terms of permitting voluntary emigration to the U.S.—and he clearly was referring at the time to white Europeans—Jefferson maintained that there should always be room for one more. He went so far as to assert in his manifesto *A Summary View of the Rights of British America* that our forebears "possessed a right, which nature has given to all men, of departing from the country in which chance, not choice, has placed them, of going in quest of new habitations, and of there establishing new societies, under such laws and regulations as, to them, shall seem most likely to promote public happiness."

Today's immigrants are not establishing new societies in the way the original settlers were, but rather are venturing to established ones. Even so, when we welcome immigrants, our society will invariably change, just as those who come to America will be transformed to some degree.

## Loyalty Oath

*Article VI, Section 3, of the Constitution:* "**The Senators and Representatives . . . , and the Members of the several State Legislatures, and all executive and judicial Officers, both of the United States and of the several States, shall be bound by Oath or Affirmation, to support this Constitution; but no religious Test shall ever be required as a Qualification to any Office or public Trust under the United States.**"

"We've just sworn not only to 'renounce and abjure all allegiance and fidelity' to the country of our birth, but to 'support and defend the Constitution and laws of the United States of America against all enemies, foreign and domestic,'" says Naji. "It's a little intimidating even to pretend to redo a Constitution we've just given our undying loyalty to."

Even so, he and the other recently naturalized citizens on hand have agreed to consider participating in my project. I'd gotten to know Naji, an information technology specialist who came to the United States from Syria twelve years ago on a work visa, over the course of several Socrates Café gatherings. He'd invited me to attend his citizenship ceremony the previous week. The others taking part had become friends with him during the months they'd spent in classes preparing for their citizenship exam. After the ceremony, Naji said to me, "I can't believe I'm now an American citizen, just like you."

Eventually, Jimena—one of the increasingly rarefied illegal immigrants from Mexico who succeed in gaining citizenship—says to us, "It occurred to me, as I was studying for my citizenship test, that even those born on U.S. soil should have to make a loyalty oath of some sort. The fact that they're born here doesn't mean they'll be loyal to the Constitution. On the other hand, taking an oath as we had to do is no guarantor of loyalty either. But it is a solemn and moving event. It makes you really think about, and feel, what it means to be an American citizen, and what your privileges and duties are."

"If Americans born here took part in such an event, they might even be inspired to know their own Constitution," she goes on.[8] "Once, I was at a café poring over the Constitution as part of my study regimen for my citizenship exam, when it suddenly struck me that your"—Jimena checks herself—"*our* Constitution, *my* Constitution— I have to get used to saying that—does not once mention the word 'democracy.' Democracy should ring loud and clear from every page. I told a person sitting next to me at the café about my shock over the lack of the 'd-word' in the Constitution, and she said, 'Really? I've never read the thing myself.' What does that say if some Americans don't care, or don't have to care, to know about the document that enables them to live so free? Aren't they sure to lose the most important part of who they are and what they're all about?"

"People born in the U.S. shouldn't have to pass some test about the Constitution to be citizens, but they should of course want to know and appreciate it," says Zhang, from China.

"I'm a literacy volunteer. When I told one of my students a couple years back that I'd begun the process of becoming a naturalized citizen, she congratulated me and then recited to me passages of the Declaration of Independence that she knew by heart. And she

---

8. A nationwide poll conducted in 2010 by the Center for the Constitution revealed that few Americans—less then one-third—have actually read the Constitution, though the same comprehensive poll reports that the overwhelming majority of Americans recognize the enormous impact of the Constitution on their everyday lives.

said, 'Young man, before you give your oath, I will be able to read to you the entire Declaration, and the Constitution too.' From then on, she and I worked on reading them as part of her literacy instruction. The week before I became a naturalized citizen, she read both of them to me."

Then he says, "Some segments of American society throughout this country's history have been intentionally kept down and out—and by people who could read the Declaration and Constitution, but couldn't care less that they were betraying its ideals in the cruel way they treated fellow Americans. This student of mine may not have to give a loyalty oath like we did, but she's loyal to the American dream, to making it come true for herself and her children."

After a pause, Naji says, "Elected federal officials are required by the Constitution to give a loyalty oath. Article VI requires all federal and state legislators, as well as all executive officers and all judges, to give an oath or affirmation in support of the Constitution. The oath is similar to the one we had to take to become citizens."

He reads from a copy of the congressional oath that is currently administered: "'I, [name], do solemnly swear (or affirm) that I will support and defend the Constitution of the United States against all enemies, foreign and domestic; that I will bear true faith and allegiance to the same; that I take this obligation freely, without any mental reservation or purpose of evasion; and that I will well and faithfully discharge the duties of the office on which I am about to enter.'"

Then Naji says, "Even though this constitutional clause regarding the oath they must take says that 'no religious test shall ever be required as a qualification to any office or public trust,' most elected officials being administered the oath add 'so help me God' at the end. It's not part of the oath, but it's clearly important to them that their constituents know they're not only loyal to the Constitution, but to God."

"On the other hand, in the loyalty oath that naturalized citizens are administered, even if we're atheist, we're required to say at the end, 'so help me God,'" says Jimena.

Then she says to me: "Did you know that the oath we take in order to become naturalized citizens isn't even a constitutional requirement? It's only a mandate of the Immigration and Nationality Act of 1952 and can be done away with at any time by an act of Congress. I'll read it to you: 'I hereby declare, on oath, that I absolutely and entirely renounce and abjure all allegiance and fidelity to any foreign prince, potentate, state, or sovereignty of whom or which I have heretofore been a subject or citizen; that I will support and defend the Constitution and laws of the United States of America against all enemies, foreign and domestic; that I will bear true faith and allegiance to the same; that I will bear arms on behalf of the United States when required by the law; that I will perform noncombatant service in the Armed Forces of the United States when required by the law; that I will perform work of national importance under civilian direction when required by the law; and that I take this obligation freely without any mental reservation or purpose of evasion; so help me God.'"

"Should the oath administered to naturalized citizens be made a constitutional requirement?" I ask.

Jimena thinks this over. "Except for the 'so help me God' part, yes it should." And then: "Everyone who becomes a naturalized U.S. citizen has a special status, though not quite like that of an elected official. We have 'elected' to become citizens of the United States. For those of us fortunate enough to pass through all the citizenship hurdles, we're sort of like official goodwill ambassadors for the U.S."

Then Zhang says, "Many of us naturalized citizens undoubtedly appreciate the promise of this country more than many born here. We appreciate that the rights in the Constitution are guaranteed, and that if you're denied them by anyone, you have real recourse to have them restored. Many of us come from countries with constitutions in which guarantees of rights and liberties are just empty words. China's constitution mentions again and again that it is a 'democracy,' and that all citizens are equal, and have all sorts of freedoms that can never be denied to them. These empty words in my native country's constitution make it a hurtful one, a betrayal of what a constitution is supposed to stand for."

*Constitution Café Article, Section 1:* Senators and Representatives, and the Members of the several State Legislatures, and all executive and judicial Officers, both of the United States and of the several States, shall be bound by Oath or Affirmation, to support this Constitution; but no religious Test shall ever be required as a Qualification to any Office or public Trust under the United States. The oath they shall give shall say: "I, [name], do solemnly swear (or affirm) that I will support and defend the Constitution of the United States against all enemies, foreign and domestic; that I will bear true faith and allegiance to the same; that I take this obligation freely, without any mental reservation or purpose of evasion; and that I will well and faithfully discharge my duties and responsibilities."

*Constitution Café Article, Section 2:* All naturalized citizens of the United States shall be administered the following oath: "I hereby declare, on oath, that I absolutely and entirely renounce and abjure all allegiance and fidelity to any foreign prince, potentate, state, or sovereignty of whom or which I have heretofore been a subject or citizen; that I will support and defend the Constitution and laws of the United States of America against all enemies, foreign and domestic; that I will bear true faith and allegiance to the same; that I will bear arms on behalf of the United States when required by

the law; that I will perform noncombatant service in the
Armed Forces of the United States when required by the
law; that I will perform work of national importance under
civilian direction when required by the law; and that I take
this obligation freely without any mental reservation or purpose of evasion."

## Oath of Allegiance

The oath that all immigrants are required to take before they become
naturalized citizens is officially called the Oath of Allegiance. General Washington administered the first such oath at Valley Forge on
February 3, 1778, before the military campaign against the British
began in earnest. With the aim of ferreting out British sympathizers, Congress had passed a law requiring all officers to profess and
sign an oath swearing their allegiance to the cause set forth in the
Declaration of Independence.

All the officers who stood before Washington placed their hands
on the Bible and recited the oath. One officer, General Charles Lee,
withdrew his hand. When Washington asked him to explain himself, Lee replied, "As to King George, I am ready enough to absolve
myself from all allegiance to him; but I have some scruples about the
Prince of Wales." His reply elicited a great deal of laughter, but "covered a deeper motive . . . Lee was then playing a desperate game of
treason, and probably had some conscientious scruples about taking
such an oath which he would probably violate." Lee was eventually
dismissed from the army for direct disobedience of Washington's
orders.[9]

Today's Oath of Allegiance taken by naturalized citizens is not

9. Benson Lossing, *Our Country* (Kessinger Publishing, 2004).

a constitutional requirement, as Jimena pointed out during our gathering, but rather is stipulated by an act of Congress. At other times in our nation's history, Congress has mandated the administration of loyalty oaths to American citizens themselves, typically during times of fear or uncertainty. Congress did so during World War II, and again in 1947, when increasing tension between the United States and the Soviet Union generated anticommunist hysteria, leading President Harry Truman to launch an initiative aimed at determining the loyalty of the federal workforce. Truman's Federal Employee Loyalty Program included "an examination of any files held by any government agency, from the FBI to schools." If an employee refused to take part, he was charged with disloyalty and dismissed from his position. If he did participate and was charged with disloyalty, he could defend himself at a Loyalty Review Board hearing. Following Truman, individual states launched their own loyalty programs, and in particular investigated teachers at schools and universities. Out of principle, many teachers refused to participate and were usually fired.[10]

Georgia still has "loyalty legislation" on its books, requiring all job applicants to fill out a loyalty form, and Oklahoma requires employees to sign a loyalty oath after thirty days on the job. California is also among the states that require such an oath.[11] In 2008, an employee at a California university was temporarily dismissed for refusing to sign it. But Marianne Kearney-Brown, a Quaker, was reinstated after signing an oath tailored especially for her, which stated that if she had to defend her state and country, she only had to do so in nonviolent ways.

---

10. Peter Knight, *Conspiracy Theories in American History* (ABC-CLIO, 2003).

11. As is New York, where I had to sign an oath of allegiance to the Constitution before I could teach at New York University.

...

Would Jefferson believe that one best demonstrated one's loyalty to the nation by solemnly swearing to always support and defend the Constitution?

Newspaper editor John Colvin once asked Jefferson whether there were occasions when one could act outside the letter of the law in good conscience. Jefferson replied that while the "strict observance of the written laws is doubtless one of the high duties of a good citizen . . . it is not the highest." He believed there were "laws of necessity, of self-preservation, of saving our country when in danger, [which] are of higher obligation" even than constitutional law. "To lose our country by a scrupulous adherence to written law, would be to lose the law itself, with life, liberty, property and all those who are enjoying them with us; thus absurdly sacrificing the end to the means."

Thurgood Marshall, the renowned civil rights lawyer and first African-American appointed to the Supreme Court, echoed this view of Jefferson's in his autobiography. Marshall believed that

> there is something 'higher' than the Constitution—that is, quite simply, the people. I do not mean that 'the people' are not bound to live under our system of laws. . . . But what I do mean is what Thomas Jefferson said in the Declaration of our Independence—that just governments derive their authority from the consent of the governed. And because of this, you have not only the right but also a responsibility to the government of this country.

By this perspective, all U.S. citizens have a civic responsibility to make sure that the government is working in a way that does right by everyone, and by democracy itself. To that end, Marshall contended that Americans must be loyal above all else to embracing "all of the qualities that Jefferson embodied: commitment to difficult projects, confidence in the soundness of one's own vision, and perseverance in working through a problem."

But did Jefferson in fact embody these qualities?

John Dewey acknowledges that political expediency compelled Jefferson "to deviate on special points," and that, moreover, Jefferson was "disposed to be conciliatory and compromising." Even so, Dewey asserts, "there are few men in public whose course has been so straight," even as Jefferson demonstrated "inconsistency between professed principles and actual behavior:"

> [I]f Jefferson is better known for his political ideas and his public acts than as a human being, it is just what he would have wished for himself. Considering his times and the difficult and important part he played in them, there remains the image of a magnanimous, high-spirited public gentleman who subordinated himself with complete devotion to what he conceived to be the welfare of the country he loved.[12]

But the "special points" on which Jefferson deviated were crucial ones, and they eventually had to be addressed if public life in the New World was going to be revolutionized. Aside from the fact that Jefferson's professed views on the equality of all were contradicted by his prejudice toward blacks, he was hypocritical in his stance on women's rights. "Jefferson assumed without argument that women were by their very nature excluded from the public realm," notes the important Jefferson scholar Joyce Oldham Appleby. In Jefferson's worldview, women "think naturally of home and hearth, of husband and children, and rarely (if at all) of wider public concerns."

12. Dewey's encomium to Jefferson is from his *Living Thoughts of Thomas Jefferson* (David McKay Co., 1940). Jefferson even insisted that the public not celebrate his birthday, Dewey notes, "on the ground that the only birthday he wished to have recognized was 'that of my country's liberties.'"

Albert Gallatin, secretary of the treasury during Jefferson's presidency, upon relating to Jefferson that there was a dearth of qualified applicants for a number of posts in his department, suggested the names of a number of qualified women. Jefferson dismissed out of hand Gallatin's recommendations, replying, "The appointment of a woman to office is an innovation for which the public is not prepared, nor am I." The enlightened view of his own cabinet secretary makes it clear that in important respects Jefferson's own mind lagged behind the most progressive minds of his times.

It would be up to others to embrace the promise of the Declaration and advance the cause of women and of blacks. Touching on the issue of slavery in an 1814 communiqué with Edward Coles, a Virginia aristocrat, Jefferson reflected, "the hour of emancipation is advancing in the march of time." He was honest enough, however, to acknowledge that he would not be the one to lead this advance: "This enterprise is for the young; for those who can follow it up and bear it through to its consummation. It shall have all my prayers, and these are the only weapons of an old man."

In judging Jefferson's character, as Jefferson critic Joseph Ellis stresses, one should not divorce Jefferson's actions from the times in which he lived: "Lifting Jefferson out of that context and bringing him into the present is like trying to plant cut flowers." But even when considering Jefferson's deeds firmly in the context of his times, Ellis chastises Jefferson for the fact that his "utter devotion to great principles" was compromised by "a highly indulged presumption that his own conduct was not answerable to them."

Yet Jefferson did believe that he should be held accountable for his deeds by future generations. Jefferson described how he judged others: "by their lives. For it is in our lives, and not from our words," that one must gauge one's character. "By the same test," he held, "the world must judge me."

## Radical Character

The astute Jefferson biographer Fawn Brodie was intrigued by the fact that Jefferson managed throughout his career to be a consummate political insider while remaining on the radical fringe: "rarely if ever has a man with such a radical bent won so many elections from such an electorate." Yet back then, it was not as rare as it is today for someone to be part of the mainstream yet have the temerity to propose drastic changes that would challenge the status quo. Indeed, the argument can be made that the only Americans who were not inclined to radicalism were the minority of entrenched power brokers among them, including the Framers.

Even Joseph Ellis—who characterizes Jefferson as "a flawed creature, a man who combined massive learning with extraordinary naïveté"—asserts that the one element of Jefferson's character that was unchanging was his inveterate radicalism. Ellis notes that "no one, . . . including the ever-skeptical Adams, ever doubted his radical credentials." Jefferson showed that there didn't have to be a contradiction between working diplomatically with the mainstream in government and endorsing radical ideas.

Yet today, it is widely assumed that a radical is necessarily an outsider, even an extremist. But what seems to characterize those labeled today as "radicals" of the left, right, or center is a dogmatic mindset; they are convinced that their respective viewpoints are beyond reproach or debate. Yet a "Jeffersonian radical" today would assert that if the original American character is to be revived, much less to evolve, then we must slough off the dogmatism so pervasive today and replace it with an enthusiastic openness to new points of view. Such a radical would actively seek out compelling objections and alternatives to her own view, recognizing both that no one has a monopoly on wisdom and that diversity and differences of opinion are good for public life.

# VI

## Money Matters

"No taxation without representation!" This indelible slogan of the American Revolution, crafted by Boston patriot James Otis, still rings in our national consciousness. There's no more eternal nor potentially irresolvable political argument than that between those who see taxes as a necessary way to fund public goods—including infrastructure, education, police, public health, and national defense—and those who see taxes as a chokehold on individual liberties.

The agony of taxpaying is of course part of our birth story, since as every schoolchild knows (or should know), the New World colonies revolted against England in large measure because its empire-expanding agenda left it drowning in debt, and so to raise money, the British Parliament enacted loathsome levies on the colonists without their advice or consent.

Yet most colonists remained victims of taxation without representation even after winning the Revolutionary War, since in almost all cases, only property holders could vote. Even the constitution for the new state of Massachusetts, where colonists had been the most militant when it came to protesting taxation without representation, did not grant voting rights to those who did not own property. As a consequence, many were still denied the right to participate in public affairs.

Nonlandowning citizens of Massachusetts were angered and insulted by the fact that the wealthy landowners and industrialists had created a state constitution that disqualified them from voting or holding office. Two militia captains, Samuel Talbot and Lemuel Gay, took the lead in airing their complaints publicly. In resigning their commission as officers in the militia, they expressed their bitterness over how they and the soldiers serving under them had been "by the Constitution disenfranchised, for want of property." The state's first governor, John Hancock—president of the Second Continental Congress, and a signer of the Declaration—upon learning "how bitter it was for men who had put their lives on the line to find that they were voteless and ineligible to hold office," might have been expected, as a leading revolutionary figure and patriot, to insist to the state legislature that the constitution be changed on their behalf. Instead, he ignored their appeals.[1]

The Framers of our national Constitution also failed to fully address the issue of taxation without representation: they gave Congress the power to tax all those living in the United States, even though women, blacks, and taxpayers who didn't own property were usually denied at both the state and federal level the right to vote for those who supposedly represent them in Congress and would have authorization to tax them. To this day, those who live in U.S. territories and possessions, and in Washington, D.C., are subject to federal taxation even though they have no direct representation in Congress.

Congress took its taxation powers to new, constitutionally murky heights in 2009 when it passed a stimulus package that cost taxpayers nearly a trillion dollars. Yet while it added dramatically to the rampant spending and borrowing that triggered the recession

---

1. Gary Nash, *The Unknown American Revolution: The Unruly Birth of Democracy and the Struggle to Create America* (Penguin, 2006).

in the first place, there's little indication that it has helped abate our ongoing economic crisis. Jefferson believed government's wasteful ways encouraged its citizens to be copycats. Would Americans be more responsible spenders and savers on a personal scale if they could exert more influence over stemming federal profligacy? Would Americans have more clout if they all enjoyed taxation *with* representation? What if even noncitizens who paid federal taxes could vote for members of Congress?

## Taxation with Representation

*Article I, Section 8, Clause 1, of the Constitution:* **"The Congress shall have Power To lay and collect Taxes, Duties, Imposts and Excises. . . ."**

"No taxation without representation," says Sheila. "This has to be stated point-blank in a constitutional article. It's what the American Revolution was all about, after all. Yet the only thing the Constitution says on the subject is that Congress 'shall have power to lay and collect taxes, duties, imposts, and excises.' But Congress should only have taxing authority over people who have taxation *with* representation. A revised article should say that no one can be taxed who doesn't have this right."

I'm at a small plaza in the Washington, D.C., suburb of Takoma Park, Maryland, where I once lived. About fifteen others in this municipality of 17,000, which has long enjoyed a reputation for cutting-edge politics—it was the first place in the nation to declare itself a "nuclear-free zone"—have joined me to examine Congress's taxation powers.

Sheila, a producer for a popular radio program, says next, "If the article I'm proposing were already in the Constitution, all residents of Washington, D.C., would have at least one voting representative in the House, and two in the Senate. Either that, or they wouldn't have to pay federal taxes. I moved from D.C. to Maryland a decade ago in part out of frustration over the fact that I had no voting representative."

Washington, D.C., is a federal district. While it is governed by a mayor and city council, Article I of the Constitution dictates that Congress has ultimate authority over its affairs. The district has one nonvoting member of Congress, and no U.S. senators.

Jessie, who works for the U.S. Agency for International Development, says, "This article should give all those on U.S. soil who pay federal taxes the right to vote in federal elections, just as they have the right to vote here in Takoma Park in local elections."

Takoma Park is the largest municipality in the United States to grant suffrage rights to noncitizens, including unregistered immigrants. Maryland's original constitution extended voting rights to all "inhabitants" of the state. But in 1810, during a time of widespread anti-immigrant sentiment, the state legislature rescinded this right, amending the state constitution to restrict suffrage to citizens. However, this limitation only applied at the state level of governance. Exploiting this loophole, Takoma Park activists in 1991 succeeded in passing a referendum that not only allows noncitizens to vote in local elections, but also to run for local office.

"Most of those residing in our nation who are denied the right to vote on the federal level make significant contributions to their communities, and so to our country," Jessie goes on. "They deserve representation in Congress as much as any other person who pays federal taxes."

"That's going too far," says Mason, a State Department analyst. "I agree in principle that all American citizens, wherever they may live, should have voting members of Congress, and that if they don't, they shouldn't have to pay federal taxes. But I draw the line with giving noncitizens, whether here legally or not, suffrage in federal elections. Yes, many surely are major contributors to our community and country, but they're here by choice. I've spent over half my adult life overseas, and have paid my fair share of taxes abroad. But I'd never expect, much less demand, voting representation in any nation of which I'm not a citizen. So I can't agree to extend full-fledged voting rights in federal elections to noncitizens."

"What about a noncitizen who is serving in our military, and who might risk his life to defend U.S. soil?" Jessie asks him.

"I honor his service to our country," Mason replies. "But he's doing this of his own free will, in part out of the promise of having his citizenship application expedited. I don't feel anyone should be able to vote in federal elections, and have voting representation in Congress, unless he's an American citizen."

"I've been a permanent resident of Singapore for nearly three decades, and of course I'm not allowed to vote there," says David, an architect who is here visiting his parents. "As a U.S. citizen, I take advantage of my right to vote in my country's federal elections. My voting precinct is Takoma Park, the place in the U.S where I last voted. My children are twenty-two and twenty-five, they both have good jobs, and pay lots of federal taxes. Though American citizens, they've never lived on U.S soil. The Uniformed and Overseas Citizens Absentee Voting Act guarantees the right to vote in federal elections to all American citizens living temporarily or permanently abroad. But—and here's the Catch-22—because my children have never lived in the U.S., they don't have a designated voting precinct. So they're effectively denied their right to vote.

"So until we make sure that all U.S. citizens not only have the right to vote in federal elections, but actually *can* vote, I'm not prepared to consider extending this right to noncitizens. Ideally, the more than four million expatriates should have their own voting representative in Congress. We're taxed at a much higher rate than

Americans living on U.S. soil, because we don't have a voting representative standing up for us."

"Many people born on U.S. soil aren't U.S. citizens," Jessie says in due course. "Only those born in the fifty states, in the District of Columbia, and in Puerto Rico, automatically are citizens.[2] Those born on the other island territories that are U.S. possessions have never been given the right to citizenship—and it's a right that can be taken away at any time from Puerto Ricans; they were granted citizenship by an act of Congress, but there's nothing in the Constitution that automatically guarantees this to them."

"As it is, Puerto Ricans are treated like second-class citizens," she goes on, "just as D.C. residents are. They're taxed by Congress, though they have no voting representation in either chamber. Only those American citizens who reside in states have the guaranteed constitutional right to vote for members of Congress."

"All the more reason to stipulate, in a revised article, that those Americans who don't have voting representation in Congress should not have to pay federal taxes," says Sheila. "Or—and this would be better—the article could state that all those born on U.S. soil, whether a state, territory or other U.S. possession, are automatically U.S. citizens, and as such, must have the right to voting representatives in Congress."

"Well, those who live in 'nonstates' that are under United States jurisdiction receive a lot of federal dollars that are used for building and running schools, hospitals, infrastructure development projects," says David. "Above and beyond that, the residents of Puerto Rico and Guam choose not to be states; they prefer to be independent entities. And at least in the case of Guam, though citizens do

2. In 1917, almost two decades after American forces ousted Spanish troops from the Caribbean island, President Woodrow Wilson signed the Jones-Shafroth Act, which extended U.S. citizenship to Puerto Ricans.

pay federal taxes, I believe all that money is returned to their government." He thinks some more. "But even so, they're as much a part of this nation as the rest of us, and I agree they deserve to be treated as if they are in a 'statelike' place when it comes to having taxation with representation, so they have elected officials who look out for their particular interests. So until they have voting representation, they shouldn't have to pay federal taxes."

"Article IV of the Constitution gives Congress the power to create new states," says Jessie. "This new article can give Congress an additional authority: to grant all those born and raised in U.S. territories and possessions the statelike right to have voting representation in Congress."

"That has my vote," says Sheila, then adding, "If the patriots of the American Revolution knew that so many Americans today still are victims of taxation without representation, they might wonder if their sacrifices were worth it."

Her son Chad, 14, has been sitting silently during the entire exchange. But now he says: "Many states refuse to allow prisoners convicted of felonies to vote either in state or federal elections—not only while they're in prison but even after they're released. So this article maybe should see to it that they get voting representation before any noncitizens are granted it."

And then he says, "But where do you draw the line? I mean, I'm a citizen and I've been paying federal taxes for the last two years, since I started working as a dishwasher at a restaurant. But I can't vote for four more years. There's eighteen-year-olds I know who don't work, and so don't pay taxes of any kind, but they get to vote. Why can't I?"

*Constitution Café Article:* The Congress of the United States, comprised of a House and Senate, shall have power to lay and collect taxes, duties, imposts, and excises over American citizens, and over all others who are both born and residing on U.S. soil, who are represented by voting members of said Congress.

## Suffering Without Suffrage

While Jefferson did succeed in reforming Virginia's legal codes as they pertained to inheritance, he was not uniformly progressive when it came to the issue of taxation. When he was a member of the Virginia House of Delegates, he did propose a bill (which was defeated) that would have created a system of taxpayer-supported free public education. But all in all, he did not believe that elected officials should have the power to spread the wealth by taking from the rich and giving to the poor. "To take from one, because it is thought his own industry and that of his father has acquired too much, in order to spare to others who (or whose fathers) have not exercised equal industry and skill, is to violate arbitrarily the first principle of association," he maintained in a letter to the French Enlightenment aristocrat Antoine Louis Claude Destutt de Tracy.

Jefferson approved of the Framers' decision to give Congress taxing authority. As he told Francis Hopkinson—fellow Founding Father and delegate to the Continental Congress—in 1789, he "approved from the first moment of . . . the power of taxation" granted to Congress in the new Constitution. But he didn't support all the taxes they enacted. Since members of Congress were elected directly by voters, he believed that taxation authority should reside with them, because in a sense it gave the people themselves oversight, at least in theory. In practice, Jefferson didn't always abide by Congress's decisions when it came to levies. As president, he repealed all so-called internal taxes that had been approved by his Federalist predecessors, eliminating federal excise taxes on everything from whiskey to land.

In his first inauguration speech—considered one of the most

memorable in our nation's history (not to mention the first)—
Jefferson stressed that the "suffrage of the people" was a fundamental right. Yet most who'd supported the Revolutionary War were
denied the right to vote in local, state, or federal elections. Only the
State of New Jersey came close to granting universal suffrage; its
founding constitution granted "all free inhabitants" the right to vote.
From 1776 until 1807, women, free blacks, and noncitizens residing
in New Jersey could vote in local elections. But in 1807, the state
legislature backtracked and passed a new law that restricted voting
to "free, white, male citizens," eliminating any chance that what had
been by far the most democratic approach to suffrage might eventually be emulated in other states. Meanwhile, noncitizens who were
property holders—wealthy white males, in all cases—continued to
enjoy a right that was denied to most U.S. citizens, along with the
right to run for public office. Not until 1926 did Congress rescind the
right of noncitizens to vote in federal elections.

## Debt Be Not Proud

*From Article I, Section 8, Clause 4, of the Constitution:* **"The
Congress shall have Power . . . To establish . . . uniform
Laws on the subject of Bankruptcies throughout the
United States."**

"A section in Article I of the Constitution gives Congress sole
authority to establish 'uniform laws on the subject of bankruptcies
throughout the United States,'" says Simone, a credit counselor. "But
'uniformity' doesn't even enter the equation. Congress's bankruptcy
laws are bankrupt."

Simone, a friend from my high-school days who'd moved to the
area over thirty years ago, is chiefly responsible for spreading the
word about this Constitution Café gathering, which has mostly

attracted participants who have been impacted by the debt and credit crunch.

"The article needs to be retooled," she goes on. "It should direct Congress to establish 'a uniform law *for* the *subjects* of bankruptcy throughout the United States.' That way, all bankrupt 'subjects'— whether a megabank, one of the big car manufacturers, a farmer, a financier, a single mom struggling to make ends meet, or a blue-collar worker—are treated exactly the same."

I'm in a diner of a medium-sized town located in what is known as the Southern Auto Corridor. Over the past decade and a half, auto and auto-parts assembly plants have sprung up, attracted to this stretch of the Deep South in part because of strong antiunion laws. Many have closed or have laid off a large percentage of their workforce in the last several years. Vast stretches of farmland stand shoulder to shoulder with enormous exurbs built during economic boom times. Many tracts are half-developed, the projects abandoned. A number of the buildings near the diner, which has been in the same family's hands for over a century, stand vacant.

Dell, a local car dealer who has had to close two of his three franchises since the economic downturn, says to Simone, "Your suggestion would be a big improvement, though there's no guarantee Congress will follow it. As you pointed out, our representatives don't properly exercise the constitutional authority they already have. They've mandated all these different bankruptcy 'chapters' with a crazy quilt of laws. How these laws are applied differs according to whether you're a big or small business, whether you're poor or middle class or rich. And the new comprehensive financial reform law that Congress passed does nothing to address this hypocrisy."

"As we all know," he goes on, "Congress refused to allow some of the biggest banks, investment firms, insurance companies, car manufacturers, to go under. Though their problems were every fault of their own, they were considered indispensable to the American economy. But most small businesses were allowed to go under, even though most were operating responsibly. That can technically be considered 'uniform treatment' on the part of Congress, in the sense that it has uniformly enacted bankruptcy laws that favor the largest corporations. But that's surely not what the Framers of the Constitution had in mind."

Beverley, a certified public accountant, then says, "Unfortunately, the Supreme Court itself, which is supposed to make sure the Constitution is followed to the letter, contributed to this 'un-uniform'— and in my opinion unconstitutional—treatment of Americans in bankruptcy when it gave corporations all the rights of individuals. Bankruptcy laws are skewed towards the interests of corporations because they have the resources to influence Congress in a way we mere mortals can't even dream of."

In the 1886 case *Santa Clara County* v. *Southern Pacific Railroad Company*, the Supreme Court ruled that corporations could lay claim to the same rights as individuals, including the right to political and other noncommercial free speech. Our Constitution makes no mention of corporations. The Framers hadn't anticipated the central role they would come to play in the development of our economy. But by the nineteenth century, corporations were at the forefront of raising the vast sums of investment capital needed to undertake large privately financed projects, such as the building of the private railroad system, including the portion spearheaded by Southern Pacific. In the Supreme Court ruling in this case, corporations were accorded all the rights of individual persons. Opponents then and ever since have argued that this decision has undermined the democratic process: since corporations have exponentially more resources at their disposal than individuals, they not only can control commercial speech, but political and other noncommercial speech as well.

Beverly says now, "At least with a revised article, we can stipulate that bankruptcy laws must be applied evenly to individual persons and corporate persons alike."

"At its origins, this constitutional article we're discussing was a revolutionary attempt at fairness by our Framers," says Elena, a university professor whose particular scholarly interest is the history of debt in America. "It gave Americans the right to enter bankruptcy proceedings and to emerge with a fresh beginning. Prior to that, if you were in debt, you were put in a debtors' prison, usually ruined for life. When this article became part of the ratified Constitution, bankruptcy became a right for every American."

"Though there were, just as now, financial panics triggered by irresponsible borrowing and lending, the great majority of Americans back then who went bankrupt were honest and frugal, but through hard luck still fell on difficult times," she continues. "This constitutional article was meant to protect both creditors and debtors equally, to make sure both sides—or 'subjects'—were treated fairly in bankruptcy proceedings. The Framers understood that creditors and debtors both had an important role in growing the economy.

"Most everyone profited by this article's intent, including democracy itself. It created a thriving middle class and built an economic engine that had to be reckoned with by other nations. But in the generations since our founding, Congress has distorted its intent, to the extent that bankruptcy laws today almost entirely favor creditors and the big conglomerates. While predatory practices by lenders and banks may be curbed somewhat by the new financial reform laws, the fact remains that when an individual or small business enters bankruptcy, few protections are afforded from Congress's bankruptcy laws."

The *New York Times* reports that debtors' prisons are on the rise again in America: "It comes right from the pages of 'Little Dorrit,' Charles Dickens's scathing indictment of Victorian England's debtors' prisons. Unfortunately, it is happening in 21st-century America."

For instance, in the state of Minnesota, arrests and imprisonment of people unable to pay their debts—often for amounts of less than $100—had risen 60 percent in the last four years.[3]

"But it's not Congress's fault that creditors and debtors forgot the purpose of credit and went on a borrowing and lending frenzy," says Abby, owner of the diner where we're gathered. "No one forced people to borrow like there was no tomorrow. In my parents' and grandparents' time, you'd do anything to keep from going bankrupt, because you were looked down on for being careless with your or other people's money. Now there's no stigma attached to being financially irresponsible. If people can't pay their loans, they just walk away from them with the attitude, 'I'll just file for bankruptcy.' I'm not sure a constitutional article can do anything to remedy this."

"It looks like I'm the only farmer in attendance, so I'll speak up," says Curtis after a pause. "The early rain and cold weather this year really hurt area farmers. I only got 30 percent yield on my crop. Some farmland has been declared a federal emergency, but all that means is I can qualify for a low-interest federal loan—putting me more deeply in debt.

"Family farms are still the backbone of this country. Congress recognizes this, and that's why there's a special bankruptcy chapter for farmers. While the types of federal loans I qualify for under this chapter may ensure that I can continue to barely stay afloat, they also ensure that I stay in debt for life. On the other hand, the big agribusinesses that play with the same funny money as any other conglomerate somehow manage to thrive in bad times; the more debt they get into, the more their stock value seems to go up. It leaves me scratching my head."

Then Dell says, "Maybe bankruptcy laws *should* give special treatment to businesses considered indispensable. The problem is that

3. This according to a June 9, 2010, report in the *Minneapolis Star Tribune*.

Congress considers indispensable the wrong businesses—the relative handful of big corporations rather than the more than 27 *million* small ones that keep America strong. It should be giving special treatment to all the small businesses in this country that play by the rules and have real connections to their communities—especially to the small-town banks that refused to lend one irresponsible dime, while the big boys were giving anyone and everyone a loan who wanted one without reviewing their application, yet now find that they're as much impacted as the rest of us by the economic crisis brought on by the large banks."

"Because our largest banks have played such a central role in triggering bankruptcies," Elena says to us, "a new constitutional article on this subject needs to state specifically how Congress can make sure that from here on out, they play only a positive role in helping businesses of all sizes thrive."

"That sounds good on paper," Curtis chimes back in, "but the thing is, nowhere in the existing Constitution is Congress given the authority to regulate banks. But Congress does so anyway—and it does a miserable job at that. If any entity has this authority that Congress has assumed, it's the states. Yet only one state has a bank of its own. North Dakota."

Started in 1919, the Bank of North Dakota (BND) is a state-owned and -run financial institution, the only one of its kind in the nation. All state and local government agencies are required to place their funds in the bank. North Dakota started a state bank in order to prevent predatory lending, particularly to farmers. Today, while most states are experiencing enormous deficits, North Dakota enjoys a surplus.

"The Constitution should say outright that the states, rather than Congress, regulate banks. That would do away with the Federal Reserve, which has brought on so much of this mess by playing enabler of financial irresponsibility to our largest corporations."

Finally, Simone says, "Congress's authority for creating a uniform bankruptcy law has to be aimed at ensuring that bankruptcy hardly ever happens. As has been pointed out, there are times and circumstances when, no matter how careful a person is, she might still default on her loans. In such cases, bankruptcy laws should serve as a safety net. For that to happen, the powers granted to Congress by the Constitution have to be such that all involved in the 'debtor-creditor transaction' are responsible and accountable, just as the Framers envisioned."

> *Constitution Café Article:* Congress shall have Power to enact legislation that treats impartially all the subjects and objects of bankruptcy throughout the United States, and shall have Power to sustain and perpetuate a creditor-debtor system of responsibility and accountability. The States shall charter and regulate banks.

## Bank Rupture

As governor of Virginia, Jefferson helplessly looked on as the state's economy collapsed. Shortly before he took office, as he relates, the legislature repealed "so much of an act as makes it penal to offer or pay, ask or receive, more in paper bills of credit of this commonwealth or Congress, for any gold or silver coin, or more in the said paper bills for any property, real or personal, than is asked or offered in gold or silver." In other words, the legislature had opted to quit tying the dollar's worth to the gold standard, which had long held the value of paper money steady. When inflation struck, the value of paper bills plummeted. Since Virginia's constitution had established a weak governor, giving virtually all power to the legislative assembly, Jefferson could do nothing to stop this.

As critical as Jefferson was of the legislature's financial folly, he mostly blamed the nation's money problems on banks. He distrusted private financial institutions, which had the power to issue currency and credit, and to control interest rates. Writing to his friend John Taylor, Jefferson remarked, "banking establishments are more dangerous than standing armies," what with their "demoralizing" lending practices.

He believed that only financial austerity would enable the United States to remain independent. Even before the Revolution was won, he lamented to fellow Virginia patriot Richard Henry Lee in 1779 that the "inundation of money appears to have overflowed virtue, and I fear will bury the liberty of America in the same grave. . . . It is a cruel thought, that, when we feel ourselves standing on the firmest ground in every respect, the cursed arts of our secret enemies, combining with other causes, should effect, by depreciating our money, what the open arms of a powerful enemy could not."

No matter how decisive a victory America might achieve on the battlefield, Jefferson contended that if banks were allowed to continue utilizing unsound fiscal practices, from predatory lending to flooding the market with paper bills, Americans would never achieve real independence, since their fortunes would be vulnerable to the banks' whims.

Exacerbating the problem, Jefferson believed, was the fact that individual banks received money from a congressionally authorized private national bank—called the First National Bank of the United States. "The idea of creating a national bank I do not concur in," Jefferson asserted soon after it was founded. To him, the national bank was nothing less than "an institution of the most deadly hostility existing against the principles and form of our Constitution." "If the American people allow private banks to control the issuance of their currency, first by inflation and then by deflation, the banks and corporations that will grow up around them will deprive the people of all their property until their children will wake up homeless on the continent their fathers conquered."

Jefferson insisted that Congress was straying from its designated constitutional parameters in authorizing the creation of a national bank: the "incorporation of a bank and the powers assumed have not . . . been delegated to the United States by the Constitution. They are not among the powers specially enumerated."

Jefferson tried to nip in the bud the central banking system of his day, contending that money's "issuing power should be taken from the banks and restored to the people to whom it properly belongs." If banks were to play a responsible role in American society, he argued that they shouldn't be in private hands or in quasi-private hands, but rather owned by the public, which would be shareholders and would delegate the responsibility of issuing currency and credit to elected federal officials.

As president, Jefferson succeeded in having the national bank's charter revoked. But James Madison renewed the bank's authority in 1814 after becoming president. Since then, presidents that include Andrew Jackson (the only president to pay off the national debt) and Abraham Lincoln, both of whom shared Jefferson's belief that the national bank's machinations were ruinous to democracy's long-term prospects, have tried to do away with it. But it has withstood all such attempts. In 1913, the national bank morphed into the Federal Reserve. Though its stated mission is to stabilize the economy, the Federal Reserve's monetary policies arguably have been at the root of every modern financial crisis.

The Federal Reserve's managers have relentlessly discouraged savings by propping up low interest rates and have hidden how high inflation is in real terms, ruining not just millions of middle-class families, but saddling future generations with an insurmountable burden of debt. Even most Americans who locked into fixed-rate low-interest loans during the latest real estate frenzy also locked themselves into deep debt, as their properties have turned out to be worth far less than the loan amount. And because lenders failed to scrutinize the borrowers' credit history and their ability to repay these loans, millions have had to default, with millions of defaults looming.

What if our nation's borrowing and lending system had taken a different approach from the outset? Just after the Revolutionary War era, when our financial system was in a more molten state, financial and economic theorists were positing alternative systems. For instance, Edward Kellogg, a prominent American financier who amassed and lost fortunes during the financial panics triggered by unsound borrowing and lending practices in the early and mid-nineteenth century, proposed a Jeffersonian-type system that would provide fixed, uniform, low-interest loans to the general public. The loan (or debt) issuer, public credit banks, would supplant private banks under this scheme. The size of the loan would be based on such factors as a prospective borrower's amount of collateral, his previous history of repaying loans, but also on his prospects for using the loan to fruitful economic advantage. The money used to repay the loans would be put right back into the public bank, in order to finance still more loans. To keep this system uniform and fair, and also to ensure a stable currency, Kellogg proposed that congressional legislation set the interest rate. But powerful banking interests saw to it that this and kindred proposals, which would have treated all potential borrowers equally, never gained serious attention.

## It's the Economizing, Stupid

"Every discouragement should be thrown in the way of men who undertake to trade without capital," Jefferson wrote in 1785 to Nathaniel Tracy, a patriot and thriving privateer who was one of the chief financiers of the Revolution. Yet by this time, trading without capital was widespread.

Jefferson lamented that so many Americans were operating from the "miserable arithmetic which makes any single privation whatever so painful as a total privation of everything which must necessarily follow the living so far beyond our income." He believed the best remedy was one of economic tough love, in particular "the abolition of all credit" for individuals. As Jefferson told Archibald Stuart, who studied law under him and went on to serve in Virginia's House of Delegates, "I own it to be my opinion, that good will arise from the destruction of our credit. I see nothing else which can restrain our disposition to luxury, and to the change of those manners which alone can preserve republican government."

Yet Jefferson himself was a poster person for irresponsible individual consumption; he habitually made extravagant purchases far beyond his means, and his debt woes were exacerbated by a string of ill-advised investments. By the time his second term at the White House ended, he was over $20,000 in debt, a sizable sum for the times.

Jefferson was so deeply in debt at this time that he had to apply for a loan at a Richmond bank in order to keep his outstanding accounts in Washington solvent. When in 1814 the British burned the public buildings at Washington, Jefferson saw an opportunity to pay down some of his personal debt; he offered to sell his collection of some thirteen thousand books to Congress. The sale—in which Congress purchased the books for perhaps half their worth—did temporarily stave off financial disaster, but Jefferson continued spending far beyond his means.

Before the American Revolution got underway, Jefferson regularly sold parcels of his property in order to reduce his personal debt burden. But the paper money he received as payment plummeted in value as inflation soared during the war years. When the Revolutionary

War ended, British creditors resumed their efforts to collect the money he owed them. Further, Jefferson suffered enormous investment losses—exacerbated by the fact that he had cosigned a note for a relative who was insolvent—during the financial Panic of 1819. When Jefferson died in 1826, his debts amounted to about $107,000. His beloved Monticello, and all his personal possessions, including his 130 slaves, were sold at auction.

## The Joys of Privation

After the United States won independence, Jefferson was wont to wax nostalgic about the shared deprivations willingly endured by patriots on behalf of the war effort. "I look back to the time of the war, as a time of happiness and enjoyment," when everyone lived "amidst the privation of many things not essential to happiness," Jefferson recounted in a letter to his cousin Fulwar Skipwith. Doing without for the sake of a greater cause, in his estimation, "lays the broadest foundation for happiness." Yet after the war ended, he was no more willing than anyone else to practice financial parsimony, even as he continued stressing that it was an integral ingredient for personal and national autonomy.

Would Americans today be willing to drastically cut back on consumption for the promise of greater individual and national liberation? Author Benjamin R. Barber is not optimistic. He believes consumerist capitalism has infiltrated every dimension of our existence to such an extent that it diminishes and even perverts the promise of our democracy, making almost oxymoronic such terms as "corporate responsibility" and "civic responsibility." In *Consumed: How Markets Corrupt Children, Infantilize Adults, and Swallow Citizens Whole*, Barber contends that the "logic of democracy may begin with the positing of rights and of a theoretical 'natural condition' in which women and men are born free, but it depends for its implementation on civic learning, public participation and common consciousness," which to him are critical criteria for practicing "competent citizenship."

Barber asserts that even when Jefferson and John Adams were staunch political adversaries, they nonetheless agreed that "in the absence of competent citizens, bills of rights were but pieces of paper." However, Barber overlooks the great divide between Jefferson's and Adams's respective notions of what a competent citizen amounted to. Adams was an adherent of ambitious expansion of commerce and industry, which he believed was not an impediment to but rather a facilitator of the development of competent citizenship. Adams apparently forgot the fact that the American Revolution was sparked in large measure by a revolt against the world's first multinational, the British East India Company and its monopoly on trade in the New World. On the other hand, Jefferson favored at home a more agrarian-based economy that put first the interests of yeomen, artisans, and shopkeepers, who to him best exemplified both self-reliance and civic virtuousness (and so, in his estimation, were the polar opposite of industrialists, bankers, and financiers).[4]

## Neither a Borrower Nor Lender Be

*From Article I, Section 8, Clauses 1 and 2, of the Constitution:* **"The Congress shall have Power To . . . pay the debts . . . of the United States . . . [and] To borrow money on the credit of the United States."**

---

4. Jefferson further believed that an agriculture-based economy would give the United States strategic commodities for international trade. His vision on the international front, as Joseph Ellis puts it, was of "a liberal international community, comprised of open markets and national cooperation." It was a vision that "foundered on the rocks of European intransigence."

I am on Ellis Island. My handmade Constitution Café sign is perched beside me. I'd planted myself hours earlier near the entrance to the building that had once been the primary entry point for immigrants to the United States. Though Ellis Island was closed long ago as an immigration-processing facility, New York remains the primary port of call in the United States for immigrants. Nowadays, however, they typically arrive here by plane rather than ship, and usually stay with relatives or in temporary housing rather than sleep on bunk beds without blankets in a drafty hall at the processing facility, where all told, more than 12 million immigrants passed through.

I had been trying to engage school groups with meager results. Teachers informed me they were on a strict schedule, much as some indicated they might have wanted to allow their charges to have an exchange with me. Before calling it a day, I decide to take a tour. In a section with an exhibition featuring the wave of immigration from Greece and Italy starting in the late nineteenth century, I happen upon a woman staring at a photo display. She sighs audibly.

"They were desperately poor when they arrived," she says, more to herself than to me. "But most of them succeeded here, although there was no social security, no health or life insurance, no totally reliable banks. If there's such a thing as rugged individualists, they were them."

The woman, who eventually introduces herself as Mariangela, tells me that her father and his family came to the United States from southern Italy, from the village of Bernalda in the province of Matera, which to this day is an agricultural center.

I mention that my father's parents first passed through Ellis Island on March 29, 1910, arriving on the SS *Chicago*. They were among the first large wave of immigrants from the Dodecanese ("Twelve") Islands region, and hailed from the tiny volcanic island of Nisyros. Though ethnic Greeks, they were officially Italian citizens at the time they immigrated: the Dodecanese denizens recently had come together and declared independence from the Ottoman Empire, only to be promptly invaded and occupied by Italy.

"I probably have some Greek blood," Mariangela tells me. "I'm from the region where Pythagoras opened a secret religious school." The Greek philosopher and mathematician Pythagoras (c. 572–500 b.c.), was founder of the mystical and cultish Pythagorean Society. Their belief in transmigration of the souls, and that numbers represented nature's true essence, were considered heretical. Pythagoras and many followers fled to southern Italy from his native Samos, a Greek island, to escape persecution.

"Your grandparents, and my grandparents' siblings, got here in the nick of time," Mariangela says. "Congress and their constituents didn't want 'southern Europeans'—read: 'poor Greek and Italians'— coming any more." Indeed, the U.S. Congress, concerned by the flood of immigrants from southern Italy and Greece, passed the Immigration Act of 1924, which placed severe restrictions on the number of southern Europeans that could enter the United States.

Mariangela then tells me, "My own parents arrived from southern Italy in 1953, the year before Ellis Island was shuttered for good. They were among the final groups processed here. My grandfather's brothers and sisters all had come in the 1920s. But my grandfather, my *nonno*, stayed put in Matera. He was a tenant farmer, dirt-poor. According to family legend, he grew the most delicious apricots and peaches. He never scraped enough together to own his own land.

"No matter his hardships, he refused to leave Italy for hope of a better life here. He may not have owned his own land, but the land was part of him. Generations of family had been born and raised and died there, and to him it would have been sacrilege to leave. He felt like he would be abandoning them."

"My pop worked side by side with Nonno since he was a toddler,"

Mariangela says next. "He was the youngest, the only one of his eight brothers and sisters to stay on in Italy. But when Nonno died in 1952—less than three months after my grandmother passed—Pop got set to immigrate with Mom. He wanted to be a parent, and he didn't want to raise a child there, in poverty."

She smiles at a memory. "When Pop arrived here at age twenty, he 'didn't have a pot to piss in,' as he put it. He worked seven days a week, two and sometimes even three shifts, at his cousins' restaurants, until he saved enough to open up his own place—with 100 percent cash on the barrelhead. Pop never owed a penny to anyone.

"I was born nearly fifteen years after they got here. Mom was in her late thirties, old by Italian standards—or any standard back then—to be a first-time *madre*. By then, Pop had his own restaurant. It was doing well—his veal dishes were known as among the best in the city—and he felt secure enough that he could provide for a family. Four years after I entered the world, my little brother Michele was born. Pop was determined that we have everything he didn't.

"But I didn't have *him*. One day, when I was about twelve, I took the bus into Manhattan from Long Island. I went to his diner in Midtown. I walked straight back to the kitchen, where he practically lived. I said to him, 'I am your daughter, and my name is Mariangela. I love music and math and modern dance. I have a boyfriend, but I'm not sure I'm in love with him.'

"He looked at me with tearing eyes. He wiped his hands on his apron and took it off. We came out front, sat in a booth, and had a meal together and a great conversation, for the first time since I don't know when. We had so much catching up to do! After that, we went out every Sunday, just him and me.

"We came here a good bit of the time when it opened up for tourists. Some kids go bowling or on picnics with their dads; I accompanied mine to Ellis Island. I didn't mind; I had him all to myself. Pop liked to 'meditate' here, think about all the people like him who came without a pot to piss in, yet more often than not made their dreams come true."

I finally tell Mariangela about my Constitution Café project. She is intrigued.

"Isn't there a section in the Constitution about debt?" she asks me.

I show her the Constitution and point to Section 1 of Article VI, which says, "All Debts contracted and Engagements entered into, before the Adoption of this Constitution, shall be as valid against the United States under this Constitution, as under the [Articles of] Confederation."

"So we've been a debtor nation from the beginning," she says.

She eventually goes on to say, "Pop loved to quote Shakespeare. 'Neither a borrower nor lender be' was his all-time favorite. 'For loan oft loses both itself and friend, and borrowing dulls the edge of husbandry.'

"My mom and pop lived by this saying: they were frugal when it came to their own needs, and generous to a fault with everyone else's. To them, it wasn't just 'Do not borrow or lend,' but 'Be a saver.' Not a hoarder, a saver—because the more you save, the more you're able to give to others in need, and to needy causes. Savings was independence. So was giving. Pop was constantly helping relatives get back on their feet. He only gave gifts, never loans, because he didn't want anyone ever to feel indebted or beholden."

"We have to go back to Shakespeare's, and Pop's, philosophy," she then says. "Make that Shakespeare quote a constitutional amendment, just in those words. It's impossible to put it better. We need more than a balanced-budget amendment. That would still leave us with trillions and trillions in debt. We need a 'no debt amendment.'

"Pop believed we should go back to the good old days, of 'pay as you go.' In 1993, when Italy became one of the founding members of the European Union, I thought it was fantastic. Pop didn't. 'Just wait,' he said. 'Sure, in good times, everybody will think easy credit is the best thing since the discovery of pasta. But when times get rough, it will be a disaster.' He was right, as usual. All these people who'd long lived by 'pay as you go' all of a sudden had credit cards by the bushel. Now they don't have a prayer of paying off the heaps of debt they've taken on."

"Pop rarely got riled," she tells me, "but this taxpayer-funded bailout was driving him bonkers—an unjustifiable giveaway to irresponsible people. All these bankers awarding themselves billions after accepting a government bailout, all those CEOs laying off thousands of employees, yet getting bigger 'performance bonuses' than when they were actually running successful businesses . . . He considered that high treason."

Then she says, "After you know my history, you'll accuse me of being the pot calling the kettle black. I got my M.B.A. from Harvard. Then I worked my way up in real estate investment firms. The more I made, the more I spent. I was a workaholic, just like Pop. I've had a marriage, divorce, several other relationships. Never had gotten around to having children. I'm Italian. I'm supposed to have children."

She rubs her abdomen. "Now I'm pregnant. Four months. Pop was so happy, even if he didn't understand why I'm not marrying the father."

She then says, "Pop died two months ago today. By the time he was diagnosed with stomach cancer, it was inoperable."

Both hands resting on her abdomen, she says, "I'm worried about the world I'm bringing little Paola into. Most of all, I fret over being a responsible parent and good role model. I would give anything for her to know Pop, absorb his values better than I did.

"Pop never said so outright, but he wasn't so proud of my career. He was proud of my little brother Michele, who just scraped by—or so I thought. He worked until recently for a nongovernmental organization as a conflict mediator."

"My firm went bankrupt last year," she then tells me. "Our shareholders lost everything. I filed for personal bankruptcy not long afterwards. My investments all became nearly worthless. My home is being foreclosed on." She shakes her head. "In my heyday, I thought lowly of Pop for never taking some of his money and splurging, seeing the world, living the high life with Mom. Now I'm too guilt-ridden to ask Mom for money."

She then laments, "I never let Pop's wisdom on financial matters sink in, no more than our government has."

And then: "Why should my child, or anyone else's, be responsible for the unchecked greed of people like me and so many others of my generation? The next generation should have an automatic 'get-out-of-debt-free card.' Under no circumstances should they have to pay for our mistakes. That's why there has to be a 'neither a borrower nor lender be' constitutional article."

In due time, Mariangela says to me: "Last week, I unburdened myself to my brother. Michele handed me on the spot a check for a huge sum. He said he'd been saving up in case he had a child, but never met the right woman. I told him he would one day, but he pressed the check into my hands and said if he did, he still had enough left in his savings to send four more to college. He refused to consider it anything but a gift. I was staggered when he told me how much he had saved over the years. Needless to say, he'd taken Pop's financial philosophy to heart."

"Michele is going to take early retirement," she then tells me. "We're going to open a restaurant, Paolo's and Paola's, named after Pop and my daughter.

"Yesterday, I opened up a bank account for my little one. I'll put something in it every week. When she's old enough, I'll tell her about the beauty of 'neither a borrower nor lender be,' and of being a saver and a giver."

We exit the museum. From our perch at the mouth of the Hudson River, Mariangela looks out over the New York Harbor. "I was reading a book about the philosophy of Native Americans," she tells me. "A Sioux tribal chief from the eighteenth century is quoted as saying, 'We don't inherit the earth from our ancestors, we borrow it from our children.' Pop and Shakespeare would agree with that. But if we keep borrowing from our children at a breakneck pace, there'll be so much to pay back that they'll have no future."

*Constitution Café Article:* The Congress shall neither a borrower nor a lender be. For loan oft loses both itself and friend, and borrowing dulls the edge of husbandry.

## Brother, Can You Spare a Trillion?

Like Mariangela's father, Jefferson was an outspoken advocate for "neither a borrower nor a lender be" when it came to federal spending. Although Jefferson never exhibited self-control over his personal spending habits, he was careful to a fault with the nation's money. By the time his tenure as president ended, Jefferson had left the United States close to debt-free. But he was alarmed by the reckless spending habits of his predecessors.

In an exchange with James Madison, Jefferson suggested the enactment of a constitutional article that would outlaw the long-term accrual of public debt. He believed that the Constitution should make clear that no debt obligation held by the federal government could be for more than nineteen years. Jefferson arrived at this specific time limit for federal indebtedness after consulting a colonial era version of actuarial tables and finding that "the half of those of

21 years and upwards living at any one instant of time will be dead in 18 years, 8 months, or say 19 years at the nearest integral number." Therefore, it would be "wise and just for [a] nation to declare in [its] constitution that neither the legislature nor the nation itself can validly contract more debt than they may pay within their own age, or within the term of 19 years," with all future contracts "deemed void as to what shall remain unpaid at the end of 19 years from their date."

Joseph Ellis, in *American Sphinx: The Character of Jefferson*, takes a pejorative view on this proposal of Jefferson's. He claims that "Jefferson was engaged in magic more than political philosophy. For there is not, and never can be, a generation in Jefferson's pure sense of the term. Generational cohorts simply do not come into the world as discrete units. There is instead a seamless web of arrivals and departures." Yet Ellis misunderstands Jefferson's proposal: Jefferson knew perfectly well that there were not discrete units of generational cohorts. His point was that the federal debt load at any given moment should never amount to more than the federal government could demonstrably pay off within nineteen years, in order to prevent the "seamless" arrival of ever more debt.

Jefferson became so appalled by irresponsible federal spending that at one point he wanted to go to a much greater extreme to prevent financial mismanagement. As he told his friend John Taylor in 1813, "I wish it were possible to obtain a single amendment to our Constitution. . . . I mean an additional article taking from the Federal Government the power of borrowing."

Jefferson acknowledged to Taylor that he did not deny that "to pay all proper expenses within the year would, in case of war, be hard on us. But not so hard as ten wars instead of one. For wars could be reduced in that proportion." In Jefferson's view, a government that could no longer launch pell-mell into military incursions, due to constitutionally imposed financial constraints, would be more pre-disposed to mediating or avoiding conflict.

Jefferson held that one need look no further than the country from which the new nation had recently severed ties to see the wisdom of ratifying such a constitutional article. Britain had gotten itself mired in debt through rampant empire-expanding, which prompted it to levy taxes against the colonists. As Jefferson emphasized in an 1809 correspondence with Albert Gallatin, his former secretary of the treasury, Jefferson considered "the fortunes of our republic

> as depending, in an eminent degree, on the extinguishment of the public debt . . . that done, we shall have revenue enough to improve our country in peace and defend it in war, without recurring either to new taxes or loans. But if the debt should once more be swelled to a formidable size, its entire discharge will be despaired of, and we shall be committed to the English career of debt, corruption and rottenness, closing with revolution. The discharge of debt, therefore, is vital to the destinies of our government.

If the U.S. government continued emulating Britain by proceed-ing along an increasingly out-of-control career of debt, Jefferson pre-dicted that U.S. citizens would revolt again, this time against their own government. Mounting public debt would "bring on us more ruin at home than all the enemies from abroad against whom this army and navy are to protect us." If those in charge of the federal purse strings had no choice but to steer clear of unmanageable debt, he opined to his nephew John Wayles Eppes, it would serve as a "curb on the spirit of war and indebtment, which, since the modern theory of the perpetuation of debt, has drenched the earth with blood, and crushed its inhabitants under burdens ever accumulating."

One might of course contend that Jefferson himself was con-
tradictory, even hypocritical, in taking such a stance. After all, he
supported Article VI of the Constitution, which considers valid all
debts entered into before the Constitution was ratified, and sets no
ceiling on further borrowing. Indeed, both Jefferson and his political opposite Alexander Hamilton threw their support behind this
amendment. Both agreed that if the new United States was to have
credibility, it would have to assume the debts incurred by states in
the period since the Articles of Confederation had been formed, as
well as all the debt amassed by the colonies during the war effort.

Yet Hamilton supported the article out of the belief that ever-
increasing amounts of capital borrowed by the government from a
national bank with carte blanche authority to create and dispense
money would serve as the driving engine for economic growth. By
this scheme, the national bank's debt securities were guaranteed by
private profiteers, who stood to amass fortunes on the interest paid
back to them. Hamilton believed this practice would best realize his
vision of building up American empire. His operating premise was
that an always-accumulating national debt would ensure that the
federal government had staying power, by giving wealthy creditors
a personal stake in propping up the institution that was in debt to
them. If the government became insolvent, these creditors would
not recover their loans, much less continue to earn liberal interest
on them, and so it was in their best interest to keep supporting the
federal government. "A national debt," asserted Hamilton, "attaches
many citizens to the government who, by their numbers, wealth, and
influence, contribute more perhaps to its preservation than a body
of soldiers."

Jefferson, on the other hand, supported the amendment with
the expectation that all government debt would be paid off in
short order. The United States then could focus on becoming a
self-sufficient, agrarian-based, pay-as-you-go society. In contrast to

Hamilton, Jefferson's operating premise was that only a frugal national government and citizenry could foster the virtues needed for a vibrant democracy.

Yet all signs indicated that the nation would continue taking on onerous debt. Jefferson predicted that by the time it realized the error of its ways, and tried "calling the mismanagers to account," it would be too late, and the only recourse would be to "obtain subsistence by hiring ourselves to rivet their chains on the necks of our fellow-sufferers."

# VII

## Hail to the Chief

One might be forgiven for thinking our foremost champion of participatory democracy was also a bit of a control freak. In addition to designing the University of Virginia, his Monticello home, the new Virginia capitol at Richmond, and his Italian-style retreat Poplar Forest, Jefferson even designed his gravestone himself. It reads, "Here was buried Thomas Jefferson, author of the Declaration of American Independence, of the statute of Virginia for religious freedom, and father of the University of Virginia."[1]

Conspicuously absent is any mention of the fact that he was our nation's third president. Clearly, Jefferson himself did not consider his eight years in the highest office in the land to be his finest political hour. During his two terms as president, he was continuously at war with his own principles. As much as he ballyhooed states and individual rights, he was at times a staunch advocate of federalism; as much as he spoke out against the dangers of a standing military, he came to recognize its necessity; and while in balance he kept the country on stable footing, he did not make inroads in furthering the radical democratic ideals he'd long professed.

---

1. Conceived of in 1800, the University of Virginia was the first institution of higher learning in the United States whose charter excluded religious doctrine.

James David Barber[2] has identified four presidential types: "active-positives" who exhibit healthy self-esteem, adaptability, and a goal-oriented approach to the office; "active-negatives" such as John Adams, who are compulsive and covet power as an end in itself; "passive-positives" like James Madison, who demonstrate a thin skin coupled with a desire to be liked by all; and "passive-negatives," who shy away from political battles at the same time as they emphasize their civic virtue.

According to Barber, of all our presidents, no one was better suited for the office than Jefferson, an active-positive type who "knew the importance of communication and empathy." While Jefferson "had his troubles and failures" as president, he nonetheless "combined a clear and open vision of what the country could be with a profound political sense, expressed in his famous phrase, 'Every difference of opinion is not a difference of principle.'"

Yet Jefferson was relieved when he was no longer the nation's chief executive. "I have never been so well pleased as when I could shift power from my own, on the shoulders of others," he told the liberal French nobleman A. L. C. Destutt de Tracy. In the same correspondence, he indicated that he'd never been comfortable with the powers bestowed to the president by the Framers: "nor have I ever been able to conceive how any rational being could propose happiness to himself from the exercise of power over others." Maybe so, but he liberally took advantage of the powers bestowed to him during his time in office—and of some not clearly enumerated in the Constitution.

What should we demand of our chief executive? Should he mostly champion the interests of those who voted for him? As our only nationally elected official other than the vice president, should he

---

2. The late political scientist's research into the psychology of our nation's chief executives continues to resonate widely among presidential scholars.

take into account just as faithfully the views of those who opposed him? Or, should he devote his energies to implementing policies that he considers best for the nation, even if they're not the expressed will of a majority of citizens, or even of a significant minority? How did Jefferson navigate this tension, and how should we today?

## State of the Disunion

*From Article II, Section 3, of the Constitution:* **"[The President] shall from time to time give to the Congress Information of the State of the Union, and recommend to their Consideration such Measures as he shall judge necessary and expedient. . . ."**

The 6th-graders have been preparing for my visit since the beginning of the school year, well-versed by their teacher in the ins and outs of the Constitution. I'm at a magnet elementary school with specialized courses in history and government. I'd held philosophical dialogues with Mrs. Ladson's charges in school years past but had not had occasion to visit her classroom for over two years. Even so, she's confident enough in my abilities to keep her students engaged that she leaves me alone while she goes off to copy lesson plans.

"My father is a congressman," Elizabeth informs me. "He was going over the Constitution with me last night, after he got back from hearing the president's State of the Union address. He shook President Obama's hand afterwards, though my father didn't think his ideas are in line with those of the American people."

The precocious preteen scrolls her finger down her copy of the Constitution. "Here," Elizabeth says. "The Constitution says that the president 'shall from time to time give to the Congress information of the State of the Union, and recommend to their consideration such measures as he shall judge necessary and expedient.' But my father says most of the recommendations and measures our president talked about for improving the state of our Union—for how to cure global warming, cool off the financial meltdown, stuff like that—were 'way out in left field.' He says that the president should not be recommending to Congress measures that are 'necessary and expedient,' but only ones that are 'the will of the people.'"

"Can't something be necessary and expedient and also the will of the people?" I ask.

"It *can* be, but only if the president can prove, like by a poll, that the measures he recommends are the ones the people really and truly want. Like, most Americans may be all for health care for everyone, but against the measures he recommended. He didn't listen to the will of the people as expressed. My father said the polls showed that most wanted health care tax credits rather than all the new laws and regulations and taxes and layers of bureaucracy that the president and the Democrats forced through."

She takes a breath. "So when it comes to the State of the Union, the Constitution should require the president to explain himself—to not just say why his measures and recommendations are necessary and expedient, but how exactly they're the will of the people. I mean, sure, if he does stuff the people oppose, they'll vote him out if he dares run for a second term, and vote out all those in Congress who went along with him. But the Constitution should still demand that, when the president paints his picture of the State of the Union, he explain why his recommended actions to make the Union's state stronger and brighter than ever are also fulfilling the people's will."

"It shouldn't say he *has* to follow the will of the people," says Maria, after Elizabeth is done. "It should say that when delivering the State of the Union, the president has to explain what he thinks the will of the people *should* be. After all, he's our main leader, not a follower. He shouldn't have to do what the polls say he should do.

He can make his case for why he believes something should be the will of the people, no matter what the polls say. He can outline his visions and dreams for our nation, maybe ones we ourselves can't imagine because we're too shortsighted. As a wise leader, maybe he knows better when it comes to things that are in our best interests and that should be our 'will,' even if we don't know it ourselves right at that moment."

Then she says, "I bet Tyson here would agree with me. He was elected our class president, and that's pretty much how he operates." She points to an unassuming child in the row across from her who does not seem to want to draw attention to himself.

"Tyson ran against Elizabeth," she goes on. "The class president gets to do things like help choose field trips, decide the order in which we stand in line at the classroom door when going out to recess or lunch or leaving for the day, decide how we'll be punished if we misbehave as a class, things like that. Tyson and Elizabeth each gave a speech telling us why we should vote for one or the other. We liked better Tyson's ideas for improving the state of the classroom. He promised he would consult with us whenever he could before making big decisions. But he also told us that when unexpected situations arose and he had to think fast—like if the fire alarm went off unexpectedly, or it's the teacher's birthday and we forgot to buy her a gift—he might have to make a decision without asking our opinions first, but that he would always try to make ones that create more of an 'all for one and one for all' classroom spirit."

"Well, anyway," she goes on, "Carl's not here today, because he has a cold, but he came to school last Tuesday wearing a hat. Mrs. Ladson doesn't approve of hats on heads inside the classroom. It's against school rules, which come from way up high, from the principal or maybe even the superintendent. So Mrs. Ladson told him to take off his hat. But Carl wouldn't. She looked to Tyson to back her up, since he's the class president. Tyson asked Carl, 'Why don't you want to take off your hat?' Carl told him he didn't like his haircut, and he got kind of sniffly. So Tyson put his hat on, and he told us all to do the same."

"You could tell Mrs. Ladson was steaming," Elizabeth interjects.

"If Mrs. Ladson really had been steaming, she would have made us take our hats off. But she didn't," says Maria. "She said that while she normally didn't approve of such things, since they're technically against the rules, she admired that Tyson wanted the class to show our . . . what're those words we learned?"

"Sympathy and accommodation," several say.

"Right. She admired him for the fact that we all wanted to go along with his idea and show our sympathy for Carl by accommodating him in these . . ." Again she is at a loss for the words she is searching for.

"Extenuating circumstances," several say.

"Right. Tyson even had convinced Carl's enemies—I mean, people who aren't his friends—to wear hats. Even they know what it's like to have a bad hair day."

"Tyson did impose his will on us, but he didn't threaten or intimidate us. Well, no, he didn't really impose his will. What he did was inspire or convince us to make our will and his one and the same," says Felicity.

"But there's a rule that forbids hats," says Elizabeth. "Imagine if he'd been president of the United States and he'd broken the rules of the Constitution! If he really wanted to be 'presidential,' he should've inspired us to work together to change the school rule about hats, rather than do something illegal or unconstitutional that maybe would have put his classmates and teacher in a situation where they'd face harsh consequences, even if it did help Carl feel better."

"Carl was afraid people would've made fun of him," Tyson says, finally speaking up for himself. "I had to make a snap judgment, before he started crying and carrying on. It seemed like the right thing to do. And almost everyone gladly put on their hats. They were willing, like me, to take the heat."

Speaking of taking the heat, as cold as it is outside on this wintry day, the state of the classroom is a stuffy one; the radiators are turned on full blast. I see that some of the students are as uncomfortable as I am, tugging at their shirt collars and mopping sweat from their brows.

"Can you vote on whether to open or close the window?" I ask.

"We *can*," Maria replies, "but what would that do? Some in here will complain that it's too cold rather than too hot."

"Maybe we can all figure out a way that we'll all be comfortable," Tyson says. He goes to the window and pulls it up about halfway.

Then he asks his classmates, "Are you more comfortable now?" Some say yes and some no, with the rest noncommittal. He lets more time pass, so the cold air can waft further inside. Then, just as Maria predicted, the complaining begins.

Tyson seems at an impasse. Then he perks up and commands, "Those who like it kind of cold, move to desks closest to the window. Those who like it real warm, move to desks farthest away from the window and closest to the radiator." Seeing that some appear confused, he says, "What I mean is, move to a desk located wherever in the classroom you'd feel the most comfortable."

"But we're not allowed to move from our desks to another person's desk," Elizabeth protests. "If you want to improve the state of the classroom, then you should take a poll and find out what we want you to do before you make a decision."

Tyson, in deep thought, doesn't seem to hear her. "How about this: let's lift up our own desks and move them to the place where we're most comfortable with the room temperature."

Even as Elizabeth is set to register another objection, the rest of her classmates enthusiastically follow this directive; apparently they can see nothing about it that is technically against the rules. There ensues a good deal of jostling and screeching of desks and chairs along the floor. All at last manage to arrange themselves where they are most comfortable. Those hardy few who bask in the cold sit by the half-open window. About two-thirds are as far from the window as possible, and there is a thread of desks more or less clustered right in the middle.

"Are you all comfortable?" Tyson asks.

Every student except maybe one indicates that she is.

"The people have spoken," Felicity says with a slightly tongue-in-cheek air of triumph. "The state of our classroom is strong, thanks to our president."

Mrs. Ladson materializes. Her mouth drops open. While her students may have spoken, she remains speechless.

> *Constitution Café Article:* The President shall from time to time give to the Congress information of the State of the Union, and recommend to their consideration such measures as he shall judge necessary and expedient to achieve what he believes should be the will of the people.

## Man of the People

Jefferson claimed in 1801, the year he became president, that the "will of the people is the only legitimate foundation of any government, and to protect its free expression should be our first object."

Hannah Arendt, the social philosopher and political theorist renowned for her studies on the problematic nature of power, observes that at our country's founding, the notion of "the people" never "became a singular," but rather retained "the meaning of manyness, of the endless variety of a multitude whose majesty rested in its very plurality." Indeed, "to such an extent was the American concept of people identified with a multitude of voices and interests that Jefferson could establish it as a principle 'to make us one nation as to foreign concerns, and keep us distinct in domestic ones.'"

Jefferson is frequently given the sobriquet "man of the people." According to Jefferson scholar Merrill D. Peterson, Jefferson possessed the dual "traits of the man-of-the-people and the man-of-vision," and this led to his apotheosis over time as "Father of Democracy": "the man whose iconoclastic theories were received as truths by posterity, and whose lofty mental perch did not keep him from cherishing the people and mingling with them." But it can be argued that Jefferson's theories only seemed iconoclastic to those whose status was threatened by them. Max Lerner, in his book on Jefferson, supports the idea that Jefferson's notions were familiar and quite palatable to most: "the ideas Jefferson drew upon were part of the climate of opinion of the time, and lay all about him." More often than not, Jefferson was simply giving eloquent expression to the views and hopes of ordinary people.

## Treaties Treatise

*Article II, Section 2, Clause 2, of the Constitution:* **"[The President] shall have Power, by and with the Advice and Consent of the Senate, to make Treaties, provided two-thirds of the Senators present concur."**

"The treaty-making power granted by the Constitution to the president is way too open-ended," says Dinesh. "All that the Constitution's 'advice and consent clause' says on the subject is that the president 'shall have power, by and with the advice and consent of the Senate, to make treaties, provided two-thirds of the Senators present concur.'"

I'm with a group of students who attend a leading law school. Our exchange was arranged by a professor who regularly holds Socrates Café dialogues. All with me are currently taking a class on treaty law.

"But constitutionally requiring the president to seek the advice and consent of two-thirds of senators is a significant check and balance," says Jennifer. "It forces a president to secure the support of at least some of his opponents. I don't see what's so open-ended about that. If anything, it's onerous."

"*Theoretically*, this stipulation requiring the Senate's advice and consent can serve as a decent check on the chief executive's treaty-making powers," says Dinesh. "Which is why most presidents these days don't even attempt to put treaties they negotiate to a vote requiring approval by a two-thirds Senate majority. Instead, they circumvent this constitutional requisite. So a revised article must forbid a president to enter into any binding agreement with another nation or entity unless he follows to the letter the protocol outlined in the existing constitutional article."

He goes on, "A treaty is any formal, binding agreement between one or more entities, usually countries. Even if it's not called a treaty, that's what it is. So, for instance, the 'Kyoto Protocol' falls into this category."

The Kyoto Protocol is an international accord that emerged out of the United Nations Framework Convention on Climate Change and that sets binding standards for significantly reducing greenhouse gas emissions. It went officially into effect in 2005. To date, 187 nations have signed and ratified the enforceable agreement, and the United States is making overtures to sign it.

"Kyoto is a binding agreement, a treaty," Dinesh says. "It contains enforcement mechanisms that are carried out by a governing or judicial body outside the scope of the United States. Yet the president is acting as if he can finalize an agreement on it by merely issuing an executive order. He has no intention of even putting Kyoto to a majority vote in Congress, much less treating it like the treaty that it is and seeking the input and approval of two-thirds of our senators. If it was presented to the Senate, its members would have to reject it. Because the U.S. would first have to have laws of its own regarding the regulation of carbon emissions standards that mirror those of the Kyoto Protocol."

"I would go further than Dinesh," says Roya. "I would have this article contain an additional clause that prohibits the president from entering into any formal and binding agreement that has rights or laws that supersede or conflict with those enumerated in our own Constitution. An example where such a transgression has occurred is with our nation's signing of the Universal Declaration of Human Rights."

The United States was among the forty-eight nations that approved this Declaration in 1948. It was developed under the auspices of the United Nations in order to clarify and elaborate on the concepts of "human rights" and "fundamental freedoms" set forth in the United Nations Charter.

"This Declaration enumerates thirty articles, which grant unprecedented rights and freedoms," she says, "including rights to housing, universal employment and health care, leisure and vacation time, rights to security in the event of sickness, disability, widowhood, old age, among many others that are not included in our own Constitution.

"When it was ratified in 1948, Eleanor Roosevelt, who served on the committee that drafted it, stated that she hoped the Declaration would 'become the international Magna Carta[3] of all men every-

---

3. The English charter, known as the Magna Carta—its full name is the Magna Carta Libertatum (the Great Charter of Freedoms)—originated in 1215. Though it is not technically a constitution, it guarantees that all British citizens "have and enjoy all liberties and immunities of free and natural subjects." Its array of codified rights includes the right to self-rule, to endorse or reject taxation, the right to a trial by jury of their peers, to habeas corpus (a legal action that prevents unlawful

where.' Her unequivocal aim was for it to be a binding, enforceable international constitution. And in fact, the Universal Declaration's preamble makes it clear that all the nations that ratify it are committed to securing its listed rights and freedoms for its own people and for people everywhere."

Then Roya says, "Let me be clear: I'm personally all for the Universal Declaration of Human Rights. It's a beautiful, humanistic document. But such a treatylike Declaration can only be entered into by the United States if we first have parallel rights via amendments to our own Constitution, and we have our own procedures in place for enforcing those rights that parallel the international judicial body the Universal Declaration calls for."

"But a document like the Universal Declaration of Human Rights doesn't in any way diminish or conflict with our own Constitution," says Lloyd. "It makes the nations that bind themselves to it more connected to one another because they supposedly share the same high human rights standards. And it makes them more accountable, as individual nations and as a group, for realizing these foundational laws on human rights and freedoms."

To which Roya replies, "But let's say one country's government that has entered into this agreement, supposedly committing itself to securing the Declaration's rights for its people, actually deliberately denies these rights to its people. And let's say its people protest. A hawkish U.S. president might then use the fact that there was a violation of this agreement as a pretext for declaring war against such a nation. He can claim he's doing so on behalf of freedom lovers in that country, and that he's only trying to uphold the Universal Declaration, even if he really has other motives."

Turning to Roya, Dinesh says now, "I disagree that this provision

---

detention). It also establishes that the king of England himself is not above the law, and is beholden to obey and carry out the dictates of the Magna Carta.

in the treaty clause needs the additional language you suggest, but for far different reasons than those Lloyd states. If the Senate is allowed to perform its job as 'treaty watchdog,' it has shown that it will make sure that any binding agreements signed by the U.S. with other entities don't exceed their bounds. Whenever given the opportunity, it has made sure that the U.S. doesn't commit itself to enforcing rights, or violations of rights, that its own citizens don't enjoy. That's precisely what the Senate did when a two-thirds majority approved the Geneva Conventions, and if the Senate's advice and consent was sought for the Universal Declaration,[4] I'm sure it would have included a similar proviso."

"Though called conventions," Dinesh continues, "this clearly was a treaty, and it was dutifully submitted by the president to the Senate for its advice and consent. The Senate approved the Conventions because they were in line with the Eighth Amendment of our Constitution, which prohibits 'cruel and unusual punishments.' *But* the Senate only approved the Conventions conditionally: it included a proviso that stated that if there was anything in it that contradicted our own Constitution, that that part of the treaty was null and void. This is a textbook example of the Senate carrying out its rightful role in forging a treaty agreement that advances humanity, without ceding any rights not in the Constitution. So as long as the Senate is allowed to fulfill its constitutional function, Roya's concern that rights will be granted in treatylike agreements does not need to be addressed in the article we're writing."

"Then we have to make darn sure that any treatylike document, no matter what it is called, always requires the approval of two-thirds

---

4. Signed in 1949 in the aftermath of World War II, the Geneva Conventions are a combination of several treaties and protocols that dictate a set of international standards for treatment of victims of war. The Conventions were ratified, in their entirety or in part, by 194 nations.

of the Senate," says Roya. "The North American Free Trade Agreement, or NAFTA,[5] was a treaty through and through, with intricate
enforcement mechanisms. Yet it was approved as an 'agreement'
between our legislative and executive branches, and passed with just
a simple majority of both chambers. From a constitutional stand-
point, that completely invalidates it."

"NAFTA might have been well intentioned," Roya goes on. "The
U.S. might have been trying to advance its trade interest while at
the same time elevating labor rights and environmental standards
in Mexico. But first and foremost, it was a treaty. Yet only sixty-one
senators voted to approve it, though the Constitution required the
approval of sixty-seven for it to become law. So in this case, the Senate was derelict along with the president, because it didn't insist on
carrying out its powers of approval by the constitutionally required
two-thirds majority. Why wasn't the Senate protesting, as 'treaty
watchdog,' that its 'rightful role' was being circumvented?"

"If we go by the route you're suggesting, and require all binding agreements to be treated as treaties," says Jennifer, "we'd rarely
have any protocols or covenants, declarations or agreements, much
less treaties. That would seriously set back progress in advancing
human rights the world over. The U.S. presidents who enter into
these binding agreements recognize that we live in a global world. I
admire them for approving these agreements, even if they have to go
around Congress to do so, because they're for the greater good of the
nation and the world. If we adopted the constitutional article with
the language being suggested here—requiring all such agreements to
receive the blessing of two-thirds of the Senate, and maybe further

5. An expansive trilateral trade agreement signed by the governments of Can-
ada, Mexico, and the United States, and put into force in 1994, NAFTA governs all
facets of trade between these nations, and includes parallel agreements on environment and labor issues.

mandating that they contain no rights not specifically set forth in
our Constitution—we'd never have signed on to such groundbreaking human rights documents as the Universal Declaration."

After a pause, Lloyd says, "Well, I guess maybe I can come around
to some extent to the view of Roya and Dinesh when it comes to
requiring that presidents follow proper treaty protocol when entering into any binding agreement with another nation or entity, and
submitting it to a two-thirds majority vote. But I believe it's getting
carried away to say that all rights contained in any such agreements
first have to be specifically included in our own. After all, the Ninth
Amendment in the Bill of Rights says that 'the enumeration in the
Constitution, of certain rights, shall not be construed to deny or
disparage others retained by the people.' This was included because
the rights granted in the Bill of Rights weren't meant to be exhaustive. I believe most of the rights Roya mentioned were in the Universal Declaration are ones that most Americans would want, and that
many would argue are owed to them."

This brings Jennifer to say, "What if this Constitutional clause
says that when the president enters into a treaty, or into a 'treatylike agreement,' if the rights granted exceed those enumerated in
our Constitution—or at least are not clearly enumerated in our
Constitution—then all Americans automatically enjoy those additional rights. Like Lloyd, I doubt that a majority of Americans would
mind having the rights in the Universal Declaration, or the right to
breathe cleaner air that adhering to the Kyoto Protocol would give
them."

Dinesh shakes his head. "Thomas Jefferson said in his first inaugural address that the reason the president's treaty-making powers
are meant to be used sparingly is in order to keep our nation from
entering into 'entangling alliances.' It's easy to see the good in documents like Kyoto and the Universal Declaration, but not the draw-
backs. But if the Senate is required to carry out its designated role

when it comes to making sure that the only entangling alliances we enter into are ones that advance our own interests, we'll be okay."

"I'm not convinced we'll always 'be okay,'" says Jennifer. "Former president George W. Bush clearly violated the Geneva Conventions' rules on torture when he approved of waterboarding of war detainees. Every attempt to try all those who were allegedly complicit in carrying out this regimen of torture for crimes against humanity has been rebuffed. Our three branches of government have prevented the international tribunal in the Hague from seeking justice. In this case, all our constitutional and treaty watchdogs have failed us."

*Constitution Café Article:* The President shall have Power, by and with the advice and consent of the Senate, to make treaties, provided two-thirds of the Senators concur. The President shall not enter into any binding agreement or compact, alliance or confederation—be it a treaty, protocol, convention, or covenant—with another nation, foreign power, or international entity, without the advice and consent of two-thirds of the Senate.

## Treaty Powers

The first treaty that the United States entered into after the Constitution replaced the Articles of Confederation was the Jay Treaty. Put into effect in 1794 during the administration of George Washington, the treaty was arranged by Washington's secretary of the treasury, Alexander Hamilton, and his principal negotiator, John Jay. It was intended to stem yet another potentially explosive conflict between the United States and Britain. As a result of the treaty, Britain agreed to withdraw its troops from the Northwest Territory, among other things, and there followed a decade of mostly peaceful trading between the two nations.

But Thomas Jefferson, who was Washington's secretary of state at the time, strongly opposed the treaty. He believed that the strengthened economic ties it forged between Britain and the United States came at the expense of alienating France, the most critical U.S. ally during the Revolutionary War. Jefferson argued that even though the Washington administration had obtained the consent of a two-thirds majority in the Senate, it had nonetheless exceeded its authority, because the treaty included settlement and trade provisions that, to him, blatantly exceeded the constitutionally designated parameters for treaties. "I say the same as to the opinion of those who consider the grant of the treaty making power as boundless," asserted Jefferson. "If it is, then we have no Constitution."

In most instances, Jefferson found voluntary agreements far preferable to fixed treaties. In a letter he wrote during his presidency to his friend Philip Mazzei, an Italian physician and promoter of liberty, he stated: "On the subject of treaties, our system is to have none with any nation, as far as can be avoided. . . . We believe that with nations as with individuals, dealings may be carried on as advantageously, perhaps more so, while their continuance depends on a voluntary good treatment." On the other hand, Jefferson maintained, if a treaty has fixed terms over a specific number of years, and a term in it "becomes injurious to either [party]," the treaty "is made by forced constructions to mean what suits them and becomes a cause of war instead of a bond of peace." Consequently, to Jefferson, "it is against our system to embarrass ourselves with treaties" except in the most extenuating circumstances.

"I see . . . not much harm in annihilating the whole treaty-making power except as to making peace," Jefferson told James Madison in 1796. Given his views, Jefferson would likely have opposed agreements like Kyoto and the Universal Declaration of Human Rights—not because he would have been against them in principle, but because they go beyond the bounds of what is constitutionally permissible. And yet Jefferson put his strict constructionist principles on the back burner and acted outside the Constitution when he used his treaty-making authority to purchase the Louisiana Territory for very little money despite his inability to get a two-thirds majority support in Congress. Jefferson was, in the end, a canny politician, and presented a strong justification for acting outside constitutional parameters.

## American Idle

*Twelfth Amendment to the United States Constitution (which replaces Article II, Section 1, Clause 3):* "The Electors shall meet in their respective states, and vote by ballot for President and Vice-President, one of whom, at least, shall not be an inhabitant of the same state with themselves; they shall name in their ballots the person voted for as President, and in distinct ballots the person voted for as Vice-President, and they shall make distinct lists of all persons voted for as President, and all persons voted for as Vice-President and of the number of votes for each, which lists they shall sign and certify, and transmit sealed to the seat of the government of the United States, directed to the President of the Senate;—The President of the Senate shall, in the presence of the Senate and House of Representatives, open all the certificates and the votes shall then be counted;—The person having the greatest Number of votes for President, shall be the President, if such number be a majority of the whole number of Electors appointed; and if no person have such majority, then from the persons having the highest numbers not exceeding three on the list of those voted for as President, the House of Representatives shall choose immediately, by ballot, the President. But in choosing the President, the votes shall be taken by states, the representation from each state having one vote; a quorum for this purpose shall consist of a member or members from two-thirds of the states, and a majority of all the states shall be necessary to a choice. And if the House of Representatives shall not choose a President whenever the right of choice shall devolve upon them, before the fourth day of March next following, then the Vice-President shall act as President, as in the case of the death or other constitutional disability of the President.—The person having the greatest number of votes as Vice-President, shall be the Vice-President, if such number be a majority of the whole number of Electors appointed, and if no person have a majority, then from the two highest numbers on the list, the Senate shall choose the Vice-President; a quorum for the purpose shall consist of two-thirds of the whole number of Senators, and a majority of the whole number shall be necessary to a choice. But no person constitutionally ineligible to the office of President shall be eligible to that of Vice-President of the United States."

I now set out to connect with American slackers, new-millennium version, whose country, community, families neither ask nor expect anything of them, and who neither ask nor expect anything of themselves. In the ostentatious coastal community of Orange County, California—or the OC, as it has become known after the former hit TV show of that name—I contacted a teacher at a high school where I once held a dialogue with a group of graduating seniors. He was still in touch with some of them and sent out an email informing them of my project. Several replied that they'd be happy to talk with me, with the proviso that we meet at their favorite haunt, Laguna Beach.

When I arrive at the designated meeting place, the erstwhile students are leaning against their surfboards, smoking and sending text messages, looking disconsolately at the waveless ocean. All of them still live at their parents' home, or at apartments subsidized by their parents, and none have jobs. Surfing is all.

Two are holding pocket-sized copies of the Constitution. "We actually read this thing, I'll have you know," says Duane.

Then he asks me, "Are we mistaken, or does the Constitution stay silent on how presidents are elected?"

"It stays silent," I say.

"The only requirement is that presidents are elected by 'electors,' a certain number of which are allotted to each state? That's it?"

"That's it. There's not even mention of an electoral college, though most people today take it for granted that the Constitution specifies one. The Constitution only mentions that we vote for 'electors' who in turn pledge to vote for the presidential candidate who wins the majority of votes in each state."

Duane and company consider this. "So all this political party stuff, all this primary stuff, is not required by the Constitution?"

"That's right."

"So we could change that. There's nothing in the current Constitution that could keep us from doing so, right?"

I nod and wait for what's to come.

"Okay, here's our idea," says Duane. "Let's keep the elector stuff in the Constitution, just like it's already worded. We still vote for electors, and they still vote for the president. But let's change how presidential candidates are chosen, change how front-runners are made, and change how one among them is elected. What's cool about this is that we're not changing anything that's already in the Constitution. We're just adding to it in a way that'll do away with the need for political parties and primaries."

Mickey jumps in. "Okay, well, what we propose is that there be a presidential pageant or contest or however you want to term it. It would be run in a way that's sort of a cross between *American Idol* and a beauty pageant, only it'd be taken more seriously.

"As we see it, this constitutional article will give each state, plus the District of Columbia, the right to send two contenders to the presidential pageant—one of them chosen by some sort of election process of each state's choosing, and the other one chosen by lottery from all those who put their names in a lottery basket or whatever who aspire to be a candidate. That'll really mix things up, keep things interesting."

"But some states have a much greater population than others," I say. "They shouldn't have the chance to send more contenders?"

"Well, there's only one contestant per state when there's a Miss America or Miss Universe pageant, so we're being twice as fair as that," he reasons. "So anyway, moving on: At the beginning of the national presidential pageant season—which would start when fall TV season starts, in order to make sure that the presidential election can still be held on the first Tuesday in November—all the candidates from the fifty states, and the federal district, will face off against each other."

Keith picks up where Mickey leaves off. "The candidates would get to make their case straight to the American people. The show would air on all channels, for one or two hours each week, so that any TV-watching American—which basically means all Americans—would be tuned in. These two candidates from each state would have plenty of airtime to get their message out and demonstrate how bright or dim-witted they are. Each week, we the TV viewing audience would vote out a certain number of candidates until only two finalists are left standing, just like we eliminate performers on *American Idol*."

Taylor jumps in. "That's better than how nationally televised presidential debates are held now. The major networks have ruled that the only candidates who can take part are those who already have

15 percent of the voters' support, based on the latest polls, before the televised debate is set to begin. But how can anyone else get that kind of support, except the two main party players, and maybe from time to time a wealthy independent with pockets deeper even than my father's? So this process we propose is much fairer. It gives a lot more people the opportunity to be a possible finalist candidate, because they'll have a chance to get a lot of exposure and really get their message out."

Duane then says, "Anyway, a group of panelists would ask these contenders questions, some of them pitched by experts, some by regular Americans like us. They'd be asked questions like those posed in Miss America pageants—things like, 'What is your stand on world peace, starvation in Africa, steroids in sports, instant replay in baseball, a National Surfers Holiday, do you mind answering the phone at 3 a.m., as long as it's because there's a national emergency?'"

"And we TV viewers would judge them each week," says Taylor, "picking winners and losers, using an *American Idol*–style process of elimination, voting by phone ballot. The number of contenders would be narrowed down week by week, until just the top two are left standing. They'll compete in one final head-to-head match. To make sure that the vote is legit, each registered voter will have to enter a specific code when he calls in. Maybe there'd also be some sort of voice authentication device to ensure it's really him, and that he only votes once."

"So then," Mickey says, "the presidential contestants would be put through a series of simulations where they'd have to show how they'd act under certain scenarios—and they wouldn't be tipped off beforehand about what these scenarios will be, so they have to show whether they've got the right stuff and can react 'presidentially' on the spur of a moment. Like, each would have to show what he'd do if he was at a school reading a children's story to elementary students to promote literacy, when suddenly he was interrupted by the head of the Pentagon and told there's just been a terrorist strike. If he freezes up, obviously he's not the guy to lead us."

"The last part of this plan," he goes on, "is that the voting tallies for the finalists on *American Idol: The Presidential Version*, would be taken state to state. So whoever wins the majority of votes in each state wins all the electors, just as they do now."

"With this approach to electing the president," says Keith, "we'd really care about voting, and care enough to really learn about the issues. Our vote would really count, because we'd have a real range of choices. I bet the percentage of registered voters who actually end up voting would skyrocket.

"We don't vote these days because we can't relate to the candidates from the big parties. Look what they do to the country once they're elected. They allow the companies that finance them to pollute the sea and air. This global-warming thing is so serious, soon I'll be able to surf in Antarctica."

"Are all of you registered to vote?" I ask the group.

"No way," says Taylor. "I don't want them to have my name, in case there's a draft."

"You idiot," says Duane, "you had to register at eighteen, just in case there ever is one."

"Anyway," Taylor says, ignoring Duane, "with this proposal of ours to pick a president sort of the *American Idol* way, there'll probably be at least some candidates we can relate to. This constitutional article would really rock the vote."

*Constitution Café Article:* Every four years, in a process that will end on Labor Day, each of the 50 states, and the federal district, one by a general election and the other by random drawing, will present two candidates to contend for the Office of President of the United States. These 100 candidates will then compete against one another weekly, for at least two hours per week, on a program to be aired in the evenings on all television channels and all other forms of mass media. They will be interviewed by a group of expert panelists, who will ask them questions pertinent to the office they aspire to, as well as by the viewing audience. The candidates will also perform simulated segments in which they demonstrate how they would act as president when confronted with various and sundry situations requiring a presidential response. Each week, ten candidates will be eliminated by direct voting from the viewers, until there are two remaining finalists. On the final episode, to be held on the first Tuesday of November, the finalists will be put through one more grueling grilling followed by a continuous series of simulated activities designed to demonstrate their presidential capacities. The viewers will then vote one final time, with the votes tallied by each state. Registered voters shall vote by telephone. They will each have a special voter's pin number, and there will also be a voice recognition mechanism to prevent voter fraud. The candidate who garners the most votes in each respective state will be the candidate for which that state's Electors are pledged to vote for President. The runner-up candidate shall be Vice President. The Electors shall then meet in their respective states and vote by ballot for President. Each Elector shall have one vote. The person having the greatest number of votes for President shall be the President. There shall be a total of 538 electors. This number is equal to the total membership of both Houses of Congress (435 Representatives and 100 Senators) plus the three electors allocated to Washington, D.C., totaling 538 electors. Each state is allocated as many Electors as it has Representatives and Senators in the United States Congress. Each state shall decide how it chooses its Electors.

## Party Animals

The Constitution makes no mention of political parties because the Framers hadn't anticipated their advent, much less the inordinate influence they would come to have over the political process. Likewise, nowhere in the Constitution are primaries mentioned as the way to elect presidential candidates, though it is now taken as a given that voters choose their principal contenders for the highest office in the land through this process. But the system to elect presidential contenders could have developed in any number of ways, considering the vague constitutional parameters on the topic.

The two earliest political parties were the Federalists, who favored a powerful centralized government, and the Democratic-Republican Party, which originated in the 1790s in opposition to the Federalist platform and favored limited federal government so that states' and people's rights would predominate. Thomas Jefferson was the first presidential candidate to run under the banner of the Democratic-Republicans, the "party of the common man."

Jefferson believed parties were inevitable: "In every free and deliberating society, there must, from the nature of man, be opposite parties, and . . . one of these, for the most part, must prevail over the other for a longer or shorter time," he told John Taylor.

According to Jefferson, "Men by their constitutions are naturally divided into two parties. Those who fear and distrust the people, and wish to draw all powers from them into the hands of the higher classes"—namely, the Federalists—and those who "identify themselves with the people, have confidence in them, cherish and consider them as the most honest and safe, although not the most wise depositary of the public interests," namely, the Democratic-Republicans.

While we may be "party animals," Jefferson claimed that it also was our nature to transcend to some degree our inherent disposition to belong to a party. He for one resisted being pigeonholed into any party mold, and claimed he "never submitted the whole system of my opinions to the creed of any party of men whatever, in religion, in philosophy, in politics, or in anything else, where I was capable of thinking for myself. Such an addiction is the last degradation of a free and moral agent. If I could not go to heaven but with a party, I would not go there at all."

Despite such rhetoric, Jefferson's Democratic-Republicans demonstrated that they were nearly as adept at mudslinging and fear-inducing sensationalism as his Federalist opponents, and the party frequently strayed from debates on the very real issues that divided the two camps.

Jefferson claimed that a political party best served a useful purpose when it was formed in order to take a concerted stand to advance democratic principles. As a case in point, Jefferson contended that the Democratic-Republican Party took shape in response to the Federalists' encroachments on constitutionally guaranteed rights. Whenever there is such an occasion, he maintained, with the "principle of difference as substantial and as strongly pronounced as between the republicans and the monocrats of our country, I hold it as honorable to take a firm and decided part and as immoral to pursue a middle line, as between the parties of honest men and rogues, into which every country is divided."

When it comes to the two major parties of our own era, the "principle of difference" is no longer nearly as pronounced as it was during Jefferson's time: both Democrats and Republicans are beholden to corporate contributions, and both often go to equally unprincipled lengths to gain an advantage. Additionally, both betray what Jefferson would call "monocratic" tendencies, in that they are increasingly heedless of the will of most of their constituents. This is likely due in part to the fact that leaders of both the right and the left have become more extreme, leaving mainstream Americans without a candidate they can identify with.

If Jefferson were alive now, he would surely believe that the time has come for a new party to be formed—one made up of ordinary Americans of many political backgrounds who nonetheless agree that the existing parties are destructive to democracy's ends.

## Pardon Me

*From Article II, Section 2, Clause 1, of the Constitution:* **"The President . . . shall have Power to grant Reprieves and Pardons for Offences against the United States, except in Cases of Impeachment."**

"The Constitution anoints the president with 'power to grant reprieves and pardons for offenses against the United States, except in cases of impeachment,'" says Gary. The congressional staffer helped arrange for a number of people to gather with me at a majestic bar near the U.S. Capitol to explore whether the president's pardoning powers should be retooled.

"As things stand," he continues, "a president can pardon anyone for any reason whatsoever, or for no reason at all. That kind of latitude may be appropriate for a monarch or dictator, but not for a president in a democracy."

"For our Framers' purposes, this authority was meant to give the president discretion to pardon someone who'd committed a crime against the U.S., but only if it would be of great benefit to the nation," says Anne-Marie, an administrative assistant with two master's degrees who works for an Obama political appointee. "For instance, he might pardon someone who committed treason if, in exchange, he was given information that revealed other enemies of the state and that led to their arrests. In such a case, the pardon was a necessary evil that prevented even greater damage being done to U.S. interests.

"The Framers also believed the president needed the authority to pardon leaders of rebellions or insurrections as a means for restoring the peace. Like, after President George Washington had troops put down the 'Whisky Rebellion' in the 1790s,[6] and its two principal leaders were sentenced to death by hanging, he pardoned them as a gesture towards restoring tranquility.

"But like Gary said, modern presidents go far beyond this very limited scope for issuing pardons. So I agree that a refashioned article should make explicit what the Framers had thought was implicit. Presidents were never meant to have unlimited pardoning power."

"This article should state that pardons can only be made when they're for a demonstrated public good," says Jason, who works for a political action committee. "At least then, there can be a healthy debate over whether any particular pardon has served that purpose. After the Civil War, President Andrew Johnson pardoned thousands of former Confederate officials and military personnel. This was controversial at the time, but it proved to be a healing act for the nation. On the other hand, it was a crime itself that Bill Clinton issued an eleventh-hour pardon of the billionaire fugitive-from-justice Marc Rich. Rich's ex-wife had made a timely $500,000 donation to his presidential library, and voilà, he's pardoned."

"Despite good intentions," says Gary, "Jimmy Carter's amnesty to draft dodgers was unjust because he didn't also pardon those who fought in the war but eventually deserted, and he didn't pardon conscientious objectors who were convicted and served time in prison.

6. The rebellion, launched in the western frontier over general dissatisfaction with government policy, came to a crescendo after an excise tax was placed on whiskey. The tax was finally repealed after Jefferson became president.

Carter's pardon would only have been potentially healing, and so for the public good, if it had included all of those groups."

This brings Anne-Marie to say, "Even if this article stated that presidents could pardon people only if it furthered the public good, they still could pardon virtually anyone they wanted to and just claim that it was in the public's best interests, even if 99.9 percent of the public disagreed. I propose an article that gives the Senate authority to be 'pardoning gatekeeper,' so to speak. It can say that if three-fourths of the Senate opposes a pardon, it will be rescinded. Whenever the Senate is successful in getting this super majority, it clearly would mean that it—and its constituents—believes the president's pardon served no public good."

Then Walter, a staffer for a notoriously liberal congressman, says, "I've been disappointed that so far President Obama hasn't issued a single pardon,[7] though he's received more requests for pardons than any other previous president by this stage of his term. I had expected him to use his pardoning powers to right blatant wrongs in our criminal justice system. For instance, there are many youth offenders incarcerated for life today who've been convicted for a third time of a criminal but nonviolent offense. A presidential pardon could right this wrong with a pardon. It would highlight how the law itself can be unjust in such a case, in which the punishment is way out of proportion to the crime, and hopefully lead to the law being changed."

"I'm going against the grain here, but I wish that the power to pardon were used even more randomly and arbitrarily than it is now," Walter says next. "Perhaps this article could state that each year a certain number of people, incarcerated for virtually any offense, will

7. Soon after this dialogue took place, President Obama granted his first pardons, to nine people convicted of crimes such as drug possession, mutilating coins, and counterfeiting.

be picked randomly and will receive a presidential pardon. It would show that we're a merciful and forgiving nation.

"There's an ancient Hebrew tradition called a Jubilee that used to take place every twenty-five to fifty years. Debts were forgiven, prisoners released, slaves freed, seized property restored to the original owners. It allowed individuals to start again, and really, gave the entire society a clean slate. A contemporary Jubilee—held, say, every twenty or twenty-five years—might go a long way towards fulfilling Thomas Jefferson's stated dream of giving each generation in American society a fresh start."

"That kind of random forgiveness is too bleeding heart for me," says Anne-Marie. "If possible wrongdoers knew they were going to be forgiven every twenty years or so, they might be more inclined, instead of less, to break the law. While I want our criminal justice system to be equitable and fair when it comes to punishment, I certainly wouldn't want anyone pardoned outright who's been convicted of a crime. Where's the public good in that?"

*Constitution Café Article:* The president shall have power to grant reprieves and pardons for offences against the United States, except in cases of impeachment, in those exceptional instances in which it can be compellingly demonstrated that such reprieves and pardons further the public good. A vote of three-fourths of the Senate shall be sufficient to rescind a presidential pardon.

## Constitutional Absolution

In 1798, the Adams administration, in pushing through the Alien and Sedition Acts, claimed that this legislation would ensure stability and safety by making it a crime for anyone to produce "false, scandalous, and malicious writing" against the government or its

officials. After the acts were passed, a string of newspaper printers were rounded up, fined, and imprisoned for publishing essays
and articles critical of the president. Shortly after Jefferson replaced
Adams in the White House, he pardoned the journalists; they were
freed from jail, and Congress returned the fines they'd paid.

As was pointed out in the Constitution Café exchange, the Framers believed that endowing the president with pardoning authority
would help stem potential insurrections by giving the president the
power to restore the peace on occasion by forgiving outside agita-
tors. Jefferson, though, aimed to end an insurrection from within—
one he believed was orchestrated by the very people who'd sworn to
uphold the Constitution, and yet unpardonably, seemed determined
to undo it.

## Vested

*From Article II, Section 1, Clause 1, of the Constitution:* "**The
Executive Power shall be vested in a President of the
United States of America.**"

"Any new article that enumerates the president's designated
powers has to weigh in on whether he does or doesn't—or should
or shouldn't—have authority to issue executive orders and signing
statements and to assert executive privilege," says Karen.

The grassroots environmental activist is among those who
responded to one of my social networking summonses to attend this
Constitution Café gathering to devise an article dealing with executive power. We're meeting in Seattle at a boutique coffee shop that is
managing to thrive among the city's famous chains.

Karen goes on: "The 'general vesting clause' states, 'The executive
power shall be vested in a President of the United States of America.'
But what is meant by 'executive power'? Does it constitute those

powers specifically designated to the president in the Constitution? Or does it mean the president can exercise a general sort of power that might go way beyond them?"

"To me, this vesting clause is meant to give the president a good deal of leeway to deal with the unexpected," says Judy, a hospital administrator. "The Framers knew they couldn't anticipate every future contingency when it came to detailing how the president should best carry out his duties. If we refashion this clause now, all we need do is make clear that when the circumstances warrant, the president has some 'wiggle room,' as long as he uses such power responsibly and furthers the interests of our democracy."

"A president might make blustery claims to the effect that he's being responsible and has democracy's best interests at heart, but that doesn't make it so," says Trish, a doctoral student in political science. "A president shouldn't be allowed to exercise any authority whatsoever that exceeds what's specifically vested with him by the Constitution."

Nodding, Timothy, who works for the world's largest software developer, says, "Take executive privilege. It's an abuse of executive power, designed to keep the White House, the 'People's House,' a house of secrets instead of transparency. A president invokes it whenever he doesn't want himself or his staff to obey a congressional subpoena—even or especially if there's good reason to believe that the actions of the executive branch that are under investigation are willful violations of the Constitution.

"The executive branch shouldn't be privileged in this way. The only way we can make sure that this branch engages in responsible and ethical conduct is if we deny executive privilege to the president and those working directly for him. What this article should do is state unequivocally that executive power is precisely the powers granted by the Constitution to the president, nothing more or less."

"Executive power," he goes on, "constitutes all the powers the

Framers enumerated to the president: the power to sign legislation into law and veto legislation, to make treaties, appoint ambassadors and other ministers and councils, appoint a cabinet and other high-level bureaucrats, nominate Supreme Court justices, grant reprieves and pardons, serve as our commander-in-chief, among others. And most of all, as the Constitution says, he has the special power to 'take care that the laws be faithfully executed.'"

"I would have a new constitutional article explicitly support a broader interpretation," says Judy. "And I believe it's justified. There have been enough times when use of executive power, above and beyond the authority specifically given to the president, has advanced the public good. For instance, when Obama proposed legislation for creating a bipartisan panel for exploring ways to tackle the national debt, Congress rejected it. So the president used an executive order to create the panel. It's for the good of the nation to have such a panel. It hopefully will rise above politics and come up with the needed solutions to bring our debt under control."

"But good uses of unenumerated executive powers are the exception," says Karen. "Signing statements, for example. A president signs a piece of legislation into law, but then attaches a written statement saying that even though he endorses the law, he's modifying elements of it that he finds disagreeable. By doing so, in effect he's turning himself into a one-person supraconstitutional legislative chamber who has endowed himself with the power to alter legislation as he sees fit.

"The fact is, the Constitution doesn't even mention the word 'veto'—rather, it says that the president must either sign every bill presented to him by Congress, or return it. No wiggle room. As George Washington put it when he was president, 'I must approve all the parts of a bill, or reject it in toto.' But then Thomas Jefferson made things murky during his term. He signed an appropriations bill, approving it 'in toto.' But then he refused to spend $50,000 allotted to him by Congress to purchase gunboats because, as he explained it, he thought it was an unnecessary extravagance. So that was sort of the official precursor to signing statements."

"Before Ronald Reagan took over the Oval Office," she goes on, "in the entire history of the presidency, only about seventy-five signing statements had been issued, and they were rather harmless, more like proclamations than attempts to modify existing law. But then Reagan, the first Bush, and Clinton, used them almost 250 times total, with the specific intent of modifying or altering a law passed by Congress. Then George W. Bush issued well over 150 of them, upending more than 1,000 provisions of federal law. The American Bar Association called his actions 'contrary to the rule of law and our constitutional system.'"

"Now Obama is carrying on the signing-statement tradition," she goes on. "While he pledged to 'consult' with his attorney general before issuing any signing statements, he's made it clear that he intends to issue them whenever he believes they're warranted." She passes out copies of a document. "This is the issue paper Obama distributed about signing statements: 'In exercising my responsibility to determine whether a provision of an enrolled bill is unconstitutional, I will act with caution and restraint, based only on interpretations of the Constitution that are well-founded.' Well, if he's going to act with caution and restraint, he should recognize that signing statements are prohibited by the Constitution.

"But he refuses to recognize this. For instance, he approved an omnibus spending bill passed by Congress, only to issue a signing statement declaring he'd ignore those provisions that he found disagreeable, such as the sections restricting U.S. involvement in U.N. peacekeeping, and congressional claims of authority over certain areas of spending."

"The former U.S. senator Arlen Specter twice introduced a bill instructing all branches of government to ignore signing statements," says Trish. "But both times it was allowed to die in committee without debate. Congress has no interest in taking on the president's use and potential abuse of executive power. The only way all of our nation's chief executives will exercise this power properly is if the Constitution makes explicit, in a way that can't be misinterpreted or open to multiple interpretations, what executive power amounts to."

"This article shouldn't hem in a president overmuch," says Judy. "There are just too many unexpected circumstances that may crop up that'll require him to use authority that's not specifically designated. That's not the same thing as saying he should be able to operate unchecked. I believe an article should state that the executive power is not a privilege but a responsibility, and that any use of powers not specifically enumerated must be demonstrably in the public interest and for the good of democracy. President Obama, for instance, has made clear that he plans to make broad use of executive power to advance his energy, environmental, fiscal, and other domestic policy priorities. I support this, and believe it's for the good of democracy."

"Well, I have to admit that in the case of Obama, I don't see anything detrimental to democracy about that," says Karen. "He tried to have enacted legislation that would advance these priorities, but they've stalled in the quagmire of Congress. He's our only nationally elected federal official, and he believes he has to use whatever powers are at his disposal to advance the priorities the people elected him to realize. On the other hand, whenever his predecessor did this, I was up in arms about it, because his priorities weren't mine."

"Maybe they weren't your priorities," says Judy, "but they reflected those of the majority at the time. And it just goes to show why a president needs some ever-so-slight, constitutionally sanctioned latitude if he's going to realize the people's priorities."

*Constitution Café Article:* The Executive Power, which shall be vested in a President of the United States of America, constitutes those powers enumerated in this Constitution, and those that enable a President to take care that the laws are faithfully executed.

## Strong and Weak Chief Executive

Jefferson's views on whether the chief executive of government should be strong or weak changed over time. When he wrote his first draft for a new Virginia constitution in 1776, he advocated a weak executive and granted nearly all power to the legislature. This draft called for Virginia's assemblymen, rather than the people themselves, to elect the chief executive, who he merely called an "Administrator." Among the many limitations that Jefferson placed on the administrator's power, one that he decreed in his draft was that the administrator "shall have no negative [veto power] on the bills of the Legislature." Further, Jefferson's administrator couldn't dissolve or adjourn the legislature, muster the military, declare war, nor conclude a peace agreement. "Such powers," Jefferson wrote, "shall be exercised by the legislature alone." For all intents and purposes, the legislature *was* the chief executive.

But after serving one term as Virginia's governor in 1779, Jefferson dramatically changed his views. At that time, Virginia's existing constitution resembled his own draft version: the chief executive was so hamstrung that he was at the mercy of the General Assembly. Jefferson's political enemies criticized him relentlessly for his decisions as a 'war-time governor' during the Revolutionary War, when the state capitol was overrun by British troops and Jefferson nearly was captured. Yet a subsequent inquiry exonerated Jefferson, whose limited authority would have made a different outcome improbable even if he had been a competent military strategist.

After this experience, Jefferson about-faced and argued that a strong chief executive endowed with powers equal to the other two branches of government was vital if the will of the people was to be carried out. Jefferson later explained his initial reluctance to bestow significant power on the chief executive to the historian Samuel Kercheval, claiming it sprang from the fact that "the abuses of monarchy had so filled all the space of political contemplation." Determined to ensure that the leader of the commonwealth could never become a despot like King George III, Jefferson went to the opposite extreme and created a chief executive so weak that not only could he never become kingly; he could never take on any sort of leadership role whatsoever. In subsequent drafts of his model constitution, Jefferson made Virginia's governor into an executive with an array of powers.

While Jefferson also came to conclude that the nation's president should be a strong executive, he also believed certain limits had to be placed on him. For instance, he argued that one of the greatest flaws in the Constitution was its failure to place term limits on the president. To him, this meant that the president could potentially gain unlimited rule and essentially become a monarch or autocrat. As he wrote in 1807, "if some termination to the services of the chief Magistrate be not fixed by the Constitution, or supplied by practice, his office, nominally four years, will in fact become for life." Jefferson voluntarily imposed on himself a two-term limit as president, and the subsequent two presidents were inspired to do the same.

Jeremy Bailey, in *Thomas Jefferson and Executive Power*, explores Jefferson's use of executive power during his two terms in office and concludes that Jefferson's overarching views on executive power centered on the principle that "the president unifies the will of the nation and thereby embodies it." Because the president is the only nationally elected federal official besides the vice president, Jefferson believed that he would most effectively serve as the conduit for the people's will. But it is inevitable that, as supreme "caretaker of the public good," there will likely arise occasions in which he "must sometimes act outside the law, or even against it, on behalf of the public good."

But if a president does act extraconstitutionally, Jefferson told newspaper editor John Colvin, he must then "throw himself on the justice of his country and the rectitude of his motives," justifying his actions and assuring his constituents that he had acted in their best interests. To enable the people to assess whether he has done right by them, Jefferson believed that the president must attempt, as Bailey puts it, to "gather the national will around a set of declared principles" and establish his reputation as a sound "caretaker of the will of the nation." According to Bailey, Jefferson believed that this approach would best "allow for political change but also preserve constitutional limitations on power by enabling the people to judge executive discretion." By this process, a president would plainly admit when he had gone beyond his constitutionally delegated powers and try to explain why he'd had no choice but to do so to those who'd voted him into office. Jefferson preferred this honest and humble approach to presidents making what to him seemed the untenable claim that the Constitution delegated the chief executive powers above and beyond those specifically enumerated.

Jefferson believed that his predecessor, John Adams, in signing into law the Alien and Sedition Acts, had used specious claims to support the view that the president had broader powers than those explicitly ceded to him. Adams did try to explain himself; he claimed that the impending war with France made these laws just and necessary. The U.S. military, Adams argued, was woefully outmanned by that of the French. He further maintained that there were many sympathizers of the French Revolution in the United States. While there most assuredly were such sympathizers (including the Democratic-Republicans), the question is whether those in America who supported the French Revolution, because they believed it was being waged for similar reasons and objectives as the American Revolution, posed any sort of danger to security. With the U.S. and French navies embroiled in skirmishes in the Caribbean, Adams warned that if this conflict escalated and France invaded American soil, some such sympathizers, U.S. citizens and aliens alike, might create civil unrest at a time when the nation was at its most vulnerable. Democratic-Republicans contended that Adams was using the naval battle as a scare tactic for clamping down on constitutionally guaranteed freedoms, what with his virtually unlimited power under these acts to claim that just about any criticism of his government could be considered seditious. But the Adams administration claimed that the Alien and Sedition Acts, by making it possible to prosecute those who spoke out against its strategems, would ensure that the federal government had all the tools needed to win its conflict with France.

Adams was soundly defeated when he sought to serve a second term as president. A majority of voters agreed with Jefferson's counterclaim that Adams was in fact buttressing his own power at the people's expense when he pushed the acts through. In the Virginia and Kentucky Resolutions of 1798 and 1799 that he penned with James Madison to protest the Alien and Sedition Acts, Jefferson claimed that Adams had taken on the airs of a monarch, and was using the provocation with France as a pretext for silencing Republican critics of his policies. He argued that the Alien and Sedition Acts were the antithesis of the people's will, and "so palpably against the Constitution as to amount to an undisguised declaration that that compact is not meant to be the measure of the powers of the General Government. . . . This would be to surrender the form of government we have chosen and live under one deriving its powers from its own will and not from our authority."

After Jefferson succeeded Adams, he noted—surely referring to his predecessor—that sometimes a president may make what amounts to an unprincipled declaration of principle "in moments of passion or delusion," and that it is up to a wise and "watchful" public to discern when this is the case.

But was Jefferson any more principled as president? Did he himself ever argue for a broad interpretation of the Constitution when it came to use of executive power?

Three of his actions while in office shed light on an answer.

Jefferson peremptorily passed the unpopular Embargo Act in 1807, which prohibited American ships from entering foreign ports. It was particularly aimed at restricting American trade with Britain and France, which were engaged in the Napoleonic Wars, in an effort to prevent American involvement in this conflict. This was disastrous to the U.S. economy, since it brought American trade to a standstill. Leonard Levy, one of the most caustic modern critics of Jefferson, in *Jefferson and Civil Liberties*, has this to say about the embargo: "To this day, it remains the most repressive and unconstitutional legislation ever enacted by Congress in time of peace. No peacetime president ever sought or received such a vast concentration of power as did Jefferson and at the expense of provisions in the Bill of Rights which he himself once advocated as necessary checks against tyranny."

Jeremy Bailey is less harsh, but does acknowledge that Jefferson did not follow his own procedure for justifying executive privilege in this notorious case: Jefferson "did not explain the policy to the national electorate and therefore lost the battle of public opinion."

Soon after his inauguration as president, Jefferson sent U.S. military forces to fight the Barbary Pirates of North Africa, who routinely captured U.S. merchant ships and their crews in the Mediterranean and held them for ransom. Jefferson refused to pay any further tributes, and instead deployed forces to fight the pirates. But he did so without congressional approval, though he was constitutionally required to obtain it. Even members of his own party criticized him for this action. In the end, U.S. forces won out in the four-year conflict, and a treaty was signed. Jefferson did at least follow his own protocol this time around; he used his annual message to Congress to issue a declaration of principles justifying his decision to act outside of constitutional dictates.

> To this state of general peace with which we have been blessed, one only exception exists. Tripoli, the least considerable of the Barbary States, had come forward with demands unfounded either in right or in compact, and had permitted itself to denounce war, on our failure to comply before a given day [to pay tribute]. The style of the demand admitted but one answer. I sent a small squadron of frigates into the Mediterranean . . .

Still, Jefferson failed to explain why he'd neglected to ask Congress to declare war before he deployed troops, as was required—showing he was just as capable as any president of skirting the Constitution and using less than plausible rationales for doing so.

Only Jefferson's famous "Louisiana Purchase" was in line with his professed views on how to go about justifying extraconstitutional use of executive power. Though the negotiations were initially conducted in secret, Jefferson did at first act within constitutional parameters. Since the Constitution did not clearly authorize such a purchase, Jefferson at first tied to muster Congress's support for an amendment that would allow him to acquire over 800,000 square miles of French territory. Jefferson was convinced it would promote the nation's general welfare: it would double the size of the United States, allow for great expansion of settlements, take territory on the North American continent out of the hands of a European government with which it had had serious run-ins, and provide a vast new trading port on a different ocean, generating a much-needed economic boost.

But when it became evident that Jefferson wouldn't be able to garner the support of a two-thirds majority in both chambers of Congress to approve the purchase via a constitutional amendment, he went ahead and acquired the land anyway, fearful that if he didn't act with haste to clinch the deal of the century, Napoleon would change his mind and rescind the offer. On October 20, 1803, the United States purchased the Louisiana Territory for $11,250,000, after the Senate approved the purchase as a treaty, voting 24 to 7 in favor of it.

Jefferson then made his case to the people for why his actions, though undertaken in a constitutional twilight zone, were nonetheless necessary in order to carry out what he believed was the people's mandate to fortify the nation. He argued that it was his duty to purchase the Louisiana Territory come what may, and maintained that this both demonstrated his obedience to a higher law and to an expression of the people's will. Whether this was actually the case is an open question. What is hardly debatable, though, is that the acquisition was a masterstroke. Jefferson was easily reelected for a second term.

Few presidents seem to have considered whether their refusal to adhere to the Constitution that they've sworn to uphold faithfully might constitute in itself a refusal to submit to the nation's will. All too often, those who skirt the Constitution and who then justify it by claiming that they're trying to save our country during dangerous times, not only succeed in sacrificing far more life, liberty, and property than if they had not acted at all, but also, in losing sight of the law itself, succeed in chipping away at democracy's foundations. As Jefferson was the first to recognize, use of executive "prerogative" was "easy of solution in principle, but sometimes embarrassing in practice."

# VIII

## And Justice for All

"Trial by jury" is usually understood to be one of the great pillars of American justice and democracy in general. In his first inaugural address, Jefferson called for a redoubling of the nation's commitment to "equal and exact justice to all men, of whatever state or persuasion, religious or political." He hoped to right the wrongs that had been committed as a result of the Alien and Sedition Acts, which had undermined the constitutional guarantee to a trial by an impartial jury: judges partial to the Federalists had repeatedly influenced jury proceedings by issuing rulings on the law that blatantly favored attempts by the Adams administration to curtail any criticism of the government.

Adams's rationale was that, at a time when America faced potential outside threats, it was better to restrict or suspend constitutional rights in order to make the nation safer, even if democracy itself was endangered in the process. Similarly, the Patriot Act, passed by a compliant Congress following the tragic events of September 11, 2001, was a response by the government to security fears. Civil libertarians argued that the Patriot Act's restrictions on some due process and privacy rights undermined the Constitution, in much the same way that Jefferson's Democratic-Republican Party protested the "unconstitutional" Alien and Sedition Acts.

One might take heart in the fact that if American citizens feel threatened by government abuses or assaults on their rights, they can vote elected officials out of office and replace them with ones who they believe will restore their rights. That's what happened to President Adams and the Federalist members of his Congress; they were ousted following the passage of the Alien and Sedition Acts. Afterward, Jefferson and the Democratic-Republicans in Congress rescinded them. The difference today, though, is that most key elements of the Patriot Act continue to enjoy the wide support of both major parties.

In his inaugural address, Jefferson promised to restore right away the justice system's fair and equitable application of the law. In a gesture to remedy the ill effects of the Alien and Sedition Acts, he called specifically for "impartial selection" of juries, asserting that this was "essential to their value." It's noteworthy that Jefferson didn't call for an impartial jury, but for impartial *selection* of a jury. But there has never been such a selection process in the United States.

In the pre-Revolutionary era, many jurors were chosen because they were deemed to have particular knowledge relating to the case to be tried (which in the South meant juries were often comprised of the wealthiest slaveholders). While the rationale was that since they were wealthy and educated, they would "know best," they were no more representative of the average local denizen than our constitutional Framers were of the average American.

Today juries are selected from voter registration rolls and driver's license records. The thinking is that such random selection makes them more diverse, and as a result supposedly more impartial. But even this method of selection excludes an enormous segment of the population.

What is more, a *New York Times* investigation reveals that "the practice of excluding blacks and other minorities from juries in the South remains widespread" because of peremptory challenges during jury selection. This gives the defense and prosecution the right to reject a certain number of potential jurors without having to give any reason. The result is "racially discriminatory jury selection."[1] In fact, throughout the United States, attorneys are allowed to issue peremptory challenges to exclude potential jurors without stating their reasons. Juries today arguably are less likely than ever to be representative of most Americans.

How can the ideal of justice for all be realized? Is there any way to ensure that justice is meted out equally and exactly to all Americans?

## Peer Pressure

> *From Amendment VI of the Constitution:* **"In all criminal prosecutions, the accused shall enjoy the right to a speedy and public trial, by an impartial jury of the State and district wherein the crime shall have been committed."**

"How many of you believe you have the constitutional right to a trial by jury of your peers?" Darlene asks.

All hands go up.

She shakes her head. "Uh-uh. It doesn't say anywhere in the Constitution that we have that right. All we have is the Sixth Amendment right to a 'speedy and public trial, by an impartial jury.' But what we really need guaranteed is a trial by jury of our peers. We need that constitutional right that everyone believes we have already."

As with most of the women inmates with whom I'm conversing, Darlene does not hesitate to participate with great enthusiasm. Her attitude mirrors that of the enlightened warden to whom I broached the idea of holding a Constitution Café (the previous ten or so had

---

1.  Shaila Dewan, "Study Finds Blacks Blocked from Southern Juries," *New York Times,* June 1, 2010.

turned me down flat); she happened to be a fan of Jefferson and was receptive to giving it a go.

"Should this be included in a new Bill of Rights section?" I ask Darlene now.

"I've been reading over the Constitution, and to me, it should be inserted in the section on the judicial branch in Article III," she says. "That's where the Sixth Amendment should naturally have been included in the first place. And this way, the federal judges know that they aren't the bosses in jury trials. All they do is make sure that the court system operates according to proper procedure. It's the true peers in the jury who preside over the system."

Gabriela nods in agreement. "A jury of our peers wouldn't be impartial. It would be partial. There's no such thing as an impartial jury anyway. Jurors are always judging the person standing trial, and not just based on the evidence presented. With a trial by a true jury of our peers, we can quit pretending 'impartial' exists."

"Who would be an ideal 'partial peer'?" I ask.

"She's someone who's walked your walk a bit," she replies, "so she wouldn't be holier than thou. She'd know something of your pain, but also have some experience of the pain you've caused others, and what you might need to go through to straighten yourself out."

"A peer is someone who is partial in the right way," Darlene says. "People think that if the jury is partial, it can't be objective. But to me, you can't be objective unless you can relate in some way.

"Sure, a juror judges, because you can't help but judge others, no matter how much you might deny it. But she judges herself first. And then, in judging you, she takes in as much of your story as she can, not just the bad and the ugly, but the good too. If the evidence speaks to your guilt, then she'd find you guilty, but she'd have a tear in her eye—like one of my jurors had, while the rest looked at me like I was nothing."

Gabriela is moved to say, "That same day I broke into a car to steal whatever I could get my hands on, so I could sell it and get my fix, I also saved a child who was getting beaten to a pulp by some gang-bangers. That doesn't make me a saint, but it sure makes cowards of all those who stood around with their hands over their mouths, in horror, or pretend horror, doing nothing. I was a good Samaritan that day, and a criminal. I'm also an addict, a person who paints and writes poetry, who tries to be a loving mom, and who has a lot of demons. A partial jury of my peers might take all these things into account."

"For me," says Cyndi, "a jury of partial peers would have to include rich brats whose parents never spent a second with them, Mom always out getting drunk and laid by afternoon at her 'socials,' Dad cheating in his personal and professional life, and looking at me, after he's had a few, in a way a dad should never look at his child."

"Even if someone is 'like you' in experiences like drug abuse, they still may be heartless, until maybe they've 'experienced' getting caught, and are in trouble big time, so they can't be in denial anymore," says Michele.

"Peers haven't done very good by me," she goes on. "Except for my kid sister, those who've been most helpful to me are people who've had almost no experiences like mine—my counselor, for one, who"—looking at Cyndi—"describes herself as a reformed rich brat. She's doing everything she can to help me straighten out my act. Same goes for one of the jurors who found me guilty. I've only been here three months, and she's already visited, and writes me letters of encouragement all the time. Jurors can be objective and partial at the same time. Somehow they can relate to me, at least in that 'there but for the grace of God' way."

Then she says, "I'm thinking, based on my own story, maybe we should leave the jury selection system random, like it is now."

"You think it's random?" says Darlene, incredulous. "You ever see any really down-and-out people on a jury? No, it's all these straightlaced folks. If it were *really* random, then yeah, I could go along with that. I'm not just talking about who you pick out of the hat is who you get, but making the Constitution say that the hat has to include everyone, and I mean everyone—every American age eighteen or over, period."

"Including people in prison?" I ask.

"Including lawmakers, lawbreakers, and everyone in between," she says flatly. "Because that would reflect the 'American peerage' as a whole."

Soon afterward, Gabriela says, "Maybe we're not looking at this 'peer thing' the right way. A peer, in the legal sense, is someone who's treated just like you under the same circumstances. Rich or poor, if your daddy's president or if he's a janitor, if you do the crime, you do the time. Same crime, same punishment. The way it is now, though, some people literally get away with murder if they have the money to get a Johnnie Cochran–style lawyer. Yet others are put away for life—three strikes and you're out—for doing pretty petty crimes in comparison, because they're represented by an overwhelmed, underpaid public defender. In a real peer-based legal system, that couldn't happen. We'd all be treated just the same every step of the way through the process—it would be *real* due process."

"We have to go back one *more* step before that can happen. Peers would have to be the ones making the laws too," says Michele. "The Constitution should say that 'all laws are by peers,' and by that I mean the real mix of Americans that Darlene is speaking about. America is all about diversity, so peers 'American style' would be a diverse group."

"I don't know if that's possible," says Darlene. "But it sure would be nice if our Congress was made up of at least some members who can relate to us and our experiences. And at least having a jury of true peers makes sure the law is applied 'peerlessly.'"

Then she says, "The Fourteenth Amendment guarantees us 'equal protection of the laws,' which means you have the same access as anyone else to the law and the courts, and to be treated equally. This is supposed to protect us from 'cruel and unusual punishment.'"

This prompts Gabriela to say, "As things stand now, people in our situation need protection *from* the laws and courts. Like, Justice Clarence Thomas benefited all his life from affirmative action. But now he can't stand it that other disadvantaged people would want that same equal protection and support. He wants to be peerless in a way that denies his history, when he should be grateful and recognize that we all need a hand up, and that the legal system needs to help provide that. Do you know that he believes it's okay for inmates to be beaten, because he says the country's founders wouldn't have found it cruel and unusual? That's how far removed he is from his own past sufferings."

As the "originalist" legal philosopher among Supreme Court justices, Thomas claims he interprets the Constitution by seeking out the original meaning or intent of the Framers. In 1992, he argued in a dissenting opinion that the beating of a prison inmate was not overly harsh; Thomas maintained that our Constitution's Framers would not have deemed it cruel and unusual punishment.

"I don't want serving on my jury any bleeding heart. I just want someone with a beating heart," Michele says soon afterward. "I know what I did was wrong, and that there's no good excuse, no matter how hard I've had it. I know people who've had it much harder than me, but they never crossed the line into the world of drugs and crime."

"I'd consider President Obama an ideal peer to have had on my jury," Darlene says. "He was truthful about his drug use, and confessed to breaking the law—and in so many words, to getting away with it, since he was never arrested, much less served any time. So in judging me, he'd have to ask himself, 'At a time when I was so low, if I could abuse alcohol, marijuana, cocaine, and get away with it, why in the world would I put this substance abuser in jail, when what she needs is treatment so she doesn't do any more harm to herself or anyone else, especially her loved ones?'"

"I'm not sure I'd want Obama as a peer," Cyndi says to Darlene. "Like you said, he was never punished for his crime. So he never walked the whole walk. He knows he got away with using illegal drugs. If he'd been punished, maybe he'd have come out in favor of legalizing drug use, so it could be controlled. Then the focus could be on prevention and treatment, and he could divert all the billions he's added to the 'war on drugs' in Mexico to these treatment programs."

"I hear what you're saying," Darlene replies. "But you know what? I wouldn't have wanted him to be imprisoned. He was just crying out for help. And now look where he is. He overcame all those lows, and is an inspiration to us all, because he was open about his troubles, and has shown great humility."

"I'm a sinner and a lawbreaker, plain and simple," Gabriela says, looking my way. "I bet you are too, and I bet the people who tried and convicted me are. People cheat on their spouses, cheat on their taxes, drive drunk or drugged—even with kids in their car—and get away with it. They hit people, hurt people, abuse them mentally and emotionally. Yet they're considered 'innocent,' because they've never been caught or found out. They serve on juries all the time."

"A jury of peers," says Darlene, "should be made up not just of people who reflect who you are now, or who you've been, but who you want to be."

*Constitution Café Article:* In all criminal prosecutions, the accused shall enjoy the right to a speedy and public trial by a jury of true peers of the State and district wherein the crime shall have been committed.

## Judge and Jury

Jefferson didn't go as far as one Constitution Café participant at the prison, who argued that all Americans should be involved in the process of making law. He did, however, maintain that if juries "think the permanent judges are under any bias whatever in any cause," they are authorized to "take on themselves to judge the law as well as the fact." So in an instance when jurors believe a judge is not issuing rulings according to the law, but rather is allowing political bias or bribery to dictate his decisions, jurors would not just determine guilt or innocence, but would also assume the judge's role in the proceedings.

John Jay, the first chief justice of the U.S. Supreme Court, ruled[2] that while typically "juries are the best judges of facts" and "courts are the best judges of law," there are instances in which "both objects are within [juries'] power of decision." Under such circumstances, juries "have a right to take it upon [themselves] to judge of both, and to determine the law as well as the fact in controversy." As a result, jurors would not only be able to override a judge, but to nullify existing law.

This right to "nullification" was first established in the New World in 1735. John Peter Zinger, a New York newspaper publisher was arrested for "seditious libel" because he criticized the royal governor of New York in print. During the trial, the royal prosecutor himself acknowledged that what Zinger had written about the governor was true, but that Zinger's arrest was nonetheless legal because such criticism was banned. The jury, though, ruled in Zinger's favor, declaring him not guilty. Zinger had indeed broken the law, but since the jury considered the law to be unjust, it found him innocent.

2. In the case *Georgia* v. *Brailsford*, the Supreme Court itself presided over a jury trial.

To this day, though it is not widely known or practiced, nullification remains a right in jury trials. A jury (or a single juror) can invalidate the law as it applies to the specific case over which it is presiding and find a defendant not guilty even if he has committed the infraction for which he is standing trial. In our nation's history, nullification has been used for both humane and destructive purposes by juries that were not impartially selected. For instance, during the Civil War, juries sympathetic to the cause of emancipation refused to convict abolitionists even when they broke laws that prohibited them from helping slaves. On the other hand, during the civil rights era, all-white juries refused to convict whites who murdered blacks.

One could argue that the Declaration of Independence established the right to nullification in the United States. After all, it asserted that England had forfeited legal authority over the colonies after committing the egregious offense of subjecting the colonies to laws enacted without their consultation or consent.

## Crime and Punishment

No one influenced Jefferson's ideas on criminal code reforms more than Cesare Beccaria (1738–1794), the Italian nobleman and iconoclastic criminologist. In particular, Jefferson was taken with Beccaria's then-novel assertion that the only meaningful criterion for determining the appropriateness of a penalty for any given criminal infraction was whether it served as an effective deterrent. Beccaria's perspective sharply contrasted with the prevailing ethos that punishment was meant primarily to be retributive in nature. Beccaria argued in his landmark work *On Crimes and Punishments* that it is

> better to prevent crimes than to punish them. This is the
> ultimate end of every good legislation, which . . . is the art

of leading men to the greatest possible happiness. . . . Do
you want to prevent crimes? See to it that laws are clear and
simple and that the entire force of a nation is united in their
defense. . . . See to it that the laws favor not so much classes
of men as men themselves. See to it that men fear the laws
and nothing else.

If the public believed that the punishment for a specific crime
was far harsher than it should be, Beccaria believed that society's
lawmakers themselves would come to be perceived as unjust, and
that over time this perception could heighten the prospects of civil
unrest.

Beccaria considered the death penalty tantamount to "a war of a
whole nation against a citizen, whose destruction they consider as
necessary, or useful to the general good." He argued that there was
not a shred of evidence that showed it prevented crime. He maintained that "the long and painful example of a man deprived of his
freedom and become a beast of burden, repaying with his toil the
society he has offended" would serve as the best deterrent.

Jefferson acknowledges in his memoirs that "Beccaria, and other
leading writers on crimes and punishments had satisfied the reasonable world on the unrightfulness and inefficacy of the punishment of crimes by death," and that "hard labor on roads, canals
and other public works, had been suggested as a proper substi-
tute." While Jefferson did not endorse the wholesale elimination
of the death penalty, he did propose to dramatically cut down on
the instances in which it was applied. In the criminal reform bill
presented to Virginia's legislature in 1778 as part of their constitutional reform package, Jefferson and his committee of Revisors
suggested doing away with most instances of capital punishment,
arguing that it served no warrantable purpose: "the reformation of
offenders . . . is not effected at all by capital punishments, which

exterminate instead of reforming." Like Beccaria, they believed that
the death penalty

> should be the last melancholy resource against those whose
> existence is become inconsistent with the safety of their
> fellow citizens, which also weaken the state by cutting off so
> many who, if reformed, might be restored sound members
> to society, who, even under a course of correction, might be
> rendered useful in various labors for the public, and would
> be living and long continued spectacles to deter others from
> committing the like offences.

However, as Jefferson relates in his memoirs, "the general idea of
our country had not yet advanced to that point"—or at least, it had
not yet advanced sufficiently among his colleagues in the Virginia
legislature. His comprehensive bill to reform the criminal justice code
"was lost in the house of Delegates by a majority of a single vote."

## Judging Judges

*From Article III, Section 1, of the Constitution:* "**The judges,
both of the supreme and inferior Courts, shall hold their
Offices during good Behaviour.**"

"The third article of the Constitution establishes the judiciary
branch of the government," Colin says, "and the first section of that
article, after establishing the federal judiciary, says that all judges
from the Supreme Court justices on down 'shall hold their offices during good behavior.' That's been interpreted throughout our history to
mean that federal judges can serve for life, as long as they behave well.

"I'm not sure the fact that they are exemplars of good behavior—or
at least, that they're adept at keeping any bad behavior on their part

out of the public eye—is enough to warrant giving them life terms,"
Colin goes on. "Basically they serve at their pleasure rather than
that of the American people or even the president who appointed
them with the Senate's advice and consent. They're like monarchs
who can only be dethroned if they do something really, really bad, or
if they choose to abdicate of their own volition. That doesn't seem
appropriate for judges serving in a democracy."

Colin, a retired high-level federal bureaucrat, whom I first met a
decade ago while on book tour, arranged this gathering in Florida.
We're joined by a number of others in the large commons area in the
retirement community in which they live.

"In our nation's early years, the federal judges didn't serve such
long terms, even though there were no limits placed by the Constitution on how long they could serve," says Eugene, a former dean at an
Ivy League university. "So all presidents typically had ample opportunity to appoint judges, since there was considerable turnover. But
since most federal judges these days choose to serve very long terms,
maybe it would be fitting to place a specific limit on their tenure."

"I personally don't mind if federal judges serve for life," says
Norma, who was a family law attorney for over half a century. "But
in the case of the Supreme Court, I also believe that each president
should have the opportunity to put his stamp on it. A revised constitutional article can give him this opportunity. Why should one
president be able to appoint one or more justices, and another none
at all? Franklin Roosevelt appointed eight, a record. Even George
Washington, our first president, who was there on the scene when
the Court came to be, only appointed seven."

"But if there's nine justices total, how is it that Washington only
appointed seven?" asks Evelyn, a retired sociology professor.

Norma smiles. "I'd wondered the same thing. But then I realized, after scrutinizing this article and doing a little research, that
it doesn't state how many justices can serve on the Court. The

numbers have in fact varied over the years. We could have a hundred Supreme Court justices if Congress passed legislation to that effect. The Framers must have had a reason for leaving the number open-ended. Maybe they thought we should have more justices as the nation expanded.

"At first I wasn't sure I agreed with the Framers, who didn't set a limit on how many justices there could be. But after thinking about it for a while, I decided that that's fine with me. What I would do, however, is add language to this article that gives each sitting president the opportunity to appoint at least one justice."

"I'm not sure I'd tamper with the existing language in the Constitution on this matter," says Colin. "Congress has the power to increase or decrease the number of justices on the Court. If a president wants more justices on the Court, he can always ask Congress to consider increasing the number. That's what Franklin Roosevelt did."

In the mid-1930s, President Roosevelt had the strong support of Congress as he launched progressive New Deal reforms, only for the conservative Supreme Court to resist. The Court dismantled one New Deal initiative after another, declaring them unconstitutional. In response, FDR proposed to Congress a law that would enable him to appoint as many as six additional justices. While Congress was considering the legislation, the Court underwent a striking about-face: the justices—fearing their individual power would be diluted if their numbers were increased—reversed their earlier decisions against Roosevelt's programs. This paved the way for the New Deal, and FDR stopped his legislative push for additional justices. There have been no further attempts to change the number of justices on the Court.

"I wouldn't be surprised if our fairly liberal president is tempted to try to add to the Court," says Evelyn. "He'll surely clash with the conservative majority on the Court on matters ranging from the constitutionality of health care reform legislation to the overhaul of the banking and finance system.

"But rather than give a president the opportunity to increase the number of sitting justices for reasons of political expediency, I'm in agreement with Norma; I'd give each president the guaranteed opportunity to appoint at least one judge and have an impact on the makeup of the bench on the nation's highest bench."

"If, in this article we're redoing, we did give a president the power to appoint a justice for each term of office he serves," Colin says, "there's no guarantee that the president's appointee will make rulings in his favor. Some justices have shown great independence, and risen above their previously partisan leanings to make a body of rulings that are far different than what anyone could have anticipated before they assumed their seat."

"The president should still be given a chance to impact the Court's makeup, even if the impact isn't the one he intended," says Eugene. "Since the Court itself is made up of unelected officials, a sitting president, as the only nationally elected federal official, would hopefully appoint someone he believes is reflective of, or at least in touch with, the sensibilities and hopes of most Americans of the times in which he serves."

"I'm not sure the fact that a justice is one of the most recent appointees necessarily means he or she is the most in touch with Americans' pulse," says Norma. "George W. Bush appointed justices who were most like him, conservative in a dogmatic way. And Obama's appointees all reflect his liberal sensibilities. Yet most Americans aren't nearly as liberal or conservative as any of the most recently appointed Justices."

"To me," she goes on, "the recently retired Justice John Paul Stevens, the third-longest-serving justice, has been most in sync with Americans over the past decades. Justice Stevens served for thirty-six years, until age ninety. He was unchanging in the best sense. As the political winds tacked one way and then another during his tenure, he continued to issue rulings in what most call iconoclastic fashion, but what I'd call just plain fair fashion. He's billed as a liberal today, just as he was billed as a moderate conservative in his early years as a judge. But he hasn't changed at all; those around him have. By fairness and evenhandedness above all political considerations, he's the epitome of judicial 'good behavior.'"

"We're back to that term 'good behavior,'" Colin says. "I'm still not comfortable with how it's included in this existing constitutional article. For one thing, it's the only qualification that this article establishes for anyone to serve as a federal judge. This article sets no professional, age, or even citizenship qualifications. At the very least, federal judges should have to demonstrate 'exemplary behavior' rather than just comportment of the 'good' variety."

"But even 'exemplary behavior' is so open to interpretation that it really becomes an empty criterion," Evelyn says.

"Maybe this article should strike the term 'good behavior' and focus instead on bad behavior," says Norma. "That way, it'd be in line with the constitutional articles that spell out under what circumstances those in the executive and legislative branches are subject for removal from office, namely for committing high crimes and misdemeanors."

"But the Constitution already does this for the judiciary branch as well," says Eugene. "The justices are civil officers. And the Constitution says that 'all civil officers of the United States, shall be removed from office on impeachment for, and conviction of, treason, bribery, or other high crimes and misdemeanors.'[3] So in order to keep their jobs, the Constitution does make clear that at the least they have to behave as well as any other civil officer, or they can be impeached."

"Maybe so," says Colin, "but in my opinion, most of them still have been judicial activists. They rule on the law in ways that mesh with their personal and political views, and oftentimes they refuse

3. From Article II, Section 4, of the Constitution.

to voluntarily recuse themselves from cases even when they clearly have a conflict of interest. For better or worse, that's about the best behavior we've been able to get out of them."

"I don't know about that," says Norma. "Some of them, like Justice Stevens, have shown not only that they are quite qualified, but have also shown that they strive to be impartial, and that they are also of excellent character.

"In approving Obama's nominee Elena Kagan to the Supreme Court to replace Justice Stevens, the Republican senator Lindsey Graham said he'd never have appointed her if he'd been president. But he still thought she was an excellent choice, because she was highly qualified and had unimpeachable character. And that's what this article should say: that federal judges should have to be exceptionally qualified, and paragons of exemplary behavior. If Kagan continues to build on her character and her professional qualities as if they're tied together, she may turn out to be every bit as exemplary as the justice she's replacing."

> *Constitution Café Article:* The judges, both of the supreme and inferior courts, shall be exceptionally qualified and of unimpeachable character, and shall hold their Offices during exemplary Behavior. The president shall appoint to the Supreme Court one Justice during the second year of his four-year term.

## The Chase Case

Only one Supreme Court justice, Samuel Chase, has ever been impeached by the House. This either goes to show just how honest and aboveboard our justices have been over the years, or how difficult it is to remove them from the bench.

Chase was a signer of the Declaration and represented Maryland in the Continental Congress. He was appointed to the Supreme Court by John Adams. None other than Thomas Jefferson, who was president at the time, sought to have Chase ousted. An ardent Federalist, Chase imposed severe sentences on those convicted of violating the Alien and Sedition Acts.

Jefferson argued that Chase let his political views cloud his judgment to such an extent that he betrayed his oath of office. In pushing for Justice Chase's impeachment, Jefferson asked Congressman Joseph Hopper Nicholson of Maryland, "Ought the seditious and official attack [by Chase] on the principles of our Constitution . . . to go unpunished?" In 1804, at Jefferson's behest, the Republican-dominated House of Representatives served Chase with eight articles of impeachment. The thrust of the charges against Chase was that his pro-Federalist bias prevented him from treating defendants and their counsel impartially. While Jefferson did succeed in having him impeached by the House, Chase was acquitted at trial in the Senate. Its members didn't agree with Jefferson that Chase's evident partisan rulings provided grounds for dismissal. Moreover, the Constitution doesn't specifically prohibit justices from becoming directly involved in partisan politics. Chase then resumed his duties on the Court.

## Upon Further Review

*From Article III, Section 1 of the Constitution:* "The judicial Power of the United States, shall be vested in one supreme Court, and in such inferior Courts as the Congress may from time to time ordain and establish."

*From Article III, Section 2, Clause 1, of the Constitution:* "The judicial Power shall extend to all Cases, in Law and Equity, arising under this Constitution, the Laws of the United States, and Treaties made, or which shall be made, under their Authority;—to all Cases affecting Ambassadors, other public Ministers and Consuls;—to all Cases of admiralty and maritime Jurisdiction;—to Controversies to which the United States shall be a Party;—to Controversies between two or more States;—between a State and Citizens of another State;—between Citizens of different States;— between Citizens of the same State claiming Lands under Grants of different States, and between a State, or the Citizens thereof, and foreign States, Citizens or Subjects."

*From Article III, Section 2, Clause 3, of the Constitution:* "In all Cases affecting Ambassadors, other public Ministers and Consuls, and those in which a State shall be Party, the supreme Court shall have original Jurisdiction. In all the other Cases before mentioned, the supreme Court shall have appellate Jurisdiction, both as to Law and Fact, with such Exceptions, and under such Regulations as the Congress shall make."

"Let's say Congress votes to give every American a turkey for Thanksgiving, or a revolver for self-defense, or good health care for self-preservation," says George, a lawyer who once argued (and lost) a case before the Supreme Court, and is one of a baker's dozen of lawyers gathered with me. "But then an American or group of Americans—maybe a disgruntled vegetarian or group of gun control advocates or Libertarians—disagrees with these acts of Congress and decides to sue. Their cases eventually make their way to the Supreme Court, where a majority rules that Congress acted unconstitutionally, and invalidates these laws. That puts an end to the matter, because the Supreme Court is the final arbiter on issues of constitutionality, right?" He shakes his head. "That may be how it is, but it's not how the Framers meant for it to be."

Then George says, "This power of 'judicial review,' in which legislative and executive actions are subject to scrutiny and possible invalidation by the federal judiciary, is a constitutional chimera. Nowhere in the Constitution is the federal judiciary ceded this authority. So every time the Court rules that an enacted law is or isn't constitutional, it itself is acting unconstitutionally. This 'new Constitution' can explicitly nullify judicial review. Because it puts the federal judiciary on a much higher footing than the other two branches, undoing the checks and balances in the Constitution that created three separate and equal powers."

Giselda disagrees. The defense attorney and adjunct law professor says, "This new article should state that judicial review *is* within the parameters of the Court's authority. It would throw the entire legal system into chaos, and create unimaginable civil unrest, if it were dismantled now. Judicial review has been legal precedent since it was established by the Supreme Court in 1803."

Giselda is making reference to the 1803 Supreme Court case of *Marbury* v. *Madison*, which stemmed from one of the first acts accomplished by Thomas Jefferson when he became president. In an eleventh-hour move before leaving office, his predecessor John Adams, in collaboration with the Federalist-dominated Congress (soon to be replaced by a majority of Republicans), expanded the number of circuit courts and filled these new judicial seats with pro-Federalist appointees. Jefferson refused to seat any of the judges who had not yet been commissioned by the time Adams left office. One of the judges, William Marbury, an Adams cohort, petitioned the Supreme Court to seat him. To Marbury's disappointment, John Marshall, the chief justice and a fellow Federalist, denied his petition, ruling that it was outside the court's purview. The matter should have ended there, but Marshall used this case to declare that even though the Court might be powerless to help seat him in this specific instance, it nonetheless "is emphatically the province and duty of the Judicial Department [the judicial branch] to say what the law is. Those who apply the rule to particular cases must, of necessity, expound and interpret that rule." Marshall claimed that the Court did indeed have the rightful authority to decide which acts of the other two branches were and were not constitutional.

Giselda says next, "Even if I grant that I'm not sure whether the Framers intended for the federal judiciary to have this authority, the fact is, it has had the power of judicial review for over two hundred years. And there's never been a single attempt by the other two branches to challenge it and declare this power untenable. So it should stay just as it is."

"Thomas Jefferson *wanted* to take on the Marshall Court and put an end to the power of judicial review before it could begin," George says in return. "And he would have if he'd had occasion to. But Justice Marshall was too clever. He technically ruled in Jefferson's favor in *Marbury* v. *Madison*, refusing to seat Marbury as a judge, even as he went on to declare that the Court was the final decider of the validity of federal statutes. Marshall didn't dare take on Jefferson. It wasn't until two decades after Marbury died that the Court exercised judicial review powers. And those powers have been inappropriately used by the court and the rest of the federal judiciary ever since."

"I'm with Giselda," says Jason, who runs what he describes as a boutique law firm. "Judicial review has served as an effective constraint on the president and Congress. The fact that the Court has only struck down 160 acts of Congress and about 1,000 state laws since our founding shows that it exercises this power with restraint."

"But in striking down even one such law," George replies, "by utilizing powers it was never granted, the Court is altering the course of our democracy, opposing the will of Americans as carried out by those they elected to enact laws on their behalf. This power has to be wrested from the Court. It's monarchical. Even the king of England was stripped of this power way back in 1688, when a provision was inserted in the Magna Carta that did away with judicial review. From then on, the king was unable to declare legislative statutes void."

Clair, a city attorney, says now, "One can argue that chaos would ensue if this power of the Court's was done away with. But I'd argue that there's been even more damage done because of its existence.

"For example, in 1996, Congress passed the Line Item Veto Act. Before its passage, the chief executive had to veto an entire budgetary appropriations package, even if he found just a few 'line items' to be objectionable. But this legislative act gave presidents the authority to cancel specific budgetary provisions, instead of vetoing a budget appropriation in its entirety. Presidents had long been clamoring for line-item veto authority. In making a memorable plea for it, Ronald Reagan said, 'I'll make the cuts, I'll take the heat.'

"And finally, Congress passed it. For a brief time, Clinton was able to exercise the line-item veto. He struck scores of pork barrel items from the budget. Goodbye, politics as usual. But two years later, a majority of justices struck down the law. They ruled that the line-item veto was unconstitutional, that it granted the president powers he wasn't intended to have. Yet in making the ruling against one of the most popular pieces of legislation in modern history, the justices exercised a power that they themselves weren't intended to have."

"If the power of judicial review is eliminated, how are conflicts between the three federal branches resolved?" I ask.

"The voters will resolve them," says Ray, who has run unsuccessfully for the U.S. Senate almost as many times as Harold Stassen once ran for president.[4] "If Congress and the president push through legislation they find objectionable, they'll vote them out. That's how the Framers meant for the process to work itself out."

Jason frowns. He says, "You make it sound like it's some great

4. The former governor of Minnesota unsuccessfully sought the presidency twelve times between 1944 and 2000.

gesture to leave all the doings of the executive and legislative branches up to 'the people' when it comes to deciding what is and isn't constitutional. We need a wiser and more objective arbiter that isn't subject to the people's whims, so that our inalienable rights and liberties are preserved. By being above the fray, the Supreme Court can rule dispassionately. With the power of judicial review, the Court ensures that the tyranny of the majority isn't the last word on any legislative subject."

To which Ray replies, "You could apply this notion of tyranny of the majority to the Supreme Court itself. The Court only needs a majority of five justices to decide as it will, as was the case when five justices handed the 2000 presidential election to George W. Bush, or when it recently eviscerated the comprehensive campaign finance reform laws enacted by Congress. I'm not comfortable with five people wielding such power. No wonder Jefferson equated judicial review with the 'despotism of an oligarchy.'"

"The fact is, rarely have our justices been paragons of 'dispassionate objectivity,'" he goes on. "Most have personal agendas when they make their rulings that have little do with constitutionality. I prefer a tyranny of a legislative majority than that of a majority of five justices. At least legislative power is dispersed among 535 people who face elections periodically, and so they're directly answerable to the voters. The more that the judiciary takes public policy matters out of the people's hands, the more apathetic Americans become, the less informed about policy, because they know that, whether informed or not, their opinion makes no difference; only that of the Supreme Court matters."

"In the Court's landmark 1973 decision on *Roe* v. *Wade* that upheld a woman's right to terminate a pregnancy," Claire says, "Justice Byron R. White, in a stinging dissent, chastised his fellow justices for stepping in where Congress, or the states themselves, had the rightful role." She opens a textbook she has with her to a chapter that discusses this decision. "Here's what Justice White had to say about this decision: 'As an exercise of raw judicial power, the Court perhaps has authority to do what it does today, but, in my view, its judgment is an improvident and extravagant exercise of the power of judicial review that the Constitution extends to this Court.' White believed this issue had to be left 'with the people and to the political processes the people have devised to govern their affairs.' He was totally opposed to judicial supremacy."

After a pause, George speaks up again. "Antiabortion activists are waiting for one more conservative justice to be seated on the bench in order to continue placing restrictions on abortions, and eventually to overturn *Roe* v. *Wade* altogether. Meanwhile, proabortion or prochoice advocates are praying that the current president will have the chance to appoint enough liberal justices so that they'll be able to reverse recent rulings that make it more difficult to have an abortion.

"But if we do away with the power of judicial review, this issue would have to redound to Congress, where it belongs in the first place. Congress would finally have to debate this and other hot-button issues, and make the tough legislatives decisions that they should have had to make decades ago."

*Constitution Café Article:* The judicial Power shall not extend to the review and possible invalidation of Legislative and Executive actions.

## The Reviews Are In

In the pre-Revolutionary days, advisory bodies called privy councils were charged with reviewing legislation passed by colonial assemblies and with assessing whether the assemblies were acting within the parameters of the powers granted them by colonial charters.

Though a rare occurrence, the councils did at times overturn legislation. Once the colonies became states, state courts (which supplanted privy councils) struck down laws passed by assemblies on occasion. While the Framers surely were aware of this practice, there is no compelling evidence that they supported judicial review at the federal level.

After the Constitution was ratified and the system of government set forth by the Framers was put into place, Jefferson was not opposed in principle to some sort of judicial oversight over legislation. However, he'd thought that such judicial oversight would be limited to ensuring that the government did not encroach on any rights granted to citizens by the Bill of Rights. But after witnessing the concerted attempts by Federalist judges to enforce any and all perceived infringements of the Alien and Sedition Acts, Jefferson changed his tune and from then on came out strongly against judicial review.

Jefferson expressed his opposition to judicial review in regard to the Alien Sedition Acts in the course of an exchange with Abigail Adams, the wife of John Adams, who supported the acts: "You seem to think it devolved on the judges to decide on the validity of the Sedition Law. But nothing in the Constitution has given them a right to decide for the Executive, more than to the Executive to decide for them."

"The Constitution," Jefferson argued, ". . . meant that its coordinate branches should be checks on each other. But the opinion which gives to the judges the right to decide what laws are constitutional and what not, not only for themselves in their own sphere of action but for the Legislature and Executive also in their spheres, would make the Judiciary a despotic branch."

Jefferson believed the Framers were wise in creating a Constitution that "erected no such single tribunal, knowing that to whatever hands confided, with the corruptions of time and party, its members would become despots. It has more wisely made all the departments co-equal and co-sovereign within themselves."

If, as Jefferson posited, each of the three branches is "truly independent of the others and has an equal right to decide for itself what is the meaning of the Constitution in the cases submitted to its action," then how are turf wars between them to be resolved?

He noted that Spain's constitution has a promising solution in stipulating that "when the three coordinate branches differ in their construction of the constitution, the opinion of the two branches shall overrule the third."

As was one Constitution Café participant, Jefferson was particularly partial to the contention that it is up to the voters to see to it that the legislative and executive branches do not overstep their bounds: "When the legislative or executive functionaries act unconstitutionally, they are responsible to the people in their elective capacity." To him, "the exemption of the judges" from voters' scrutiny was "quite dangerous enough" without compounding this by giving them judicial review powers.

# IX

# Governors and the Governed

T he country of Bhutan adopted a new constitution in 2008, after the former Himalayan kingdom held its first-ever democratic election. The new constitution included a mandate stipulating that the worth of the nation's governors must be "judged not by the economic benefits they may offer but by the happiness they produce." Prime Minister Jigme Tinley told the *New York Times* that the goal of this mandate is to require governors to "create the conditions for . . . an updated version of the American Declaration of Independence, 'the pursuit of gross national happiness.'" To that end, the government assesses whether its citizens are able to pursue happiness by gauging a range of "domains," from psychological well-being to how much time a person spends with his family.

Bhutan's range of indicators only measures happiness in citizens' private affairs. Yet the one indicator that Jefferson deemed essential for achieving happiness is a person's right to take part in guiding public affairs, and not just on Election Day. Jefferson believed that the realization of an excellent society hinges not on iconic statesmen, "no matter how 'great and virtuous,'" but on the involvement of ordinary citizens, "enlightened, peaceable and really free."[1]

1. Jean Yarbrough, *American Virtues: Thomas Jefferson on the Character of a Free People* (University Press of Kansas, 2009).

Bhutan notwithstanding, does the representative system of government devised by our own nation's Framers best encourage such involvement?

Although the opening phrase of our Constitution, "We the people," makes clear the Framers' conviction that the power vested in the federal government comes from the people themselves, a nationwide poll conducted in 2010 by the Center for the Constitution revealed that half of Americans nonetheless believe that governmental authority doesn't spring from the people at all, but from elected officials.

Clearly there's an implicit tension between "representative" and "government" in "representative government." Do we want our elected officials primarily to serve as conduits for realizing citizens' expressed will—or at least the will of the majority? If so, is the republican system devised by the Framers structured to achieve this?

## Representative Representatives

*Article I, Section 2, Clause 1, of the Constitution:* **"The House of Representatives shall be composed of Members chosen every second Year by the People of the several States."**

*Article I, Section 2, Clause 3:* **"The Number of Representatives shall not exceed one for every Thirty thousand, but each State shall have at Least one Representative."**

"The only stipulation the Constitution makes regarding the size of the House of Representatives is that the 'number of Representatives shall not exceed one for every thirty thousand,'" Jim says.

Jim served in the House for ten years; his tenure ended after he was defeated in a primary by a more conservative Republican. He and Mary, a recently elected congresswoman, agreed to speak with me (in this case, by conference call) about my Constitution Café project, but asked not to be fully identified.

Jim says now, "It used to be that the House regularly increased the number of members as the population grew. But in 1911, House members set the number at 435. Except for one brief occasion, it has remained at that number ever since.[2] In 1911, our population was less than 94 million. A hundred years later, we have a population of over 308 million people, but we're still stuck at 435 members of the House. You can't have very 'representative' representatives when the number of members hasn't gone up as the population has swelled."

"The mind-set was that if House membership got any bigger, it'd be unwieldy," Jim goes on. "But only by increasing the number of members as the population grows is genuine representation possible. Every representative today has about 600,000 constituents. No matter how punishing a schedule you have, you can't really learn the pulse of your district in an up-close and personal way.

"Instead of increasing the number of House members, the congressional staff has been regularly augmented. Each member of Congress has 22 staff members. I'd prefer having that number dramatically cut back—so there's only 2 staffers per member of Congress—and increase the number of House members by a factor of 20, so there's one representative for every 30,000 people. This would fulfill the Framers' purpose for the House, and again make it a chamber of 'representativeness.' I'd change the language of the existing constitutional article so it says, 'the number of Representatives shall be one for every thirty thousand,' rather than 'shall not exceed one for every thirty thousand.'"

2. In 1959, the House temporarily increased the size to 437, to give the new states of Alaska and Hawaii new members, before they again reduced it to 435.

Mary whistles. "That'd give us something like, calculating off the top of my head, 10,000-plus representatives. With what you're proposing, Jim, members of Congress would have to gather in what amounts to a space about the size of a big high school or small-college football stadium."

"Is that bad?" Jim says. "It would be a modern-day version of how the Greeks in ancient Athens gathered in a stadium to deal with legislative matters. Whenever an assembly was called into session, the first 6,000 men to arrive at the stadium on the top of the Acropolis Hill took part in the vote on the measure. It was a large and raucous gathering, and the people's business was accomplished. And you know, if we'd kept gradually increasing House membership all along, we wouldn't think 10,000 was so dramatic a figure any more than the Greeks would have."

"Oh, it would still be dramatic," says Mary. "Even if we'd kept increasing the number of members over the past century at the rate we had until 1911, we'd have at most about 1,800 today."

"Do you think 1,800 members would work well?" I ask her.

She thinks about this. "It might, if they were brought into the fold gradually, perhaps over a ten-year period. Maybe this new article should simply state that, from now on, with each one percent increase of population, a new member of the House will be added to the rolls. It could further stipulate that these new members would be added after the new figures from each census come in."

"But even with my proposal of having one member of Congress per 30,000 constituents," Jim says, "if you take into account that we'd also reduce sharply the number of staff members, the overall change isn't so significant. If you multiply the number of congressmen, 435, by the number of staff each has, 22, that comes to 9,750 people. Rather than having an army of unelected staffers, there'd be so many more additional elected representatives who'd really get to know and explore the issues with their constituents. And this just may also decrease the influence of professional lobbyists, since they'd have to deal with legions of congressmen."

"I'm just not keen on the retroactive idea," Mary says. "My counterproposal is that we have one congressperson for every 60,000 citizens, and that she be allowed two staff members. That still would put us at about 5,000 members in the House, a huge increase and a big step towards more representativeness."

"How would you go about redrawing congressional districts every ten years to make space for all these new members of the House?" I ask.

"You know, there's no mention in the Constitution of how congressional districts are to be drawn up, only that there shall be at least one member of the House per state," says Jim. "For this project of yours, we should come up with a constitutional mechanism for creating districts, one that replaces the politically charged way its done now. Gerrymandering usually stacks the deck in favor of one party over the other, and almost always makes types of artificial boundaries that don't serve the interests of 'representativeness.' Rather than creating districts that gibe with the contours of a region, as they should, you have these schizophrenic lines drawn that ensure one party will dominate. Often neighborhoods are split right in half to load a district with voters who'll support the House members in office there."

"I'd also agree with the idea that congressional districts be drawn up in a uniform way in each state," says Mary. "Let's have this constitutional article state that districts for the House will be determined by decennial census results, with the boundaries for each district determined by a nonpartisan group of citizens of each state. This will take the decision-making authority out of party hands."

"That gets my vote," says Jim. Then he adds with a laugh, "Of course, if an article like this really came to be, odds are greater that I may not have lasted even ten years, since my district is artificially drawn so it's stacked with Republican voters. I never imagined I'd be blindsided by my own party." He pauses. "But who knows, maybe if my district had been more rationally drawn in the first place, I'd still be in office."

I eventually say, "You both seem to think that 'representative-ness' can best be had by increasing the number of Congress's members. But the winner-take-all majority voting system encourages our two-party system. Would a parliamentary form of representation lead to better or truer representation of our diverse citizenry? Elected officials in countries constitutionally bound to use this system typically have a far greater number of political parties with elected representatives, especially in the lower chamber of government."

"I suspect that if we markedly increased the number of congressmen, it'd just about ensure there'd be more political parties represented in the House," says Jim. "For one thing, it'd make it possible for candidates of small political parties—or no party at all—to have a good chance of winning, since they'd be able to get their message out in a cost-effective way. In addition, if each member of Congress represented just 30,000 or 60,000 constituents rather than 600,000, there'd be greater voter turnout, because people would know their vote really mattered, especially if districts were drawn up in nonpartisan fashion. So that greater voter turnout would also help a really dynamic candidate who's outside the traditional two-party umbrella."

"It'd open up creative ways of campaigning," Mary says, "and probably break the grip on corporate funding of campaigns. This might take some of the sting out of the Supreme Court's recent ruling against campaign finance reform. Having such intimate representation might make candidates less beholden to the special interests that fund their campaigns, since so much less money will be needed in order to run effectively for office."

Mary sighs. "Dare I even dream of a day when I don't have to spend more of my waking hours raising money for my next campaign than I devote to my constituents?"

"Now that Mary and I are in agreement about this particular issue," Jim eventually says, "I'd also like to suggest that the Constitution state that members of the House—and of the Senate too, for that matter—rotate office every election term. Democracy would be better served if they had to sit out a term before they could run for office again. This'd prevent the advent of entrenched politicians."

"Wishful thinking," says Mary.

"Isn't that what this thought experiment is all about?" Jim says. "To imagine what, in our eyes, a 'dream Congress' would be like?"

"I suppose, in the 'dream Congress' scenario, that might be ideal for the American people," says Mary. "Nor would I be opposed to the rotating office scheme Jim proposes if a House term was three rather than two years. It would give you time to make a real mark."

"When I lost reelection, it was hard to deal with at first," says Jim after a pause, "but now there's no question it was for the best, for me and my family, and really, for my constituents too. I didn't realize until I was defeated in the primary that I was already burned out by the system."

He goes on to say, "I'm now president of a community college, which is situated in the heart of my former congressional district. I make much more of a discernible impact now. But these days *I'm* the one pounding at my congressman's door, asking for help securing more funding for my college."

He then says, "I know by name every student on my campus. When I was in the House, I tried to know the names of all my constituents, but I couldn't even know all their faces, no matter how many town hall meetings I had. When it becomes that impersonal, members of Congress shouldn't be called 'representatives,' since they can hardly know who or what they represent."

*Constitution Café Article:* The number of representatives in the House shall be one for every sixty thousand people. Representatives shall serve a three-year term in office. Members of the House and Senate can vie for re-election only after taking a one-term hiatus at the end of each term served. Congressional districts shall be drawn up every ten years, after the release of the decennial census, by a non-partisan committee of citizens in each State. The decennial census shall also determine how many additional Members of Congress will serve in the House.

## New Rules

After reviewing the newly created Constitution, Jefferson registered his disappointment over the Framers' "abandonment in every instance of the necessity of rotation in office." He believed that if there were no term limits for our elected representatives, once installed in office, each would have the potential to become a veritable "officer for life," and as such detrimental to democracy. To Jefferson, the Framers' failure to mandate an exit strategy for members of Congress was one of the Constitution's pronounced shortcomings.

He remedied this defect in his own draft constitution for Virginia, which included an article that called not just for term limits, but for rotation in elective office. While Jim made a similar proposal during our exchange, Jefferson's article was more strict: it stipulated that elected officials could serve only one term, and also created staggered terms:

One third of them shall be removed out of office by lot at the end of the first three years and their places be supplied by a new appointment; one other third shall be removed by

lot in like manner at the end of the second three years and
their places be supplied by a new appointment; after which
one third shall be removed annually at the end of every three
years according to seniority. When once removed, they shall
be forever incapable of being re-appointed to that house.

Jefferson also detailed a unique and stringent scheme to provide
effective checks and balances between the three branches: "The Legislative, Executive and Judiciary offices shall be kept forever separate; no person exercising the one shall be capable of appointment
to the others, or to either of them." Once you'd held office in one
of these branches, you were barred from holding office in another.
Jefferson believed that if a constitution allowed elected representatives to traverse the various branches of government, it encouraged
a game of political musical chairs among entrenched officeholders.
The result was that it discouraged new, worthy candidates from
aspiring to elective office. Yet Jefferson himself served as Virginia's
governor and as a legislator; but he would not have been able to do
so if his draft constitution had been implemented.

## Republic Guaranteed

*From Article IV, Section 4, of the Constitution:* **"The United
States shall guarantee to every State in this Union a
Republican Form of Government."**

Each year, the week before Labor Day, a mecca is made of a stretch
of Nevada desert as people the world over converge to attend Burning Man, named after a wooden effigy that somewhat resembles a
male and that is put to the torch on the eve of the event's final day.
Started in 1986 on a San Francisco beach as a modest bonfire ritual
during summer solstice, Burning Man has grown into an annual

eight-day extravaganza held in the Black Rock Desert. Organizers characterize it as an experiment in radical self-reliance that serves as "a specific antidote for the passivity, anonymity, and alienation of modern society."

After landing in Reno, I make the two-hour drive to the event site, traversing a dust devil–plagued dirt road for the final mile. On this seven-square-mile dry lakebed known as "the playa," almost 50,000 people are clustered. After finding a campsite, I realize that amid my mountain of gear, I somehow have forgotten the most important items: sunscreen and a pillow. No worries. People are more than willing to lend a clueless "first-time Burner" anything lacking.

Upon pitching my tent, I wend my way to one of the site's two "civic plazas," where I set up my dog-eared Constitution Café sign. The first two "Burners" who join me had read on my website about my planned gathering here. They stand out in a crowd: he calls himself Uncle Sham, and is dressed in an Uncle Sam–like outfit, superimposed with greenbacks being flushed down a papier-mâché commode; she calls herself "Lady Libertine" and leaves little to the imagination in her choice of outfit—the opposite of demure.

"Section 4 of Article IV of the Constitution has always nagged at me," says Uncle Sham, an estate planner in his life in what Burners called "the default world" that exists outside Burning Man's bounds. "It says, 'The United States shall guarantee to every State in this Union a Republican Form of Government.'

"But it doesn't guarantee that this republic will be of a democratic form. All a republic in and of itself guarantees is a constitutional government, an ordering of society under a written law. But just because you live under written law doesn't mean it'll be democratic. A republic can just as well be a dictatorial or totalitarian state. A revised article can promise the states a *democratic* republic. I suppose this is more or less the form of government under which states operate. I just want this article to explicitly guarantee that states are composed of governments that have the consent of the people, that operate by the principle of majority rule but that at the same time protect the inalienable rights of every person, not just the majority."

"This article should go a bit farther and guarantee states the option of having a direct democracy," says Lady Libertine. "That way, people can directly involve themselves in domestic policy issues if and when needed. Right now, twenty-four state constitutions give citizens the right to engage in direct democracy, by allowing them to put legislative referenda on the ballot. This article in the U.S. Constitution should guarantee what nearly half the states already let people enjoy, the right to direct democracy. Without this guarantee, the argument can be made that it's unconstitutional for states to allow us to practice elements of direct democracy, since it isn't modeled at the federal level."

Then she says, "My home state of California is the only state that has a type of direct democracy that doesn't permit the legislature to amend or repeal laws passed by a citizens' referendum. So it's *really* direct democracy. This gives California's citizens ultimate authority, so if the legislature behaves badly, we can literally take the law into our own hands."

"California's legislature has made a colossal mess of the state's budget," she goes on, "spending sums of money that were way beyond the rate of inflation and the state's rate of population growth. And it masked over the shortfalls for years with accounting tricks. But the day of reckoning finally came, leading to painful cuts, especially in education, where our once-unrivalled public university system has been reduced to a shambles.

"The problem is that the state constitution calls for a two-thirds majority to raise taxes or pass a budget. This 'super majority' leads to a 'super minority,' a tyranny of a minority. Since the majority party needs the support of some members of the minority party in order to pass a budget, legislators from the opposition party hold the budget hostage until, in exchange for their vote, they're promised all kinds of earmarks for their districts. The inevitable outcome is huge budget deficits. I've joined the effort to change this system. There's a referendum initiative right now that will make the budget approval process one in which a simple majority is needed from both houses to pass the budget or to raise taxes."

"A direct democracy is no guarantor of a responsible democracy," says Uncle Sham, also from California. "The people are every bit as responsible as our state legislature for California's budget mess. I'm supporting a referendum that'll do away with Proposition 13."

Passed in 1978, Proposition 13 dramatically lowered property taxes and also restricted any future annual increases to 2 percent, no matter how much real property values soared.

"If property taxes were at their real value," he continues, "then we'd have had responsible budgets all along. California residents have long refused to allow their property taxes to be a fair reflection of their property's value. And the state's most poor and vulnerable are the ones who suffer the most from the enormous budget cuts then needed to curb the deficits that result. There's no perfect solution, but all things considered, I believe a democratic republic—with majority rule, but protections for the minority—rather than a direct democracy, is our best chance of creating a responsible and responsive politics in state government, and this is what should be promised in this article."

"The organizers refer to this place as the 'Republic of Burning Man,'" I say eventually. "It makes no more promise of providing a 'democratic republic' to the people attending this event than the article we're discussing in our Constitution."

"Burning Man is a breakaway republic, even if a temporary one," says Henri, who drove here from southern New Mexico with seven others in a decades-old VW van, and just joined our gathering a few moments earlier. "It's beyond democracy, which is all about voting and campaigning and arguing over party platforms and all that nonsense. This is the real deal, the *res publica*, 'the public thing.' This baby breathes. Burning Man has put into place those conditions that allow for the greatest creativity. On the other hand, the republic guaranteed by Article IV suffocates, because the type of republic it promotes has distrust and disdain for real participation by real people. You can keep that original Constitution that guarantees an ossified republic cryogenically sealed in the National Archives, but all that does is keep it from dying a natural death."

"Maybe all republics have written laws," he goes on, "but the best ones keep them to an absolute minimum, as is the case with Burning Man, which has rules or laws that liberate people. Our republic here is minimalist. It's fine with me if the Constitution promises a 'minimalist republic,' and leaves it at that. I agree with Jefferson: 'That government is best which governs least.' In that spirit, we have here just a short list of written rules for governance drawn up by the organizers. As the Burning Man powers that be put it in their manifesto, there are 'no rules about how one must behave or express oneself at this event (save the rules that serve to protect the health, safety, and experience of the community at large).' Instead, it's 'up to each participant to decide how they will contribute and what they will give to this community.'"

"Which means that a minimalist republic like this allows you to decide how to contribute, but doesn't give you the option of *not* being involved?" I say.

"It probably wouldn't enter anyone's mind not to contribute," says Jan, a political science–history major at a university in Portland, Oregon, chiming in for the first time. "People come here because it's a great experiment in the art of creative governance, with this desert bed itself our canvas. As far as the eye can see, Burners have built great and not-so-great works of art as ways of expressing what this place means to them. They do it on behalf of the Public Thing, out of inspiration, not constitutional coercion."

She considers further. "So I guess this article should guarantee a libertarian republic, which is in line with what we have here. Yes, there are written rules, but they inspire us to act together out of desire rather than coercion. We try to delight and please one another and look out for one another. I've discovered I'm my most fulfilled as an individual when I'm contributing to something greater than myself. This is a far different kind of individualism than the 'rugged individualism'—which is really all about every man getting ahead at the expense of everyone else—that exists in the default world."

"When Jan gave you a pillow, after learning you forgot to bring one, it was a gift," Lady Libertine says to me. "She knew you lacked something you needed to fully experience and participate in this event. What you don't know is that she didn't give you an extra pillow. She just told you that so you'd accept it. She wanted to make sure you have a rich experience. You looked to her like a pillow would help make that happen. That's what this place does. By helping you, she helped herself too. Because if you get a decent night's sleep, you can participate with great energy; it'll benefit her and all the rest of us, and help this 'public thing' flourish."

Jan, a bit embarrassed by what Lady Libertine reveals to me, now says, "On the website for this event, it says, 'Burning Man encourages the individual to discover, exercise and rely on his or her inner resources.' But that makes it sound like we're roughing it in an 'every person for herself' way, when in truth we look to 'outer resources'—other Burners—and rely on them to help us develop the inner resources needed to thrive in harsh desert conditions. The public thing here is many hearts beating as one. That's what should be guaranteed in the default world too. That would put an end to the dominance of the 'private thing,' where the two major parties, in league with the corporations they're beholden to, pass laws that benefit a few at the expense of the rest of us."

"We Burners operate from the assumption that when we're living in a natural state, there's trust, harmony, cooperation, an innate desire to help one another. Because this is the right kind of *res publica*, people want to participate," says Henri. "Here at Black Rock Republic, it's about trusting one another to conduct ourselves in ways that inspire and elevate without coercion. We don't have any elections, which are coercive because they force you to vote 'for' someone and 'against' someone else. Instead we have committees, all made up of volunteers, that take on public works of all kinds—public safety, public transportation, public art, you name it. They're spearheaded by a bunch of people out of a shared desire to make a great spontaneous republic, and make it like the work of art it should be."

Uncle Sham has stayed silent while others rave about the joys of the Republic of Burning Man. He says now: "I for one wouldn't mind if the rules for the Burning Man event were set forth in the form of a constitution, and that it include the promise of an element of democracy. For instance, we're not allowed to bring pets with us. We're told by organizers that it's for public safety reasons, but we should be able to have debates about whether pets are or aren't a hindrance to safety but actually enhance the safety and enjoyment of this event, and then put it to a vote. But there's no process that I know of that allows for such a debate over the rules."

"There is a hierarchy," says Marlene. "At the very top, there's an executive policy-making body made up of just six people. I do find their name—Limited Liability Corporation—off-putting, but that's its name for legal reasons, I imagine. But at all the other levels of the hierarchy, you can have input." She reads from the Burning Man annual report: "'At every level of our organization, from policies created by the LLC to decisions made at the most immediate level of operations, we employ a consensus process. The interplay between consensus-making and a hierarchic structure of organization defines our Project.'"

"Maybe, both here at Burning Man and in the default world, constitutions are needed that guarantee the 'interplay' of democracy and *res publica*," Jan says. "I can understand why there has to be consensus-making, and why sometimes there have to be representatives, but a hierarchic structure isn't needed."

"I just believe that, at Burning Man and in the default world, a constitutional article is needed that guarantees democratic participation, or at least democratic representation, at all levels," says Uncle Sham. "That will help keep the experience of governors and governed alike more open and experimental. Maybe then there won't be the rise, and irreversible fall, that all other republics in human history have had. If you want the public thing in America to breathe without life support, you need an article that provides such a guarantee."

*Constitution Café Article:* The United States shall guarantee to every State in this Union a Democratic Republic Form of Government that best promotes the *res publica*, the public thing.

## Lean on Me

In a letter Jefferson wrote to his daughter Martha in 1787, he reflected, "It is part of the American character to consider nothing as desperate; to surmount every difficulty by resolution and contrivance. . . . Remote from all other aid, we are obliged to invent and to execute; to find means within ourselves."

What system of governance, to Jefferson, would best tap into and put to optimal use this singular American character? One of a decidedly minimalist bent?

"That which governs best governs least." One Constitution Café participant attributed this quote to Jefferson. This oft-quoted Jefferson saying is employed by libertarians and conservatives who lay claim to his mantle. Yet Jefferson never said it.

Even so, he certainly protested the vast bureaucratic apparatus that the Framers' Constitution bred, characterizing it as having "more machinery of government than is necessary, too many parasites living on the labor of the industrious."

Shortly before he became president, Jefferson voiced his preference for "a government rigorously frugal and simple." To John Ferling, an authority on early American history, what Jefferson meant by this was that government had to stave off "the further encroachment of the executive branch" and focus on "retiring the national debt, eliminating a standing army and relying on the militia to safeguard internal security, and keeping the navy small, lest it drag the nation into 'eternal wars.'"

While Jefferson certainly hoped government could realize these objectives, he was no more an advocate of small government than he was of big government. Rather, he favored a singular sort of self-government that he believed would unleash untapped reserves of human ingenuity. Jefferson proposed that the Virginia constitution be amended to create what he called a ward system. Of all his envisioned reform initiatives for Virginia, Jefferson's proposal for a ward system represented "the article . . . nearest my heart." He suggested dividing the commonwealth's counties into wards, each no more than five or six square miles, and so "of such size as that every citizen can attend, when called on, and act in person. These will be pure and elementary republics, the sum of which taken together composes the State, and will make of the whole a true democracy as to the business of the wards, which is that of nearest and daily concern."

Each of the wards, then, constituted a minirepublic. Every citizen would be involved in governance, though they would not all be involved in making decisions on the exact same matters. Rather, each would be delegated a specific area of responsibility and charged with representing the interests of all his other fellows to the state. Since all were involved in governing these minirepublics, Jefferson believed that taken together, this system constituted a true democracy.

The ward system, he maintained, saw to it that all the citizenry "was thrown with all its momentum into action," with each person "a sharer in the direction of his ward-republic . . . a participator in the government of affairs, not merely at an election one day in the year, but every day," with every man "a member of some one of its councils, great or small."

Jefferson further believed that this type of grassroots governmental framework presented a nearly fail-safe way of thwarting any one group's efforts to wrest self-government from the hands of the people:

> These representative organs, should they become corrupt and perverted, the division into wards constituting the people, in their wards, a regularly organized power, enables them by that organization to crush, regularly and peaceably, the usurpation of their unfaithful agents, and rescues them from the dreadful necessity of doing it insurrectionally. These little republics would be the main strength of the great one.

Rather than relying on three separate but equally powerful branches of government to keep constitutional tabs on one another, the various overlapping levels of government in Jefferson's intricate system would be equally vigilant over one another: "The elementary republics of the wards, the county republics, the States republics, and the republic of the Union, would form a gradation of authorities . . . holding every one its delegated share of powers, and constituting truly a system of fundamental balances and checks for the government."

For Jefferson, only such a system would "save the people from lethargy and inattention to public business," because all the people would be made an integral part of it."

"We had not yet penetrated to the mother principle, that governments are republican only in proportion as they embody the will of their people, and execute it," Jefferson remarked to Samuel Kercheval in 1816. He was referring to the first attempt by the framers of Virginia's constitution—"novices in the science of government"—to create a form of government that did justice to realizing the people's will but that in his view fell far short of the mark. Jefferson believed that if the ward system—to him an ideal blend of democracy and republicanism—became the modus operandi for governance in Virginia, the will of the people could at long last genuinely be exercised in the public arena.

Jefferson also hailed the ward system for the fact that, on momentous occasions such as his envisioned periodic rewriting of the Constitution, all citizens could step out of their particular representative roles and make a group decision on the same matter. When a particularly urgent matter came up and required the equal input of all, a statewide meeting could be readily called into order, with all citizens meeting "on the same day through the state." In this way, they could "at any time produce the genuine sense of the people on any required point, and would enable the state to act in mass."

"Alone among the influential political thinkers of the revolutionary generation," maintains Joseph Ellis, "Jefferson began with the assumption of individual sovereignty, then attempted to develop prescriptions for government that at best protected individual rights and at worst minimized the impact of government or the powers of the state on individual lives." Jefferson believed the ward republic both maximized citizens' impact on government and protected their individual rights by demanding everyone's involvement. As Hannah Arendt contends, Jefferson was striving to create that form of government that allowed for "an exact repetition of the whole process of action which had accompanied the course of the Revolution"—not the bloody war on the battlefield, but the peaceable and pleasurable process of joint decision-making that complemented it. Jefferson's premise was that "the revolutionary spirit was not merely the spirit of beginning something new but of starting something permanent and enduring."[3]

## Native American Way

The prominent Lost Generation author and American social revolutionary John Dos Passos, who singled out Jefferson as a principal influence behind his activism, asserts in *The Head and Heart of Thomas Jefferson* that Jefferson was "convinced that those societies (as the Indians) which live without government enjoy in their general mass an infinitely greater degree of happiness than those which live under the European governments." Jefferson's admiration for Native Americans began as a child, when Cherokees often passed by his home on their way to Williamsburg. Over the years, he observed and interacted with a number of tribes. He marveled over how they organized themselves via small and intimate councils, and expressed his admiration for how they "never submitted themselves to any laws, any coercive power, any shadow of government." He went so far as to say that they were the exception to the rule "that great societies cannot live without government." Jefferson further lauded their "vivacity and activity of mind," claiming it "was fully equal to a white man." In observing one Native American orator, Jefferson "was impressed by the Indian's use of words to make a noble display of his humanity, to move others."[4]

3. Hannah Arendt, *Crisis in the Republic* (Mariner Books, 1972).
4. Andrew Burstein, *The Inner Jefferson* (University Press of Virginia, 1996).

Richard Matthews, democratic theorist and noted Jefferson scholar, contends that Jefferson's observations of Native American societies informed his notion that man was by nature "a social, harmonious, cooperative, and just creature." To Matthews, Native American societies provided for Jefferson "an edifying counter-cultural example of how men can live in a community without the need for formal government," demonstrating their inherent "cooperation and human sociability, rather than . . . competition and human antagonism."

In fact, Jefferson did not believe competition was at odds with cooperation; rather, he held that if the two forces worked together, they could drive human sociability and creativity. He appreciated Native Americans' "superior luster at oratory, debate and persuasion, as witnessed in their councils," and observed that their impassioned exchanges, far from generating antagonism, led to the forging of stronger bonds among them. What clearly mattered to Native Americans was that each was equally recognized by his fellow tribesmen, and that each had a chance to argue his point and to try to win over the rest.

Matthews goes so far as to characterize the Native American way of living as "the empirical model for [Jefferson's] political vision." While Native American societies were certainly one important contributor to his vision, they were by no means *the* model.

## The Greek Way

While Jefferson's system of wards was also clearly inspired by the New England township model, he ultimately aspired to "resurrect the Athenian ideal in America" in order "to re-create the intimacy of thought and endeavor . . . that he was always to characterize in Greek terms." Jefferson called these Greek societies "truly Attic societies," in which "men's highest and most charitable impulses could flourish."[5]

Paul Woodruff notes in *First Democracy* that in the intimate democracy of the Athenian polis, each participant was "given a share of the ability to be citizens, and that ability is understood both as a pair of virtues and as a kind of citizen wisdom." This kind of governing was based on the shared view that "it is a natural part of being human to know enough to help govern your community." Woodruff claims that what enabled Athenian democracy to flourish was the fact that "every citizen is called upon to assist in managing public affairs," since they believed that "no expert knowledge . . . governs decisions of the state." Likewise, Jefferson believed that it was vital that all American citizens have a direct role in governing the country. To accomplish this, the government did not need to be decentralized per se, but to be universally dispersed: ". . . the way to have good and safe government, is not to trust it all to one, but to divide it among the many. . . . What has destroyed liberty and the rights of man in every government that has existed under the sun? The generalizing and concentrating all cares and powers into one body. . . ."

Jefferson's ward system was meant to be an adaptation of the polis, literally "people place," made to fit the unique conditions of Virginia, but also, he believed, replicable on a far vaster scale. Hannah Arendt claims that living in a polis is akin to living in a political community in which, as in the Native American societies that Jefferson observed, "everything [is] decided through words and persuasion and not through force and violence."[6] But Jefferson could never

5. Michael Knox Beran, *Jefferson's Demons: Portrait of a Restless Mind* (Free Press, 2007).

6. Jefferson obviously did not admire them enough to do what he could during his terms as president to make sure that their way of life was preserved. It never

persuade the Virginia Assembly to entertain seriously his proposal for a ward republic.[7]

Jefferson's great expectation was that in post-Revolutionary America, a system of governance would be developed that emulated that of the Greek polis, giving political enfranchisement to all white male citizens, and as a result doing away with the tradition of governance in which a select coterie did the ruling for everyone else. "How soon the labor of men would make a paradise of the whole earth, were it not for misgovernment, and a diversion of all his energies from their proper object—the happiness of man,—to the selfish interests. . . . If we can prevent the government from wasting the labors of the people, under the pretense of taking care of them, they must become happy."

To him, the best way to prevent government from wasting people's labors was to create a form in which all people labored in it.

---

seems even to have occurred to him to enact policies for settlement and expansion that would enable Native Americans to maintain at least part of their original territories; instead, during his years in office, the Native American diaspora began.

7. However, at the University of Virginia, which Jefferson founded in 1819— it was the first secular university in the nation, with no religious affiliation or denominational identity—he sought to implement a version of his ward system. As Joseph Ellis relates, "Jefferson was insistent that his university be devoted to the principle of 'self government,' which meant that proctors, provosts and even a president were superfluous." Jefferson's scheme for the university "almost certainly grew out of the thinking he had been doing about wards as the primal political and educational units in Virginia."

# Rights and Responsibilities

In 2001, John McCain, John Edwards, and Ted Kennedy introduced in the Senate a bill to create a Patients' Bill of Rights. The bill was aimed in part to give patients a stronger voice in decisions about which medical procedures will be covered by insurance, and about health care-related privacy issues. While the Senate approved the legislation on a roll-call vote, in which every member's vote is recorded, it was never passed by the House. Since then, a number of states have taken the lead in passing their own versions of a Patients' Bill of Rights—not to mention a Passenger Bill of Rights, to ensure we're not stranded on airport tarmacs for hours on end, a Cell Phone Bill of Rights to guarantee our calls aren't dropped in the middle of clinching a big business deal, even a Children's Outdoor Bill of Rights, to see to it that kids receive ample outdoor exercise. And Congress itself is considering a Technology Bill of Rights, to ensure that high-tech products are accessible to all consumers in the digital age.

The implication is that we'll be able to truly enjoy what's promised in our original Bill of Rights only if we spell out more nuanced rights in these new bills of rights. The more bills of rights, the merrier. But with these rights come responsibilities.

As our founding patriots knew, a bill of rights is barely worth the paper it's written on unless you're willing to defend it. Once a set of rights has the force of law, if someone—perhaps the very enforcers of the law themselves—then attempts to usurp any of these rights, you may be obliged to risk a great deal in order to preserve or restore them. That was the case when the rights guaranteed by England's Magna Carta were wrested from the New World colonists by King George. Patriots risked their lives to have them restored.

Yet once the American Revolution was won, the Framers of our Constitution had no plans to include a Bill of Rights. James Madison, for one, insisted that it went without saying that all the constitutional rights and powers not delegated specifically to the government belonged to the states and the people. In a December 1787 letter to Madison, however, Jefferson argued that a "Bill of Rights is what the people are entitled to against every government, and what no just government should refuse, or rest on inference." He argued that such a bill was vital for "providing clearly . . . for freedom of religion, freedom of the press, protection against standing armies, and restriction against monopolies, the eternal and unremitting force of the habeas corpus laws, and trials by jury in all matters of fact triable by the laws of the land and not by the law of nations." Siding on this occasion with the so-called anti-Federalists, Jefferson proved instrumental in swaying the Framers. On December 15, 1791, the first ten amendments to the Constitution, called as a group the Bill of Rights—based primarily on the Virginia Declaration of Rights drafted in 1776 by George Mason when he was a member of the commonwealth's provisional government—became part of our supreme law.

But even with this victory, as Jefferson well knew, these rights could still be undermined. Indeed, the grievances that Jefferson spelled out in the Declaration of Independence drew from the fact that the long-standing rights granted to all British subjects by the

Magna Carta were being disregarded by King George III, who among other wrongs had imposed standing armies on the colonists, levied taxes without their consent, denied their right to trial by jury, and no longer allowed them to choose their own elected officials.

The very last grievance enumerated in the Declaration was that the king and Parliament had ignored all the colonists' petitions for redress of grievances. As Jefferson wrote, "In every stage of these oppressions we have petitioned for redress in the most humble terms: Our repeated petitions have been answered only by repeated injury." This was one grievance too many, and Americans rebelled.

"With respect to our rights," Jefferson later explained, "and the acts of the British government contravening those rights, there was but one opinion on this side of the water . . . When forced, therefore, to resort to arms for redress, an appeal to the tribunal of the world was deemed proper for our justification. This was the object of the Declaration of Independence."

Today, as then, Americans of many political stripes claim that government is violating their rights, and that their complaints to elected officials have been answered only by "repeated injury"— specifically, that their petitions either prompt retaliation by the government, or fall on deaf ears.

## Redress Address

"The last right granted in the First Amendment, to petition the government for redress of grievances, was supposed to be a piece of 'democracy insurance,'" says Patricia, an unemployed auto-parts manager. "Now, it's just an empty right."

Her offering meets with nods all around, even from her ardent political opposites. I'm holding a Constitution Café near the entrance to Independence Hall in Philadelphia, the site of the original Constitutional Convention, held from May 25 to September 17, 1787. I am with a number of Tea Party and Coffee Party members who ventured here from Pennsylvania and nearby states.

The Tea Party movement got underway in the waning days of the second term of George W. Bush. It started out as a one-issue protest group voicing annoyance with the proposed economic stimulus plan, which it considered an unconstitutional subsidy. After Barack Obama took office, the Tea Party burgeoned into a much more influential movement, and now professes to be the citizens' watchdog for all unconstitutional activities on the part of the federal government.

The Coffee Party is still gathering momentum. Claiming not to be wedded to any particular ideology, it promotes reasoned deliberation in the public sphere as the means to solve public issues. Like the Tea Party, it stresses its grassroots nature, and it too considers lobbyists anathema.

I had gotten to know Patricia, a Tea Party member, well before that movement was on the political radar screen, when she and I had taken part together in a Socrates Café dialogue I'd held in the area. When I told her of my desire to hold a Constitution Café exchange between Tea Party– and Coffee Party–goers, instead of telling me right off, as had all others with whom I'd inquired into the possibility, that this was wishful (or nightmarish) thinking on my part, she said she could arrange it, and was even enthusiastic about doing so.

Patricia now looks at Dave, a Coffee Party acolyte and social worker. "Dave and I managed to have a civil conversation at—where else—a coffee shop. We'd bailed out of a 'town hall meeting' held by one of our representatives. He'd claimed the purpose of the meeting was to solicit our suggestions, but really, he was telling us what he planned to do regardless of what we thought about it. Eventually the meeting disintegrated into a shouting match. Dave said to me at the time, 'You know, I don't blame people for screaming. It's because they're totally left out of the process.'"

She goes on, "Dave and I went on to discover that we both had presented petitions for redress of grievances."

"I'd delivered to my representative a petition demanding that Congress craft a new campaign finance reform law to replace the one overturned by the Supreme Court when they kowtowed to K Street's bagmen,"[1] says Dave. "The hundreds who signed it agreed that it was important to attempt right away to make a new law that would withstand future efforts by the Court to allow big corporations and unions to again control our elections."

"While mine was a one-issue petition," he continues, "Patricia's was pages long. I actually agreed with some of the Tea Party grievances—that the federal government has burdened Americans with debts and obligations that can't possibly be repaid; that the system of taxation places unjust burdens on some Americans while exempting others; and that the executive branch has usurped Congress's authority by involving our troops in one undeclared war after another."

"Our main shared grievance was that our petitions to the government for redress of grievances were ignored, violating our constitutional right," Patricia tells me.

"I became active in the Tea Party after I lost my job—laid off permanently by GM as part of its requirement to restructure and cut costs after receiving stimulus dollars. It was bad enough that Congress had abused its taxing authority when it passed the 'stimulus package' that stimulated GM to get rid of me. But I couldn't understand why the CEO could continue to earn millions and I was expendable, and why the stimulus package—which included my own taxpayer dollars, without my consent—allowed this. I had plenty of time on my hands, and as I became more enlightened about

1. The street in Washington, D.C., where so many of the most prominent lobbying firms are headquartered.

all the government's wrongdoings, and how they were forbidden by the Constitution, I became more active.

"At first, I tried to make my grievances known as an individual citizen. I emailed the one of my senators I thought could most relate to my grievances. I got an immediate response from his email server saying his mailbox was full. I tried calling. One of his administrative assistants said he'd relay my concerns to the senator. It was only after several more fruitless attempts that I decided to seek out others who shared my concerns, so we could band together to make our views known. I collected thousands of signatures. I then went straight to Washington, D.C. I couldn't get past security to go into the Senate office building, though professional lobbyists entered and exited like it was their second home. I admit I didn't have an appointment, but surely at least one of my senator's staffers could've come outside to take my petition."

Now Mary, a Tea Party activist who'd been unemployed for two years before landing a government consulting contract the previous week (she says she had to "hold her nose" while accepting it, but that work is work, and she has three children to support as a single mom), speaks up. "This 'freedom to petition clause' in the Constitution is supposed to give us direct access to whichever authority in government we feel can best redress our grievance. It's meant to guarantee that Americans' gripes with those who govern can't be ignored.

"As I'm sure you know, it was the failure by the king of England to redress colonists' grievances that led to the American Revolution. The Magna Carta gave British subjects wherever they lived the iron-clad right to petition government for redress of grievances. But when King George III arrived on the scene, he ignored this right."

In 1215, the Magna Carta gave British subjects for the first time the right to petition the monarchy for redress of grievances. It detailed a process for realizing this right, with twenty-five barons charged with addressing a subject's petition. The Magna Carta further guaranteed that there could be no retaliation against a petitioner while his grievance was considered. In 1669, British Parliament expanded this right, giving every commoner, "in case of grievance," "the inherent right to prepare and present petitions." In this updated process, the House of Commons was charged with determining whether the petition merited redress, and if so, would have to take concrete steps to resolve it. The American Revolution was launched after the Crown prohibited its appointed governors in the New World from considering the colonists' petitions, effectively refusing to adhere to their own foundational laws.

"King George did worse than just refuse to address petitions," Dave says now. "Whenever the colonists tried to petition him, he retaliated. He directed Parliament to enact more severe restrictions, restraints, taxes, every time colonists complained that their rights were being violated."

Patricia then says, "When the Bill of Rights became part of our Constitution, the right to petition government for redress of grievances was put right upfront. At our nation's beginning, U.S. citizens could go directly to either chamber in Congress to hand over their petitions. And a hearing would be held on their grievance. It didn't mean that a decision would be made in favor of the petitioner or group of petitioners, but the petition had to be received and considered, and the legislators had to issue a thoughtful response.

"But during the Civil War era, when Congress was flooded with petitions from abolitionists demanding an end to slavery, it refused to receive any more of them. Members of Congress complained that they had so many petitions to consider that they didn't have time to conduct their regular legislative business. They said they didn't want the public to dictate their agenda. But that's Congress's job, to be steered by the concerns of the people. It used the slavery issue as a pretext to end the right of citizens to petition it directly.

"Ever since, the right to petition has been diluted more and more.

Today, it's equated with the rights to peaceable assembly and to free speech, as if there's no difference. Free speech and assembly may let you shout from the rafters, but they don't guarantee that the people in government you're directing your grievances to will be anywhere nearby listening to what you have to say. Only the right to petition the government official to whom your grievance is directed—and the right to receive a response that addresses your grievance—guarantees that you'll be both seen and heard."

To which Darcy says, "Right now, the First Amendment states, 'Congress shall make no law . . . abridging . . . the right of the people . . . to petition the Government for a redress of grievances.' I suggest we rewrite it so it says, 'Congress shall make no law abridging the right of the people to petition *directly* the Government for a redress of grievances.'"

"That doesn't go nearly far enough," says Mary. "It also has to say, following that, that 'Congress shall elaborate a process whereby petitions for redress of grievances are addressed.'"

"What sort of process do you envision?" I ask. "If Congress and the executive branch are flooded with tens of thousands of petitions for redress of grievances, how would they handle them?"

"Congress could have a well-staffed permanent committee—a Committee for Redress of Grievances—with a rotating membership to handle petitions directed at either or both chambers," says Dave. "And the White House also could set up a special office for receiving and processing grievances. This is such an important part of democracy that there should be a cabinet officer—a secretary for redress of grievances—overseeing it. And whenever it becomes clear that a broad cross-section of petitioning Americans share grievances over certain issues, the cabinet officer could inform the president, and he would personally have to respond. But whether the grievance is large or small, an appropriate government official would have to directly receive the petition and respond."

"Way back in the thirteenth century," says Patricia, referring to a book on the subject that she has on hand, "King John of England wrote that only 'when redress has been obtained' shall his subjects 'resume their old relations to us.' In other words, relations between the king and his subjects were put on hold until the petition for redress was considered. So, in line with that, a clause in the article we're composing should also state that relations between the government and those petitioning for redress of grievance are at a standstill until the grievance is considered and responded to."

"People on the left and right and everywhere in between want to revive this freedom to petition for redress of grievances at all levels of government," says Mary. "But the more they try, the harder federal and state governments come down on them. The federal government is considering a law that would require all would-be petitioners to register as professional lobbyists. As it is, over half the states have imposed restrictions on grassroots efforts to petition.

"Now, as you can imagine, I don't usually agree with the American Civil Liberties Union. But in this case, it is absolutely right in arguing that if this bill ever passes, it will be a disaster for our democracy. It would mean that if you or me or any other concerned citizen who tries to mobilize others and urge them to sign a petition related to an issue of shared concern, you'd have to register as a professional lobbyist with the government. You'd lose your status as a private citizen and be treated on a par with someone on K Street.

"We'd have to provide to the federal government all personal information—such as name and address, contact information, occupation—about ourselves and anyone who has contributed even a small amount to our effort. But what's most cause for concern is that the government wouldn't just collect and store this information—it would report it publicly. So if there's an issue that's dear to someone as a private citizen, she might not sign a petition out of fear that the government will publish information about her, and that her employer, who might differ with her stance, will find out and it could affect her job."

"It only gets worse," says Patricia. "If this bill becomes law, the government would monitor our grassroots activities. We would have to file monthly reports with the government. All of this, taken together, is retaliatory. It's every bit as much an attempt to intimidate us as what King George did to New World colonists. It makes citizens afraid to be activists. Government officials of course know that we aren't anything remotely comparable to professional lobbyists. We don't represent special interests. We represent a general interest, of taking back our democracy.

"I personally wish the Constitution would outlaw professional lobbyists, who don't petition for redress of grievances, but create further grievances for regular Americans. The Framers never anticipated lobbyists, and so of course they never dreamed they'd be the primary influence over our politicians."

Darcy sighs. "We're right back to where our original patriots were. We have a government that hates and fears ordinary citizens, and that's determined to keep us from practicing this most important right, so it can continue to act unconstitutionally."

Dave says now, "Jefferson anticipated this: 'crush in its birth the aristocracy of our moneyed corporations, which dare already to challenge our government to a trial of strength and bid defiance to the laws of our country.' Our elected officials are so tied to the moneyed corporations that they band together to defy the laws of our country."

"The media makes us Tea Party types out as fringe protesters, as if you're either part of a movement of protest or part of a movement of participation. But that's a false dichotomy," says Mary. "Protest can be the highest form of participation in a democracy. And gathering a petition to deliver to government to have grievances redressed is an act of protest *and* participation. Really, the right to petition the government for redress of grievances is the right to be recognized."

> *Constitution Café Bill of Rights, Article 1:* Congress shall make no law abridging the right of the people to petition the Government for a redress of grievances. Congress shall make laws that establish a process by which grievances are received, considered, and addressed. Until such time as grievances are appropriately addressed by Government, relations between those citizens submitting the grievance and the Government shall be considered suspended, and there shall be no retaliatory measures taken by Government against petitioners.

## Good Grief

The first attempt to eliminate the right to petition for redress of grievances took place just seven years after the Bill of Rights was ratified. In 1791, enactment of the Alien and Sedition Acts effectively eliminated this right, since citizens who expressed a grievance against the government typically were arrested, jailed, and fined by courts sympathetic to the Federalists.

Thomas Jefferson and James Madison warned in a draft of the Kentucky and Virginia Resolutions (or Resolves) that the government's breach of the most fundamental rights "unless arrested at the threshold . . . will furnish new calumnies against republican government." To them, it was especially important that, during those times when an open society was weathering putative threats from within or without, the government should redouble—not stifle—efforts to redress grievances. If it instead took the route of a King George III or a John Adams and closed off long-enjoyed outlets for airing and resolving citizens' concerns, it was only serving further to destabilize democracy.

## Let Your Conscience Be Your Guide

"Maybe James Madison didn't believe at first that there was a need for a bill of rights, but he went on to become one of its greatest advocates," Bart tells us. "He even wanted to include in it the right to exercise freedom of conscience. His initial draft of the First Amendment contained this clause: 'nor shall the full and equal rights of conscience be in any manner, or on any pretext infringed.' But it was voted down. For this new Constitution, let's vote it back in."

A first-year law student at my and Jefferson's alma mater, the College of William & Mary, and a sometimes attendee at my local Socrates Café group, Bart and several of his friends join us for this exchange. We're meeting on the William & Mary campus in an outdoor amphitheatre that was declared a 'free speech zone' by the Student Assembly, after a new regulation established by the college administration placed restrictions on where students could hold protests.

I ask the obvious: "What is freedom of conscience?"

"It's the freedom to think and believe what you want, to go your own way and never have to agree with anyone if you don't want to," Bart says. "Now, it doesn't mean you can act on those beliefs. A blanket 'freedom of expression' isn't allowed in the Constitution, only freedom of speech, which is just one form of expression. Exercising free speech in and of itself isn't a violent act, no matter how outrageous or controversial. But other acts of expression can be violent."

"Freedom of speech isn't the only way we exercise freedom of conscience," says Amy, who attends nearby Christopher Newport University in Newport News, Virginia, my father's alma mater. "The First Amendment freedoms of assembly, of religion, of the press, also are forms of free expression that encourage or at least enable us to live lives of conscience."

"You first have to *have* a conscience in order to exercise freedom of conscience," says Sasha, a cadet at Virginia Military Institute, the oldest state-supported military college in the United States, who has been silent up till now. "Too many in America today speak their minds in ways that aren't conscientious.

"Many in positions of influence use their right to free speech not to liberate people but to drum up animosity. Theirs aren't acts of conscience. So many on the right and the left have ramped up the hate, demonizing those who disagree with them. After health care reform was passed by Congress, death threats were made against Democrats who voted for it, and some had their homes and cars vandalized. Many who used this unconstitutional form of freedom of expression seemed to be incited by the extremist rhetoric of political leaders."

"Democratic leaders also have their share of blame," says Amy. "Nancy Pelosi, the former House Speaker, once characterized all who used their free speech to loudly oppose the Obama administration's health care plan as 'simply un-American.' Since when can't Americans loudly oppose something? What matters is that, for or against, you've made a free and informed and well thought-out—a conscientious—decision. On the other hand, those who try to intimidate or demean those who don't think like them, and those who intentionally incite people to carry out violent acts, are exercising lack of conscience."

"Even Obama joined the 'un-American' parade," says John, from the University of Virginia. "Once, while promising to find a way for illegal immigrants to become U.S. citizens, he warned that there are 'demagogues out there who try to suggest that any form or pathway for legalization for those who are already in the United States is unacceptable.'

"I disagree that if you oppose a pathway for legalizing the status of undocumented workers, you automatically are a demagogue, and as such merit the 'un-American' label. Even if I don't arrive at the same conclusions, I've heard some reasonable arguments for why illegal immigrants shouldn't be allowed to stay in the U.S., much less become citizens."

"Obama may have won the Nobel Prize for Peace," Sasha says, "but when he made that statement about demagogues, he wasn't being peaceable, much less conscientious; he was using his bully pulpit as president to intimidate, to discourage reasoned debate. Maybe some people who oppose naturalization of illegal immigrants are demagogues. But you can be for immigration reform, and be a demagogue. And a revised First Amendment should emphasize that the rights it includes are specifically meant to serve as the best ways to exercise freedom of conscience."

Eventually, Reed says, "The imam at the mosque where three of the 9/11 hijackers worshiped called the alleged Fort Hood shooter, Major Nidal Malik Hasan,[2] a supreme 'man of conscience.' Others in the U.S. who've engaged in violent hate-based acts—like Scott Roeder, who murdered George Tiller, a physician who performed late-term abortions—have been praised as people of conscience by extremist religious leaders. The problem with a right to freedom of conscience is that it can be misconstrued as not only the freedom to believe what you want, but to act on those beliefs, no matter how violent and hateful. Such people in my view have the worst kind of conscience, but they see themselves in just the opposite light."

"Now I'm starting to appreciate why freedom of conscience was eliminated from the final version of the First Amendment," says Sasha. "It's too easy to claim you're exercising freedom of conscience, and yet do something horrific that sets back what an open society is to be all about."

To which Amy says, "We should leave the First Amendment just

2. Hasan is alleged to have killed 12 and wounded 31 people when he opened fire at the base.

as it is. We should leave freedom of conscience out of the picture. Because it can erroneously imply that we have the right to exercise even the most violent forms of freedom of expression."

Bart isn't convinced. "Freedom of conscience is all about exercising *good* conscience, promoting reasoned debate. A person of conscience in a democracy would never act in a way that would deliberately try to negate other voices. So to be on the safe side, this article should stress 'freedom of good conscience,' rather than just a blanket freedom of conscience."

"You know," Reed says, "the people I admire most throughout our nation's history are those who didn't just feel free to believe whatever they wanted, but were willing to act on their beliefs, even when their actions were outside the law, to improve our society. They often carried out acts of civil disobedience in the name of making the ideals in our Declaration of Independence come true. They exercised all the existing First Amendment rights to one degree or another, putting their beliefs on the line, to make sure all Americans were recognized equally. Along the way, they faced down conscienceless people, many of whom committed terrible acts to try to intimidate or silence them."

Then Bart says, "Another Framer, Elbridge Gerry, also tried to insert language in the First Amendment about freedom of conscience. His proposed draft said simply, 'Congress shall make no laws . . . infringing the rights of conscience.' Like Madison's attempt, his clause also unfortunately was eliminated in the final version of the Bill of Rights, even though it made clear that 'rights of conscience' aren't unlimited, but are tied directly to the unabridged rights to freedom of speech, freedom of assembly, freedom of the press, freedom to petition for redress of grievances. Maybe people would appreciate these rights more if the First Amendment stressed that they're meant to promote those constitutionally guaranteed freedoms that amount to exercise of good conscience."

*Constitution Café Bill of Rights, Article 2:* In order to promote freedom of conscience, which celebrates human dignity and worth, Congress shall make no law respecting an establishment of religion, or prohibiting the free exercise thereof; or abridging the freedom of speech; or the right of the people peaceably to assemble, and to petition the Government for a redress of grievances.

## Conscientious Conscience

"No provision in our Constitution ought to be dearer to man than that which protects the rights of conscience against the enterprises of civil authority," Jefferson told a group of Methodists in 1809, referring specifically to the exercising of rights of conscience as they pertain to freedom of religion. Clarifying this viewpoint further in his *Notes on Virginia*, Jefferson explained, "rights of conscience we never submitted [to any authority] . . . We are answerable for them to our God." He stressed that "the legitimate powers of government extend to such acts only as are injurious to others. But it does me no injury for my neighbor to say there are twenty gods, or no God. It neither picks my pocket nor breaks my leg."

By this perspective, while one is free to believe in God or gods or no god, such rights of conscience are permissible so long as they remain in the realm of pure belief and do not inflict any real, physical harm on anyone. Jefferson elucidates his view by drawing on a quote from the Enlightenment political thinker Montesquieu's *Spirit of the Laws*: "Words carried into action assume the nature of that action. Thus a man who goes into a public market-place to incite the subject to revolt incurs the guilt of high treason, because the words are joined to the action, and partake of its nature. It is not the words that are punished, but an action in which words are employed."

Yet Jefferson's own words, in the Declaration of Independence—a manifesto for freedom of conscience if ever there was one—incited Americans of virtually every religious and political outlook to revolt against the British. If his words had not been backed up by deeds, they would have been empty.

Jefferson made clear in a correspondence with James Madison following Shays's Rebellion[3] that when people are oppressed by the very government that is supposed to ensure their liberties, they might have to resort reluctantly to violent means in order to have their grievances addressed: "I hold it that a little rebellion now and then is a good thing, and as necessary in the political world as storms in the physical." While an uprising like Shays's Rebellion may be put down, and while it hopefully is a rare occurrence, Jefferson believed it will have served a good purpose if it brought to light "the encroachments on the rights of the people which have produced them," and then leads to a just resolution.

Despite his rhetoric to the contrary, there are exceptional instances in which Jeffersonian freedom of conscience cannot be confined to the realm of pure belief; at such times, rights of conscience are converted into action in order to realize promised or hoped-for rights, or to restore those which had been taken away.

## Free the Press

"I like that the First Amendment is so general about press freedom," says Scott, one of several journalists meeting with me at a café that

---

3. Shays's Rebellion—named after the movement's leader, Daniel Shays, a farmer and Revolutionary War soldier—took place in western Massachusetts in 1786 and 1787. Poor farmers were up in arms over being heavily taxed without their consent, which put many in debt and some in debtors' prison—not exactly the kind of repayment they were expecting after sacrificing so much for the Revolutionary cause. When their pleas for debt relief were unheeded, they erected liberty poles and liberty trees to highlight their cause. The uprising was put down in February 1787 by a 4,000-man private militia supported by aristocrats.

they frequent in northern Virginia. "Sandwiched almost inconspicu-
ously between freedom of speech and freedom to peaceably assemble, it simply says that Congress 'shall make no law that abridges
. . . the press.' Very concise, but it packs a wallop. This little clause
assures broad press freedom."

"But it's only saying that Congress *can't* keep us from doing our
job," says Kathleen, an assistant editor at a daily paper. "In redoing
this clause, I'd have it state that while Congress can't make laws
abridging press freedom, it *can* make laws that better enable the
press to function optimally."

Daniel, a freelance investigative reporter, nods. "This would force
Congress to enact a blanket federal shield law. Right now, thirty-
four states have some type of shield law that affords us, to varying
degrees, some protection from being forced to reveal our sources.
But on the federal level, there's no shield law. Though the Senate is
in the process of crafting one that provides some limited protections
to journalists, even if it passes, it can be rescinded at any time. As
things stand, a reporter faces the prospect of serving time in prison
if required by a federal court to reveal his sources on a story. But if
Congress was constitutionally required to enact laws that further
free up the press to do its job, a blanket federal shield law would be
a given."

"What if someone posts classified or other sensitive government
documents on a websites like WikiLeaks.org?" I say, referring to the
websites that publishes such material typically in order to expose
alleged government or corporate misconduct, and that protects the
identities of its sources. "Would he be afforded protection under this
expanded free press clause?"

"Let me put it this way: I like that the Framers of our Constitution didn't attempt to define 'the press,'" says Daniel. "Since the
beginning of our nation's history, the press has basically been any
medium that disseminates information. So a site like WikiLeaks

would constitute 'the press' to our Framers, and so yes, it would be protected."

"The Democrats in the Senate are drafting a 'media shield bill' to protect so-called traditional news-gathering agencies from revealing their sources," he goes on. "But the bill wouldn't extend these protections to websites like WikiLeaks. That's setting a dangerous precedent. It's not just that more nontraditional sources than ever will emerge in coming years as the traditional press continues to disappear, and eventually will become the mainstream. The fact is, WikiLeaks clearly is a news-gathering source. It is applauded for giving people unexpurgated information and has earned a number of respected international media awards for advancing the cause of human rights. Without WikiLeaks, there'd be few places for the Daniel Ellsbergs of the world today to reveal government misdoings, now that corporate-owned papers are so averse to taking risks that would impact that financial bottom line."

In 1971, Ellsberg, a U.S. military analyst working as a private consultant, released a top-secret report on U.S. government decision-making regarding the Vietnam War. A retired Marine Corps officer who'd served a stint in Vietnam, Ellsberg had high level government security clearance. The documents to which he had access revealed that government officials were lying in their public statements claiming that the war in Vietnam was being waged successfully—with victory, as Secretary of Defense Robert McNamara had put it, "just around the corner"—and also that the officials had not disclosed that the war was causing far more U.S. military casualties than it had publicly claimed. The "Pentagon Papers" that Ellsberg passed on to the *New York Times* also made clear that the Johnson and Nixon administrations felt no ethical, much less constitutional, compulsion to be up front with the press or the American public.

"People should have access to a wide variety of sources of news," says Scott. "The press—whether WikiLeaks or the *National Enquirer* or a traditional newspaper—usually is disparaged when it does its job particularly well and prints uncomfortable truths that the government or a politician or other public figure doesn't want people to know, because it might change public sentiment. So this expanded article can also clarify that the press is any medium that disseminates information, to make sure that Congress doesn't limit what constitutes the press as it sees fit. Because if it doesn't define broadly what the press is, Congress will define it in the most limited way possible."

"Now, the issue with WikiLeaks," he goes on, "isn't whether it's the press—of course it is. The issue is whether, in publishing classified information about our incursions in the Middle East, it has been endangering national security, and whether the press freedom clause in the Constitution should place restrictions on this. In the latest case, it posted online a ream of classified documents about how the war against insurgents in Afghanistan and Pakistan is bleak and getting bleaker all the time."

In late July 2010 alone, 92,000 military reports from 2004 to 2009 were leaked to WikiLeaks.org as well as traditional news sources, and tens of thousands more have been leaked since.

"These reports contradict some of the spin put out by the Bush and Obama administrations that the situation there is stabilizing," he continues. "The question is whether, in its zeal to carry out its stated mission of creating more government transparency, Wiki-Leaks has compromised our national security, even putting lives of American troops at risk. If that's the case, should this press clause grant unlimited press freedom, even if the press potentially endangers national security?"

"If a member of the press, or any other citizen, passes along information that enables a potential enemy to do harm to our nation, there's an article already in the Constitution—Article III, Section 3—that states that such treasonable acts will be punished," says Kathleen. "It specifies what are treasonable acts: 'levying War against [the United States], or in adhering to their Enemies, giving them Aid and Comfort.' So the government already has the constitutional right to try a reporter or a press outlet for treason. But it would have to prove that there was an attempt to intentionally give aid and comfort to the enemy or to assist in fomenting an uprising against the U.S."

"Where in the existing Constitution does it give the government permission to have classified information?" says Christie, a reporter for a national radio program. "It seems to me that an outcome of writing a press clause that incorporates the language we're discussing is that Congress would have no choice but to pass laws that help us better do our job. So, it would have to pass a law that either prohibits classified information, or that allows some members of the press, in its special role as the eyes and ears of the public, to freely access and review such information."

"Obama is just the latest president to issue an executive order making certain government information classified, supposedly because it's too sensitive to national security to be revealed," she continues. "I believe the argument can be made that the government provides aid and comfort to the enemy when it makes ours an increasingly closed society, what with its penchant for keeping secrets just because it can. Obama is going after anyone who reveals so-called secrets to the press with a vengeance, even if they don't endanger our security."

Indeed, the *New York Times* reports that "the Obama administration is proving more aggressive than the Bush administration in seeking to punish unauthorized leaks. . . . President Obama has already outdone every previous president in pursuing leak prosecutions."

"The argument can be made that national security is even more at risk when certain classified information is withheld from the press and public," says Kathleen. "Classified information is an inherent abridgment of freedom of the press."

"If at least some members of the press had access to classified information, because of an expanded free press clause," she goes on, "one outcome would be that the government couldn't so easily mislead us in military matters. For instance, if the press had had timely access to information about the Gulf of Tonkin incidents, the U.S. might not have been able to escalate its involvement in Vietnam. This might have prevented our nation's involvement in that conflict, which I believed weakened rather than strengthened our security."

The Gulf of Tonkin incident took place on August 2, 1964. It was reported by U.S. military officials to have involved two separate clashes between American destroyers and North Vietnamese torpedo boats. The military claimed that in the initial clash, the North Vietnamese had fired first. Two days later, a second naval skirmish was reported by the Navy to have taken place. This prompted Congress to pass the Gulf of Tonkin Resolution, giving President Lyndon Johnson carte blanche authority to involve the U.S. military in defending South Vietnam against the North Vietnamese. Forty-one years later, the National Security Agency at last declassified a study that showed that the United States had in fact been the first to open fire during the initial incident, and that showed that the second reported clash simply never happened.

"You can't seriously believe that giving reporters access to any and all classified secrets is realistic," says Scott. "Clandestine activities by the CIA should only be known by a handful of government officials, or it could endanger their activities and U.S. interests abroad."

"Correct me if I'm wrong, but in the sixties and seventies the CIA's covert activities helped topple democracies throughout Latin America, setting back democracy in that region," says Christie. "It orchestrated the Bay of Pigs fiasco. In nations like Iran, it propped up dictators, allowing them to stay in power until finally the situation imploded and fundamentalists took over. Then there's the CIA's 'slam dunk' case that there were Weapons of Mass Destruction in Iraq.

"So in balance, surely it's better that some press members are kept abreast of their activities in 'real time,' if nothing else so they are constantly reminded that America is supposed to be the beacon of the free world, and as such, needs to operate as much in the open as possible."

Then she says, "There will always be information that can never be printed. But there will be times when members of the press will have strong differences with the government over what should and shouldn't be revealed to the public. For instance, the government might argue that we can never reveal secrets about our nuclear arsenals, or about spies. But even in these highly sensitive areas, if the press ever discovers what it considers clear-cut evidence of unconstitutional shenanigans, then it would be obliged to report it. If there's ever a question over which side—the press or the government—has committed treason, then there's a court system in place that can decide the matter."

"But even with the language being discussed here for a constitutional article to expand press freedoms, it doesn't mean we'll be able to more effectively sway the public," says Daniel. "It only means that the public will be better able to make more informed decisions, if it so chooses. No matter how much freedom the press has to do its job, the American public won't necessarily care more about the doings of government, even when far outside constitutional bounds. For instance, even though Watergate brought down Richard Nixon, polls at the time consistently showed that most of the public wasn't interested in Watergate."

After a pause, Christie says, "The more freedoms and protections extended to us, the fewer excuses we'll have for failing to do our job responsibly and wisely. If this expanded clause on press freedom really came to be, I believe it would enable the American public to do an even better job of keeping the government, and the press itself, more honest and aboveboard."

*Constitution Café Bill of Rights, Article 3:* While Congress shall make no law abridging the freedom of the press, it shall make laws that further enhance and secure press freedoms.

## Keeping the Peace

In 1787, as the delegates at the Constitutional Convention were meeting, James Madison and Thomas Jefferson contemplated "whether peace is best preserved by giving energy to the government, or information to the people." Jefferson argued that the government must put all information it has at the people's disposal, so that they in turn can give their energy to the government in the form of educated and enlightened opinions on public policy. To him, the people not only are "the only sure reliance for the preservation of our liberty," but they "are the most legitimate engine of government. Educate and inform the whole mass of people. Enable them to see that it is their interest to preserve peace and order, and they will preserve them."

Jefferson told his friend Edward Carrington that the best way to prevent uprisings by the people "is to give them full information of their affairs." He believed that when the government becomes secretive, the seeds for public unrest are sown. Jefferson further told Carrington that the best method of informing the public is "through the channel of the public papers, and to contrive that those papers should penetrate the whole mass of the people."

So vital was the role of the press in preserving democracy, Jefferson contended, that "were it left to me to decide whether we should have a government without newspapers, or newspapers without a government, I should not hesitate to prefer the latter. But I should mean that every man should receive those papers, and be capable of reading them." When approached by French leaders after the French Revolution for advice on framing their new constitution, Jefferson stressed the need for unfettered freedom of the press: "This formidable censor of the public functionaries, by arraigning them at the tribunal of public opinion, produces reform peaceably, which otherwise must be done by revolution. It is also the best instrument for enlightening the mind of man, and improving him as a rational, moral, and social being."

Jefferson asserted that if the French followed his counsel, they would be breaking with the precedent set by all other European governments. Not only, in his estimation, was the European press habitually "the first shut up by those who fear the investigation of their actions," but European governments regularly and deliberately spread misinformation. "Under the pretense of governing," he claimed, "they have divided their nations into two classes, wolves and sheep. I do not exaggerate."

Where would Jefferson stand if the press printed false facts—facts fed to it by the federal government itself—that damaged relations between the United States and other nations, as was the case with the Weapons of Mass Destruction episode in Iraq that prompted the U.S. to launch the first preemptive incursion in its history? In such a case, Jefferson would surely have argued that the government itself had libeled democracy.

Despite his panegyrics to the press, Jefferson changed his tune when he became president. During his first term in office, Jefferson argued that it was the press rather than the government that was deliberately spreading misinformation and dividing the nation. He considered himself the victim of a relentless smear campaign orchestrated by pro-Federalist press moguls opposed to his policies; not only had they cast his government in the worst possible light, but the notoriously thin-skinned Jefferson accused them of sullying him personally. His vitriol against the press knew few bounds during this period: "Truth itself is suspicious by being put into that polluted vehicle. The real extent of the state of misinformation is known only to those who are in situations to confront facts within their knowledge with the lies of the day."

But try as the press might to turn the public against him and his administration with its "demoralizing licentiousness," Jefferson believed that the people were not swayed. He tried to paint himself as magnanimously taking the high road, and rather than attempting to punish the press for its alleged slander, he decided to "leave to others to restore it to its strength, by recalling it within the pale of truth." He claimed to be confident that "public indignation" would bring the press back to its true calling.

While president, Jefferson boasted to John Tyler, a judge whose son would become the tenth president of the United States, that his administration was successfully testing out an idea that had been "wanting for the world to demonstrate"—namely "the falsehood of the pretext that freedom of the press is incompatible with orderly government."

Yet Jefferson was no believer in a totally unfettered press. Long before he became president, he made it clear that he was against granting absolute press freedom. The article that he composed for the final version of his draft constitution for Virginia that dealt with press freedom stated, "Printing presses shall be free except . . . where by commission of private injury they shall give cause of private action." His draft article further declared that the press "shall be subject to no other restraint than liableness to legal prosecution for false acts printed and published."

After the federal Constitution was approved, Jefferson told James Madison that while freedom of the press must be part of the Bill of Rights, he believed that such freedom should come with constraints: "A declaration that the federal government will never restrain the presses from printing anything they please, will not take away the liability of the printers for false facts they printed." In another letter to Madison, Jefferson proposed specific language for a constitutional amendment pertaining to press freedom: "The people shall not be deprived or abridged of their right to speak, to write, or otherwise to publish anything but false facts affecting injuriously the life, liberty or reputation of others, or affecting the peace of the [U.S.] with foreign nations."

This language is in one sense far more restrictive than the press freedom clause that came to be included in the First Amendment. On the other hand, it opens a potential Pandora's box, since it makes no attempt to clarify precisely what 'false facts' amount to, or a process for determining whether they are injurious, whether such injury applies in the same way to public officials as to private citizens, or whether the printed material would impact relations with another nation. Indeed, the overall tone of Jefferson's amendment is more reminiscent of the intimidating libel laws that he excoriated as part of the Alien and Sedition Acts, which were meant to keep people from speaking their minds. Jefferson's article certainly goes against his assertions as president that there was no need to level any punishments or create any restrictions against the press, since people were smart enough to see through any false claims.

## Armed and Safe

**The Second Amendment of the Constitution: "A well regulated Militia, being necessary to the security of a free State, the right of the people to keep and bear Arms, shall not be infringed."**

"We need to decide with this article whether individuals have the right to keep and bear arms. That right isn't made clear in the existing Second Amendment," says Mike, who conducts team-building seminars for businesses.

I'm with about fifteen people in a sprawling Texas exurb who agreed to join me after receiving an email blast I sent out inviting people to review the Second Amendment, with the idea of possibly revising or overhauling it.

"It *is* clear," says Fred, a barber. He reads from his copy of the Constitution, "'A well regulated Militia, being necessary to the security of a free State, the right of the people to keep and bear Arms shall not be infringed.'

"So, we have the right to keep and bear arms. *But* this right is completely tied to being part of a militia regulated by the government. In the Revolutionary era, any male could be part of a militia, so any male had the right to bear arms while serving in his capacity as a militia member. Today this amendment means that any citizen can bear arms who is part of the modern militia—the Guard and Reserve, but the other armed forces, too, I'd imagine. The right to keep and bear arms is totally tied to the defense of the nation as a whole. The Second Amendment includes no right for an individual to bear arms for his personal self-defense."

"Okay, point taken. But for our purposes here, it doesn't matter how anyone interprets the existing Second Amendment," says Mike. "People, including Supreme Court justices, have been reading into this amendment anything they want to for over two centuries, interpreting it in a way that suits their agenda or their outlook."

Looking at me, he then says, "If I understand correctly Chris's project, what we have to do is decide what *we'd* want a constitutional article today to say regarding the right to keep and bear arms. Do we want this right? If so, do we want the blanket right? Or should it depend on where we live—whether we live in an urban area riddled with gun-related violence, or a rural area where guns are used mostly for hunting?"

"This article should state, 'The right of the people to keep and bear arms on their place of residence—whether owned or rented—shall not be infringed,'" says Linda, a personal trainer. "Everyone needs to have the means to defend hearth and home.

"This would remedy the deplorable situation today in which society's most vulnerable are unable to defend themselves. For instance, in New Orleans, survivors of Hurricane Katrina protested how the New Orleans government voted unanimously to raze a housing complex where they'd lived most of their lives. No one in government cared that the residents wanted it restored. They had gone to the expense of hiring an expert who'd shown that the complex was salvageable. It was their home. When they protested against its demolition, they were subjected to pepper spray, they were gassed and tasered. What they needed was the constitutional right to defend themselves with equal force, in order to defend their property."

CBS News reported that one law professor at Loyola University involved in the demonstration held up a piece of taser wire that had been shot at another protester and asked ironically, "Is this what democracy looks like?"

"Nowadays, you might need a stockpile of weapons to defend hearth and home," says Fred, "what with federal agents raiding people's homes with overwhelming force, and in instances mistakenly raiding the wrong residence."

"I agree that law-abiding citizens have the right to defend their home by any means necessary," says Mike. "But I'm hesitant to put the word 'arms' in a modern article bearing on this issue. An arm could be taken by some to mean biological or chemical weapons, or even a handheld nuclear device.

"Even if we're talking about more conventional weapons, it's a delicate issue," he goes on. "My grandparents on my mother's side had an arsenal. They lived in mortal fear that their home would be invaded and that they'd again be removed against their will. They were interned during World War II. When they died, my parents got rid of every weapon, all of them legally registered."

"And you believe such stockpiles should continue to be constitutionally permitted?" I ask.

"I'm not sure. I don't know that their arsenal ever really made my grandparents feel safer. I'm still angry over what the government put them through, but arming oneself with weapons has never seemed to me the best way to go about addressing government abuses."

"I need to return to what I see as the original intent of the Second Amendment, since it influences my own view," says Kathy, a housewife and mother of four. "Because I take this amendment to mean that only those in the militia can keep and bear arms, and because I believe that it is an indisputable truth that America today is one of the most violent societies in the Western world—in big part because it's so easy to purchase weapons—I would have this article state that no private citizen has the right to keep and bear firearms. That way, only those in their professional capacity to keep our society safe—public safety officers, members of the Guard or Reserve, or of the armed forces—can bear them. This article should say that they can't keep arms at their homes; they have to leave them at their base or station, where they will be stored in modern versions of magazines—the places the colonists in militias stored weapons and gunpowder.

"This would build on the approach to arms-keeping and -bearing at our founding, when militias were well-regulated," she says. Then she is quick to add, "When I use the word 'militia,' I'm not talking about these self-appointed groups that are misappropriating the name and claiming to do things like protect our borders or trying to secede from the nation. The only groups that should be called militias are those highly organized units strictly controlled by the state and federal government."

"I just believe that, precisely because American society is so dangerous today, every individual deserves to keep and bear arms on her property—either on her land, or in her vehicle," says Linda. "But maybe Mike is right in that the word 'arms' is kind of a Pandora's box. So I would have an article just say, 'The right of an individual to protect and defend his property by whatever means necessary shall not be denied.'"

"Isn't 'any means necessary' a Pandora's box in its own right?" I ask her.

"It is, but it's a box that you can only keep on your property and nowhere else, so the language I'm proposing should serve its intended purpose," she says.

"I want a nation without arms," Kathy says quietly. "My neighbor's niece in Chicago was wounded several months back. Some neighborhoods in that city are war zones. Her niece was just walking to school and was caught in the cross fire of a gun battle over turf for selling drugs."

The *New York Times* reports that in 2009, "258 public school students were shot in Chicago, 32 fatally, on their way to or from school, traveling through gang-infested territory and narcotics wars."

"The best way to protect our most important property, our *selves*, is to ban all arms in private hands," Kathy continues. "A new constitutional article should say that only public safety officers can bear arms in the community they serve, and the military can only bear them on their bases or when defending the country."

She then says, "Chicago's elected officials rightfully imposed strict handgun bans to stem violence in the city, only to have this law overturned by the Supreme Court."

Just before our gathering, a bare majority of the Supreme Court issued a ruling that broadened Second Amendment rights, concluding that its protections apply to state and local gun control laws as well as to federal law.

"A new article has to take this out of the Court's hands, before our society becomes more and more like the OK Corral. I know some will say it's naïve to think we can ban guns, that the gun culture is here to stay. But for this Constitution Café project, we can imagine the world we want to have. And the one I want is one without arms of any kind in private hands. Honestly, I don't even want them in the hands of public safety officers, though it's a necessary evil."

Turning to Kathy, Mike says, "To me, what you say about the situation in Chicago goes to show that the Constitution should give local governments the right to determine gun control laws. It's an abomination that the Supreme Court struck down what for Chicago was a commonsense gun control measure to keep innocents from being victimized. I can see where there'd be lax rules in remote stretches in America. But I'm thinking now that each municipality's government officials should be able to determine its gun control laws."

"I was taught to shoot as a junior member of the National Rifle Association, and was a longtime member," says Carl, a retired high-school teacher, speaking for the first time. "I got rid of all my weapons back in 1990. Without going into specifics, let me just say that it's best if guns aren't in our personal possession. I believe that every person is capable of killing—and not just for reasons of self-defense, but out of desperation, hatred, a moment of extreme mental duress. In balance, gun possession makes us no safer. The issue of public and personal safety should be the guiding light upon which a constitutional article on this subject is based. For the sake of public safety, I'd ban them outright in private individuals' hands.

"There are no perfect solutions, and there'll always be bad guys. But hopefully we can keep guns out of the hands of most of them, and prevent further tragedies like the one in Chicago, not to mention Tucson. And if you have to defend yourself in a tight spot, for heaven's sake become an expert at one of the martial arts."

This group was evenly split between the following two articles:

*Constitution Café Bill of Rights Article 4, Version 1:* The right of individuals to keep and bear arms on their property shall not be infringed.

*Constitution Café Bill of Rights Article 4, Version 2:* Because a well-regulated National Guard and Reserve, and well-regulated federal, state, and local public safety departments, are necessary to the security of our free states and of our free nation, the right of citizens, while serving in their capacity in the aforesaid organizations, to keep and bear arms shall not be infringed.

## No Farewell to Arms

In Jefferson's day, almost all men—and many women, especially those living on the frontier—could expertly use a gun for hunting and for self-defense. Jefferson advocated gun ownership; he believed it had a moral dimension, and so was important for cultivating character. As he told his nephew Peter Carr in 1785: "A strong body makes the mind strong. As to the species of exercises, I advise the gun. While this gives moderate exercise to the body, it gives boldness, enterprise and independence to the mind. Games played with the ball, and others of that nature, are too violent for the body and stamp no character on the mind. Let your gun, therefore, be the constant companion of your walks."

A gunsmith with an extensive armory, Jefferson further contended that if all citizens kept arms and were properly trained in their use, it would actually minimize gun violence. As he wrote to George Washington, while "one loves to possess arms, . . . they hope never to have occasion for them."

When Virginia's General Assembly held a convention in 1776 to write a new constitution, Jefferson proposed an article that granted a universal right to bear arms, rather than limiting this right to those serving in a well-regulated militia, as was the norm with other state constitutions. Jefferson's proposed article stated that "no man shall be debarred the use of arms"—and he appended in brackets in his final two drafts "within his own lands or tenements," as if his article might stand a better chance with the legislature if it specified where one might keep and bear arms.

Don B. Kates, Jr., a scholar of constitutional and criminal law, argues that Jefferson's view is based on the tenet that "arming the good citizen minimized the likelihood of violence by deterring the wrongs that would provoke it." To Jefferson, constitutionally sanctioning the universal right to bear arms would put the gentry on notice that even the poorest citizen had the means to defend himself against encroachments by the powerful. "What country can preserve its liberties if its rulers are not warned from time to time that their people preserve the spirit of resistance?" Jefferson told Colonel William Stephens Smith, an American diplomat who would eventually become a congressman for a district in New York. "Let them take arms."

Jefferson's proposed article was defeated. According to historian Saul Cornell, who considers Jefferson "perhaps the most forward-looking and innovative legal thinker involved with the framing of the Virginia constitution," the defeat of the universal right to keep and bear arms on one's property reflected "a view common among members of Virginia's gentry elite that it was dangerous to arm the 'rabble.'"

## Civics Lesson

I'm at a McDonald's outside of a high school in Washington, D.C., with a group of 16- and 17-year-olds. The teacher who'd helped arrange my visit is an old friend; we attended elementary school together in the area, and we'd managed to stay in touch for most of the ensuing years. He thought his students would be more candid and comfortable if they met with me off-campus at their favorite after-school hangout.

At the outset, Natasha says to me, "As Mr. Williams, our history and government teacher, was preparing us for this meeting with you, I put a question to him that he said I should put to you: Why doesn't our Bill of Rights say a thing about the right of every American child to receive an education? It gives us the right to vote once we're eighteen, but I don't see how this right does us much good if we haven't been well educated."

"Even if the Constitution doesn't give us this right, there are laws in every community in the U.S. that make it mandatory for kids to attend school starting at about age four or five," says Hugo.

"But they can change these laws anytime they want to unless the Constitution states that we have the right to education," Natasha counters.

"*But* even if they never change these laws, the thing is, just because you have to go to school doesn't mean you'll learn much," says Zachary. "And even if there was a law that said you could never drop out of school, no matter how badly you're doing or how bored you are, it doesn't mean your life will be any more hopeful."

Natasha thinks about this. "What we need in the Constitution is the right to the kind of education where it hardly would occur to anyone to drop out."

Then she says to me, "We watched during class time the so-called 'schools speech' that President Obama delivered live via satellite from the White House to students across the country. I got envious when he started bragging about how his kids are receiving a 'world-class education.' That's the kind of education we all should have the right to."

"How would you define a world-class education?" I ask.

All the students on hand have a copy of President Obama's schools speech, which they're using to complete a homework assignment. Referring to his copy, Hugo says, "I'll answer your question like this. The president said to us students in this one passage, 'You'll need the knowledge and problem-solving skills you learn in science and math to cure diseases like cancer and AIDS, and to develop new energy technologies and protect our environment. You'll need the insights and critical thinking skills you gain in history and social studies to fight poverty and homelessness, crime and discrimination, and make our nation more fair and more free. You'll need the creativity and ingenuity you develop in all your classes to build new companies that will create new jobs and boost our economy.'"

He looks at me, "He's defining what a world-class education is all about. But our teachers don't have the resources to give us all these knowledge and problem-solving skills he talks about. And a lot of them don't have the training to give us these insights and critical-thinking skills, all this creativity and ingenuity, he says we have to have. And even if they did, they wouldn't have time to teach them to us, because they have to spend so much of class time preparing us to take standardized tests. But these tests reveal next to nothing about who we are, what we can do, what we know or can know, what our dreams are. So they sure don't provide the basis for a world-class education."

"I bet President Obama's kids don't spend all their time preparing for performance tests," says Veronica. And then: "If you want to know if a school offers a world-class education, you can tell by whether President Obama would send his own kids there. The Washington, D.C., public school officials reached out to the president when he was just moving into town here with his family. They tried to sell him on sending his kids to a D.C. public school. But you *know* that he never gave a serious thought to it. His daughters attend a private school that's surely world-class. I found out that it costs more to go there than my parents earn *combined* in a year. I'd need *four* parents at least to pay the bills if I were going to go to a school like that—two to pay for my school and two to earn pay for the rest of our expenses. I'd need even more parents if my brothers and sisters were going to be able to go there too."

"I don't blame the president and first lady for sending their children there," says Natasha. "I just want to be able to send myself there too. My kind of Constitution would give me that right."

"It's hard for me to get too pessimistic about my situation as long as I have teachers like Mr. Williams," says Zachary. "Just because you go to an expensive school with all the trimmings doesn't mean your education is totally world-class. Part of a world-class education is not learning in a bubble. If you go to a swank school, you're probably insulated from the world. Mr. Williams, though, believes a world-class education is one where the entire world is your class."

Natasha nods. "We were studying in Mr. Williams's class about the civil rights movement. I finally got up the nerve to tell Mr. Williams that as much as I appreciated what he was trying to impart, I just couldn't relate. A lot of other students said they agreed. He just stared at us, then stared out the window for a while. He finally said to us, 'You need to take a trip to a place that will bring the past to life, and show you how connected you are to it.' He told us that we were going all the way to the National Civil Rights Museum." The Memphis, Tennessee, museum is housed in the Lorraine Motel, where Dr. Martin Luther King, Jr., was assassinated on April 4, 1968.

"We got so excited," Veronica tells me. "But then he said we'd have to raise the money ourselves. School funding is so tight there isn't a penny even for local field trips, much less a trip all the way to Memphis."

"Of course, I was the first to look for the negative," says Natasha. "I said, 'Where are we going to get that kind of money from?' Mr. Williams just smiled and said, 'Where there's a will, there's a way.

And believe me, we're going to find a way, so don't even think about not having the will.'"

"We did fundraisers, washed cars, had bake sales," says Hugo. "I even played my trombone out on a street corner, and my trombone case filled up with donations. These activities really brought us together as a class. A lot of parents pitched in too. All who could, gave something, and most who couldn't, gave something too.

"We still didn't have enough funding to support the trip, even with all the effort we put into it, so Mr. Williams paid for the rest out of his own pocket. Well, he never admitted he did. He claimed that some anonymous donor had made up for the difference. But we all knew who that anonymous donor was. And last time I checked, high-school civics teachers don't make a lot of money. But it meant the world to him for us to visit that museum. We rode a bus thirteen hours to get there."

"I cried during the museum tour," says Natasha. "I stood on that same balcony where Dr. King stood when he was shot by a person blinded by hate. I listened there to his 'I Have a Dream' speech. It did just what Mr. Williams promised it would do: it brought the past to life for me, and made me feel part of it. As I stood out on the balcony where Dr. King was on that tragic day, I realized that a world-class education isn't something that's just handed to you. It's something you hand to yourself, by learning whatever skills you need so you can carry the torch for all those who tried—and in some cases, like with Dr. King, died while trying—to make your world a little more loving and helpful.

"I realized that if I don't make something good of myself, if I don't quit making excuses for not succeeding, it will reflect poorly not only on my country and myself and Mr. Williams, but also on Dr. King and all the other civil rights activists who risked everything so I could have a world-class future."

Referring to her copy of President Obama's schools speech,

Veronica says, "The president said during his talk that America's story is 'the story of students who sat where you sit 250 years ago, and went on to wage a revolution and found this nation,' and that it's also the story of all the students who 'fought for civil rights.'

"He was saying that going to school and getting your diploma in itself isn't enough, that you have to 'learn and do' at the same time, and in a way that makes the world brighter."

Natasha nods emphatically and says, "So we decided not to wait till after graduating to start making something good of ourselves."

She goes on to tell me, "In our neighborhood, a lot of people have had their homes foreclosed on, and have been evicted. One day I had neighbors, and the next they were gone for good. All over our neighborhood, there are empty and uncared-for homes.

"Well, I was walking down the street one day soon after we got back from our field trip, and I heard a lot of meowing coming out of an abandoned row house. I didn't know the family who'd lived there all that well, because their kids were so much younger than me, but I remembered they had a bunch of cats. I peeked through a front window, and sure enough, there were all these cats and kittens. They looked to be starving. I peered into some other foreclosed houses, and it was the same deal. Cats, dogs, in one case a bunch of hamsters, left behind. Now, I see to it that they're fed. I put food and water inside, usually placing it through the broken windows. Veronica and Hugo and Zack and some others here eventually began help me out."

"We paid for all the pet food out of money we earn from doing fundraisers," Hugo tells me. "We've tried to find new owners for the pets. We put ads in papers and posters on telephone poles. So far, we've found homes for five cats and two dogs. The SPCA has taken all the other abandoned pets we alerted them to."

"Now we've built on that project, in a 'prevention-oriented' way," says Veronica. "Now, all our classmates deliver pet food to people in our community who otherwise would have to abandon their pets.

We didn't have the money to buy this food ourselves. Mr. Williams showed us how to apply for a community grant. We did that as a class project. I couldn't believe it when we received a grant. I just felt so much goodness and gratitude well up inside of me. I'd never thought before that anything I might be part of might be seen to have so much value."

"And so," Natasha says, spreading her hands wide, "that's the story of how me and my classmates are already going about making a good mark in the world."

"I wrote to President Obama to tell him about this project of ours, and to thank him for inspiring me to do my part to make sure I have that world-class education," says Hugo. "Now I need to write him again and tell him about this article we want put in the Constitution. I'll emphasize to him that if he *really* wants to make sure his own children have a total world-class education, then there's no time like the present for them to start making the world a better place."

*Constitution Café Bill of Rights, Article 5:* All children of school age in the United States of America shall have the right to a world-class education.

## Natural Aristocracy

In 1812, both of them out of politics, Thomas Jefferson and John Adams overcame years of estrangement and began to engage in a rich correspondence. Though they both remained largely political opposites, they did manage to agree on one thing—that the United States' vibrancy over the long haul hinged on the cultivation of a noble and virtuous cadre of young citizens. But they parted company when it came to figuring out how this *aristoi*—Greek for "the best," when referring to the noble class—is developed. Adams maintained that you were either part of the noble class by birth or you weren't.

"Birth and wealth together have prevailed over virtue and talents in all ages," Adams insisted.

Jefferson disagreed. He believed Adams was describing an "artificial aristocracy," one "founded on wealth and birth, without either virtue or talents." Jefferson considered the version of the noble class promoted by Adams to be "a mischievous ingredient" detrimental to democracy, and argued that "provision should be made to prevent its ascendancy."

Jefferson favored a "natural aristocracy," which to him embodied the only type of noble class grounded in "virtue and talents." As he told Adams, "The natural aristocracy I consider as the most precious gift of nature for the instruction, the trusts and government of society."

To cultivate the development of a natural aristocracy in Virginia, Jefferson had introduced, as part of the statute reform package put together by his Committee of Revisors, a piece of legislation called the Bill for the More General Diffusion of Knowledge. If it had been passed, he told Adams, "work would have been complete," and the "pseudo-Aristocracy" in Virginia would have been eliminated altogether.

This legislation was designed to give all children and youth a world-class education. It was based on the premise, as Jefferson put it, that the opportunity for formal learning should "not depend on the condition of life in which chance has placed them." Jefferson's proposal would provide a well-rounded education in the arts and sciences, and teach children how to apply the knowledge gained in concrete problem-solving skills for the betterment of their community, giving them the opportunity to nurture "a good conscience, good health, occupation, and freedom in all just pursuits"[4] so they could "work out their own greatest happiness."

4. Jefferson had proposed to extend education to black youth as well. According to Fawn Brodie, in *Thomas Jefferson: An Intimate History*, Jefferson proposed "that all black youths be educated 'to tillage, arts or sciences' till twenty-one and all black girls to eighteen, 'at public expense.'"

As set forth in the bill, not only would all those of school age in Virginia be provided with a free public education, but those who displayed "the most promising genius, [yet] whose parents are too poor to give them further education" would be selected to

> be carried at the public expense through the colleges and the university. "The object is to bring into action that mass of talents which lies buried in poverty in every country, for want of the means of development, and thus give activity to the mass of mind, which, in proportion to our population, shall be the double or treble of what it is in most countries.

If this bill had passed, Jefferson felt certain that "worth and genius would thus have been sought out from every condition of life," and that the nation's children would be "completely prepared by education for defeating the competition of wealth and birth for public trusts" that Adams endorsed.

Jefferson's bill, though, was "completely defeated." The Virginia legislators, mostly made up of the planter oligarchy, were "unwilling to incur that burden" of paying taxes that would have supported the program. Their own children already enjoyed the best education money could buy, and they had no desire to extend this privilege to anyone outside their circle. They favored Adams's artificial aristocracy, since it favored them.

Donald K. Sharpes, a prominent scholar on the history of education, notes that it wasn't until 1840 that some elements of Jefferson's scheme for universal public education were at last realized, when civic leaders such as Horace Mann, head of the newly formed Massachusetts Board of Education, "fought for and won legislatively the principle of *universal public education*, and the establishment of the common school open to all children and youth." Education was "the great equalizer," Sharpes contends, and "Mann believed, like Jefferson, that ignorance and freedom in a democracy cannot survive together."

If Jefferson's premise is correct—that ignorance and freedom cannot be bedfellows in a democracy—then the Texas Board of Education's decision to eliminate all mention of Jefferson from history and social studies curricula discussing the most important political figures of the eighteenth and nineteenth centuries does not bode well. A majority of the board, taking issue with Jefferson's efforts to erect a "wall of separation" between church and state in Virginia, decided it preferred to keep students ignorant of the deeds of one of our most important Founders. The vote by the board was along party lines, with all Republicans opting to replace the study of Jefferson with material on religious thinkers like John Calvin and Thomas Aquinas. The conservative majority also demanded that textbooks used by Texas's nearly 5 million students from here on out explore major political ideas in terms of their relation to "laws of nature and nature's God." They further stipulated that any reference to the word "revolution" be deleted, and that the word "democratic" be eliminated from references to the U.S. form of government. Unlike Jefferson, they believe that students should not be given the tools to think for themselves.

## Hopi Way

I've just arrived at the Hopi Reservation, located in northeastern Arizona in the region known as the Four Corners, where the boundaries of Arizona, Utah, Colorado, and New Mexico meet. When I lived in Phoenix a decade ago, I ventured often to this captivating region. The Hopi territory, known as Hopiland, has a population of about 12,000 dispersed over thirteen villages situated on three large mesas. Many continue to live as artisans, farmers, and shepherds, and practice the traditional rites, dances, and ceremonies. Descendants of the ancient Anasazi Indians of the Southwest, the Hopi are unique among Native American tribes; they never signed a treaty with the U.S. government, and so never accepted its dominion over them.

I make my way to one of the few indigenous villages in the region that survived a devastating thirteenth-century drought. The community is governed autonomously, and refuses outside funding. The cluster of adobe homes is situated on steep cliffs overlooking stunning buttes and mesas, and seems carved out of the earth itself. I park nearby and walk to a local store in the hopes of striking up a dialogue there. On my way, I happen upon a wizened man carving a detailed figurine that looks to be a kachina, a type of religious icon used by Hopi elders to teach children about their religion. An adolescent girl is also carving. He waves me over and invites me to sit down. Then they return to their labor. "He's the best," she says. Her name is Aponivi, which she says means 'where the wind blows down the gap.' It turns out she is his great-granddaughter.

After sitting in silence for a while, I tell them about my project.

Eventually, both Aponivi and her great-grandfather, whose name is Len and who is 94, put down their work. "Would you like some tea?" he asks me. He goes inside his home and brings out a pitcher and three glasses. I marvel at the aromatic taste. "It's made from an herb called greenthread," he tells me. "It has healing properties."

Len sips his tea and remains silent. He looks around. "We need these mountains, animals, trees, water, to survive in this harsh climate. We've never written it down in a Constitution, but the Hopi believe that all things have rights, because they are all needed, all important."

"Should the U.S. Constitution give all other living and nonliving things the same rights as people?" I ask.

"I don't know about the same rights," he replies. "Maybe more rights, or different rights. Everything that 'is' is different, takes up different space, has a different role. If any part of the universe is not treated well by people, then people are not treating themselves well. They're doing damage to something put here by the Creator that we need to sustain us."

"Hopi don't have a word for 'nonliving,'" Aponivi then says. "All things are beings—stones, trees, clouds, mountains, eagles. All are alive, all have spirit. They're all sacred, and all need to be taken equally into account by humans."

"This 'taking into equal account' is a commandment of Taiowa, Creator of the Hopi people. He gave us this land to live on," says Len. "So whatever action we take as a tribe or as an individual, we have to think about how it'll impact our surroundings. We have to consider these mountains, the earth itself, but also the past, the present, and the future, since they're all part of the environment. We have to make sure our actions put everyone and everything first, not just ourselves, or harmony isn't preserved."

"Like, if we lose our most precious resource, water, we lose our way of life," Aponivi then says. "We'll suffer, the earth will suffer. There's a ripple effect of suffering."

"Millions of gallons of our water are wasted because a private energy company is allowed to divert it," she goes on. Aponivi is referring to the Peabody Energy Company, previously the Peabody Coal Company, which has a contract giving it the right to divert water from Hopi land in order to transport coal extracted from the southernmost part of the Black Mesa in Arizona. "Our springs are drying up. Without the water, we can't live our way of life as farmers and shepherds."

"If we still governed the traditional way, this couldn't have happened," says Len, "because all of the people would have been consulted, and they would have made it known that the loss of so much of our water would do too much damage to our way of life."

"Hopi have never been roamers," he continues. "We're mostly dry farmers and herders. Most other tribes, when they were forced to settle on reservations, were placed far from their traditional lands. We've always been in the same place. Our environment is semidesert. We used to all know how to live within the limits the earth here places on us. We accepted it, respected it, nurtured it, and in return, it did the same for us."

Then he says, "But our way of living and deciding took a turn for the worse in 1934, when I was 19. The Bureau of Indian Affairs produced a written constitution for the Hopi. The federal government didn't want to have to deal with each of our villages, which governed themselves separately. This constitution required all the villages to be combined. It also would force us to have a government with a chairman and vice chairman to govern Hopiland, and a council with representatives from each village.

"When it was time to vote on the constitution, most of us abstained. Our traditional ways of governing promoted harmony, and there was no reason to change them. We thought that by abstaining, we were rejecting the new constitution. But all the 'abstain' votes were counted as votes in favor, and it was approved. Like all the other villages, Old Oraibi was given a seat on the new Hopi council. But we've never put anyone on it. We don't want a 'representative.' Because democracy isn't about majority rules. You consult with everyone, hold a discussion until everyone agrees. If one person is left out, there's no harmony.

"How can one man, whether a president of a country or leader of a tribe, decide for everyone else?" Aponivi says. "Like, how can a president send men and women to war with a country far away, without consulting his people and the people there in the country being invaded?"

"In the Hopi traditional way of governing," Len then says, "one of the village elders, the *kikmongwi*, is the tribal and spiritual leader. Our *kikmongwi* are leaders because they listen to everyone, and help us find harmony among our differences. If they didn't, they wouldn't last long as leaders. Today, except for the traditional villages, the members of the tribal council are far more important than the *kikmongwi*. Harmony isn't taken into account."

Aponivi hesitates, but then says, "But the villages that have council members have all accepted government money. Those villages have nicer homes. They have a good supply of drinking water, they have sewers and electric power."

"The fight over money has divided us," Len says. "It's better not to be tempted. You forget how to use just the resources that are around you, and forget how to take care of yourself."

"Aponivi has good ideas," he tells me. "She's traditional and modern. She believes the old and new can come together to create a new and maybe better harmony. To her, the Hopi tribal council is good for dealing with outsiders and the village way is best for insiders."

Eventually he says, "Government must be faith-based. You can't separate spirit from politics. It's the only reason for politics. A Hopi's purpose for being alive is to fulfill the vision of Taiowa. A traditional Hopi doesn't try to achieve harmony for a day or a season, but for generation after generation."

Then he says, "Hopi means 'peaceful people.' Societies that practice violence and aggression, that forget harmony and ignore the practice of taking all things into account, come and go. We're still here. If we want to stay here, we have to remember who we are."

*Constitution Café Bill of Rights, Article 6:* All beings have the right to be taken into equal account.

## Harmony

Donald Lee Fixico, in *The American Indian Mind in a Linear World*, writes that traditional Native American forms of governance are imbued with the ethos "that all things are equal at creation. All things are related in the world and in the universe. Plants and animals are an important part of this Natural Democracy. Each . . . has a role and responsibility. As a result, there is a strong dependency on each and all things." Cultivating this outlook, he contends, lends itself to the creation of a "community of togetherness."

Jefferson's first term as president came on the heels of a fierce campaign during which the rhetoric that flew from both Democratic-Republicans and Federalists sparked great divisions among Americans. During his inaugural address, Jefferson made extreme rhetorical overtures aimed at bringing back some semblance of togetherness. He even went so far as to say, "We are all republicans, we are all federalists."

> Let us restore to social intercourse that harmony and affection without which liberty and even life itself are but dreary things. And let us reflect that having banished from our land that religious intolerance under which mankind so long bled and suffered, we have yet gained little if we countenance a political intolerance as despotic, as wicked, and capable of as bitter and bloody persecutions.

In a letter to Elbridge Gerry, Jefferson confided that restoring this "harmony and social love" was "almost the first object of my heart, and one to which I would sacrifice everything but principle."

Jefferson maintained that at least in theory "every difference of opinion is not a difference of principle." As long as all principled views are given the opportunity to "purify themselves by free discussion," he claimed that democracy would flourish, "leaving our horizon more bright and serene."

## Faith-Based Governance

Jefferson's controversial relationship with Christianity was grounded in the belief that only by engaging in unflinching questioning, which even included questioning the existence of God, could one arrive at truths that further revealed the will of God. Jefferson had a "life-long conviction that the God whom nature revealed and the religion which reason indicated were more believable than the God and doctrines of biblical revelation and dogma."[5] Consequently, Jefferson "hoped for the spread of a religion of reason and morality" into all social dimensions. John Dewey maintains that Jefferson's faith "had a genuinely religious quality," and that he believed he best carried out God's work by determining how the "forms of government and law, even of the constitution, might and should change" in order to better realize a society in which all men are "endowed by their Creator with certain unalienable Rights, that among these are Life, liberty, and the pursuit of happiness."

Despite his own faith, Jefferson believed this task was best accomplished by keeping religion out of the public domain.

The First Amendment of the U.S. Constitution mandates that "Congress shall make no law respecting an establishment of religion." It guarantees that government will not establish a religion itself, or sanction the establishment of an official church, and it prevents the government from interfering in religious affairs. However, there is nothing in the Constitution that requires the separation of church and state.

5. Charles B. Sanford, *The Religious Life of Thomas Jefferson* (University Press of Virginia, 1987).

Only the state constitution of Jefferson's Virginia established a "wall of separation" between church and state, as mandated in Jefferson's famous bill, the Virginia Statute for Religious Freedom. It was one of the very few pieces of Jefferson's comprehensive package to reform Virginia's legal codes that actually passed, and it was enacted in 1786.

The Virginia legislature had initially aimed to pass a bill permitting the establishment of many denominations. Jefferson didn't see a contradiction in accomplishing God's work by keeping religion out of government, and what his alternative bill indeed managed to present was "a forceful anticlerical condemnation of dogmatism and religious coercion."[6] To Rhys Isaac, Jefferson's bill had revolutionary implications; it was a celebration of "the autonomy of the individual against the moral claims" of the community and "proclaimed individual judgment as sacred, sacred against the pressure of collective coercions"—specifically coercions of the religious variety.

However, Isaac fails to mention that while this was indeed a signal victory, it was a partial one. In and of itself, this one bill did little to empower the people against the entrenched coerciveness of the established planter oligarchy. As a consequence, the far bigger wall of separation—between the powers that be and ordinary citizens—remained as impenetrable as ever.

## Alter and Abolish

I'm seated on a bench in one of the resplendent gardens of Monticello, the 1,060-acre mountaintop home of Thomas Jefferson situated outside of Charlottesville, Virginia. With me are the members

6. Rhys Isaac, *The Transformation of Virginia, 1740–1790* (University of North Carolina Press, 1999).

of the original Constitution Café group. It's July 2. We chose this day to reconvene because this is really our nation's independence day. It is the anniversary of the day in 1776 when the delegates of the Second Continental Congress, who hailed from all thirteen colonies, voted to approve the resolution for independence introduced by Richard Henry Lee. From that day onward, American colonies considered themselves legally and officially free from Britain. The Declaration of Independence was published two days later, on July 4.

After the resolution for independence was approved, John Adams, who attended the congress, predicted that the "second day of July, 1776 . . . will be celebrated by succeeding generations as the great anniversary festival. . . . [and] solemnized with pomp and parade, with shows, games, sports, guns, bells, bonfires, and illuminations, from one end of this continent to the other." Though Adams was two days off the mark, one might argue that July 4 still deserves to be our official independence day because the Declaration of Independence was published on the 4th—but in fact, most delegates didn't sign the document until August 2, 1776.

Over a year has passed since I set off on my trek to construct a new Constitution. Those with me are perusing copies of the constitutional articles I've devised with people across the United States.

"There's still something missing," says Helen with her usual bluntness. "It lacks a strong closing statement."

"There's another section of the Declaration of Independence," Sara eventually says, "besides the part that's now in the new preamble that the high-school students in West Virginia put together for the Constitution that Chris has been working on. It would make a good closing statement. It's the section that says that in order to secure the rights to life, liberty, and the pursuit of happiness, 'governments are instituted among men, deriving their just powers from the consent of the governed.' It goes on to say, 'whenever any form of government becomes destructive to these ends, it is the right of the people to alter or to abolish it, and to institute new government, laying its foundation on such principles and organizing its powers in such form, as to them shall seem most likely to effect their safety and happiness.'"

This brings Marjorie to say, "Jefferson believed that if government didn't give ordinary people the equal right to participate, then it made pointless 'the whole object of the present controversy,' meaning the American Revolution. As he said, 'should a bad government be instituted for us in future, it had been as well to have accepted at first the bad one offered to us from beyond the water without the risk and expense of contest.'"

Then Alejandra says, "That section of the Declaration that Sara referred to is basically giving people the right to rebel. Jefferson argued that all Americans—well, all white male Americans—of whatever social class, should have this right. He was the one founder who supported, at least in principle, Shays's Rebellion. In referring to it, he remarked that 'if the happiness of the mass of the people can be secured at the expense of a little tempest now and then, or even of a little blood, it will be a precious purchase.'"

"I take this to mean that if, at any point in our history, most people come to conclude that a bad government has been instituted, then they have the right to do away with it," says Stuart.

"But this section of the Declaration doesn't just give one the right to abolish government," I point out. "It also includes the responsibility to 'institute new government.'"

"Really, just having this right inserted like a closing statement at the end of the Constitution is abolishing the old government and putting in a new one," says Helen. "Because it's saying that we can and should declare our independence again and again, rebel over and over, until we get it right. Jefferson's right: it's a small price to pay, if our happiness is secured."

> *Constitution Café Bill of Rights Article 7:* Because Governments are instituted among people, deriving their just powers from the consent of the Governed, whenever a Government becomes destructive to these ends, it is the right of the people to alter or to abolish it, by creating a new Constitution that institutes a new government, one that lays its foundation on such principles, and that organizes its powers in such form, as to them shall seem most likely to effect their safety and happiness.

## Out with the Old, In with the New

"Let us," Jefferson exhorted, "avail ourselves of our reason and experience to correct the crude essays of our first and unexperienced although wise, virtuous, and well-meaning councils." This was quite a backhanded compliment: on the one hand, Jefferson characterized the Framers' efforts to create a Constitution as "wise, virtuous, and well-meaning"; on the other, he left no doubt that he considered their accomplishment little more than a "crude" and "unexperienced" first attempt that should be revisited and remedied. As Jefferson told Samuel Kercheval,

> I am certainly not an advocate for frequent and untried changes in laws and constitutions. . . . But I know also that laws and institutions must go hand in hand with the progress of the human mind. As that becomes more developed, more enlightened, as new discoveries are made, new truths disclosed and manners and opinions change with the change

of circumstances, institutions must advance also and keep pace with the times.

To Jefferson, what lent sanctity to a constitution was not its status as a virtually unchangeable document, but rather treating it as a work in progress and having faith in each generation to improve upon it.

The call for a modern-day constitutional convention of "the people" might seem an unlikely prospect. But if a critical mass comes to the conclusion that our government is failing to achieve the goals for which it was designed, the time might at last be ripe to consider Jefferson's proposal to rewrite the Constitution.

University of Virginia political scientist and popular media pundit Larry Sabato is one of our most outspoken advocates for a new constitutional convention. In *A More Perfect Constitution*, Sabato acknowledges the Framers' great accomplishment in creating a document that "would survive for centuries and produce one of the most accomplished nations in human history." However, he believes that the Framers

> might also have been surprised and disappointed that future generations of Americans would be unable to duplicate their daring and match their creativity when presented with new challenges. The evidence today that parts of the Constitution do not work well is just as overwhelming as the proof in the founder's day that the Articles of Confederation were inadequate to the needs of the growing United States.

Sabato maintains that we must "look past the current 'values' debates and hot-button issues, and consider this very real possibility: that the failure of the nation to update the Constitution and the structure of government it originally bequeathed to us is at the root of our current political dysfunction."

> The democratic theorist Robert Dahl poses this provocative question: Why should we feel bound today by a document produced more than two centuries ago by a group of fifty-five mortal men, actually signed by only thirty-nine, a fair number of whom were slaveholders, and adopted in only thirteen states by the votes of fewer than two thousand men, all of whom are long since dead and mainly forgotten?

Dahl further asks, "If our constitution is in some important ways defective by democratic standards, should we change it, and how?" While he does not echo Sabato's call for a new constitutional convention, he does ask us to decide for ourselves whether the Constitution is "the best that we can design for enabling politically equal citizens to govern themselves under laws and government policies that have been adapted and are maintained with their rational consent."

Dahl envisions "the possibility . . . of a gradually expanding discussion that begins in scholarly circles, moves outward to the media and intellectuals more generally, and after some years begins to engage a wider public."

Or it may well be the reverse—that the wider public takes the lead in pushing for revisions to our Constitution.

But Gordon Wood, leading historian of the American Revolution, is not optimistic that any of us today—not the media, not our intellectuals, and certainly not the public at large—can improve on the work of our original Framers, no matter how well intentioned and dedicated the attempt might be.

In *Revolutionary Characters: What Made the Founders Different*, Wood asserts:

If we want to know why we can never again replicate the extraordinary generation of the founders, there is a simple answer: the growth of what we today presumably value most about American society and culture, egalitarian democracy. In the early 19th century the voices of ordinary people, at least ordinary white people, began to be heard as never before in history, and they soon overwhelmed the high-minded desires and aims of the revolutionary leaders who had brought them into being.

In Wood's opinion, ordinary Americans have further diluted this high-minded thinking ever since. But one of our founders, Thomas Jefferson, would disagree. Wood's pejorative take on egalitarianism—namely, that it panders to the lowest common denominator—is the antithesis of Jefferson's, who held that all Americans must be given equal or at least ample opportunity to become standouts. This does not in any way mean that to Jefferson all citizens have to have an equal share of material wealth; however, by his conception, it does mean that all Americans do need certain essentials, like the right to take active part in public problem-solving, the right to a good education, and even the right to a modicum of property, in order to participate fully and positively in the public sphere. The fulfillment of these needs would, Jefferson believed, spur the creation of a more "egalitarian elitism."

Hannah Arendt applauds the form of egalitarianism advanced by Jefferson. Of all the founders, she considers him unique in his promotion of "a new form of government that would permit every member of the modern egalitarian society to become a 'participator' in public affairs." In particular, if Jefferson's vision for universal education had been implemented at our nation's founding, he was certain that a group of "public foundationers" would have emerged from every station in life, rather than only from the most advantaged segments of society. They would have been singled out for their exceptional "taste for public freedom," their deeds setting an example for the entire citizenry that one "cannot be 'happy'" if one does not give one's all to "the task of good government." But Jefferson's project was thwarted by entrenched gentry with a firm grip on power who either voted down his proposed reforms or refused to consider them seriously in the first place; they had no more interest in democratizing education than they did in facilitating citizen participation in governance.

Ultimately, the system of governance created by the Framers ensured that some potentially exceptional American voices would have little opportunity to be fully developed, let alone heard in the public sphere.

# XI

## Brew for a True Revolution

The Boston Tea Party is typically considered to mark the official beginning of the American Revolution. We tend to think of it as the ultimate democratic moment, in which "the people" rose up against unjust and overreaching government. In fact, it was the act of a handful of radicals who had little time for the opinions and will of the majority.

The idea for the Tea Party was hatched by 52-year-old political firebrand Samuel Adams, who had no faith that his fellow colonists would voluntarily quit drinking tea, even for the highest principles, if it was allowed to come ashore. Reverend William Gordon, one of the Revolution's first historians, remarked that to Adams and his fellow Sons of Liberty, "the virtue of the people . . . was too precarious a ground on which to risk the salvation of their country." British Parliament had passed the Tea Act, which among other things placed a tax on tea without colonists' consent. Besides leading to a significant price increase on a beloved staple, it was a breach of the colonists' rights to be taxed only by their elected representatives. Determined to teach the British a lesson, Adams made sure that the barrels of tea on British merchant ships anchored in Boston Harbor never landed on dry soil. On December 16, 1773, he and about fifty others boarded the merchant ships, broke open all 343 casks of tea, and dumped their contents into the harbor.

The Boston radicals had disregarded alternative approaches to confronting the monarchy. Their "town meetings," though held ostensibly to entertain various suggestions for responding to the Crown's abuses, in fact were intended only to advance their own position. At their final public gathering, Adams cut off discourse when some attendees opposed his recommendation to dump the casks of tea and proposed other options. "This meeting," Adams remarked, "can do nothing more to save the country." He then marched off with a group of men already dressed as Mohawks. Unbeknown to everyone else at the meeting, Adams and his cohorts had decided well beforehand to destroy the tea.

The Tea Party episode was on the verge of fracturing colonists. Many Boston merchants, dismayed by what they considered an unwarranted provocation, offered to reimburse their British counterparts. And most colonists outside of Boston felt that "Boston had gone a great deal too far in destroying the East India Company's tea." As a consequence, "Boston stood in danger of being isolated, even in New England," where colonists were typically more receptive to radical ideas for reform.[1]

Rather than promising to be, in Adams's words, a "great epocha," the Tea Party threatened to poison the nascent struggle for independence before it could properly begin. Enter Thomas Jefferson, whose intervention helped "translate the local grievance of Boston into a common cause."[2]

After the Tea Party took place, Jefferson hastily initiated a series

---

1. Neil Stout, *The Perfect Crisis: The Beginning of the Revolutionary War* (New York University Press, 1976).

2. From Dumas Malone's classic biography, *Jefferson the Virginian* (Warren Press, 2007).

of evening meetings at the Raleigh Tavern with other Virginia legislators. They debated how their colony might respond in the wake
of the event. Should Virginia side with the Boston provocateurs,
vocally oppose their action, or remain neutral?

Jefferson gave great thought to Massachusetts Bay's dilemma. He
was alarmed that the "ill-fated colony, which had consistently been
bold in their enmities" against the Crown, now seemed "devoted
to ruin." Jefferson reasoned, though, that if the Tea Party mob "did
wrong" in throwing the tea overboard, the Crown went even further by closing off the Boston port and curtailing all trade, "without attempting a distinction between the guilty and the innocent."
What's more, he feared that if no one resisted Great Britain's implementation of the draconian Boston Port Act on this occasion, then
"another and another will be tried till the measure of despotism
be filled up." The challenge, then, was for Jefferson to convince his
fellow Virginians and colonists elsewhere that they should view the
Crown's actions against Massachusetts Bay as a pancolonial threat.

Jefferson recounts how those with him at the Raleigh decided
that the Virginia legislature "must boldly take an unequivocal stand
in support of Massachusetts." But he admitted that the odds of
accomplishing this were against them, since many legislators "had
grown too conservative" and lacked "the determination that the
times demanded." Besides, the colonists themselves had let down
their guard, not having directly confronted the British since the *Gaspee* Affair of 1772.[3]

3. On June 9, 1772, a group of Rhode Islanders protesting the British schooner
*Gaspee*'s practice of pursuing cheap merchandise at the expense of colonial companies officially approved by the government of England set the ship ablaze and were
sent to trial in England. Jefferson, appalled that the colonists were being denied
a jury of their peers, took the opportunity to establish "committees of correspondence" aimed at uniting colonists in pursuit of a common cause, and succeeded in
having Parliament's decision to try the colonists in England repealed.

Jefferson and those who joined him at the Raleigh ultimately decided to craft a resolution calling for "the appointment of a day of general fasting and prayer," which Jefferson felt could turn the divisive Boston Tea Party event into a galvanizing one by serving "to avert from us the evils of civil war, to inspire us with firmness in support of our rights, and to turn the hearts . . . to moderation and justice."

The resolution calling for a pancolonial day of "fasting, prayer and humiliation" presented to Virginia's assemblymen made clear that the rights it promoted were not just for a select few, but rather were "American rights." It declared that the Virginia colony was "prepared to suffer the same punishments and indignities as their fellow men from Massachusetts," and so was ready to employ "all just and proper means" to oppose any punitive measure imposed by British Parliament. Despite Virginia's reputation as one of the most "loyal" colonies and the generally conservative mind-sets of the majority of Burgesses, the resolution appealed to the legislators' sense of piety and justice, and passed without opposition.

Jefferson's efforts to convert the divisive, rebellious actions of a few into a common cause had worked—the legislatures of other colonies promptly passed similar resolutions in support of Massachusetts, and a revolution was catalyzed.

In the wake of this success, "Aristocratic Virginia had its first taste of participatory democracy." Jefferson and his fellow Virginia legislators had called for county meetings to discuss the fate of the colony and to determine the delegates that would represent them in a future Williamsburg assembly, "welcom[ing] not only 'gentleman freeholders,' but all male inhabitants over twenty-one."[4] The wealthiest landowners and the most impoverished nonfreeholders rubbed shoulders in these meetings, inspiring Jefferson to liken the

4. Stout, *The Perfect Crisis.*

atmosphere to "a shock of electricity, arousing every man, and placing him erect and solidly on his center."

Jefferson was chosen to represent Albemarle County at the Williamsburg gathering, where the delegates would then decide on representatives for the forthcoming congress in Philadelphia. Though Jefferson would have seemed a natural candidate for participation in the congress, his publication of a pamphlet titled *A Summary View of the Rights of British America*—which among other things asserted "that our immigration from England to this country gave her no more rights over us"—branded him as a radical, and so he was notably absent among the fifty-six attending delegates of the First Continental Congress on September 5, 1774.

The fact that Jefferson—once declared "too extreme"—was ultimately invited to participate in the Second Continental Congress on May 10, 1775, that he penned our Declaration of Independence, and that he served as our nation's third president indicate that he was not actually too bold—too "radical"—but rather ahead of his time, and able to adapt his innovative ideas to the demands of his historical moment. So wouldn't it follow that another visionary proposal by Jefferson that what may currently seem a "flight of fancy"—a new constitution drafted by diverse groups of ordinary Americans—might provide a very real impetus for change?

Is it likely that a critical mass of Americans with motley political convictions will ever decide that today's Constitution is just as unworkable as our original governing document, the Articles of Confederation? Or is such a prospect too far-fetched?

Speaking of far-fetched, the progressive group MoveOn.org was considered so extreme when it was founded in 1998 that few believed it would ever have much of an impact on mainstream politics. Yet the millions it subsequently mobilized came out in droves in 2008 and were instrumental in electing our nation's first black president. Now the Tea Party has transformed from a fringe group into a king-maker in electoral politics, giving Republicans a decisive majority in Congress in the 2010 elections. Both groups show the power of grassroots activism—and the limits.

My hunch is that just as progressives came to feel betrayed when Obama abandoned the liberal agenda of his presidential campaign to engage in political compromise and accommodation, Tea Party activists will come to find that their own expectations for "change they can believe in" will be equally stymied—not just because those they supported will either have to practice politics as usual to get anything done in Washington or become irrelevant, but because the system itself that was handed to us by our Framers prevents meaningful reforms that facilitate more responsive and responsible government.

Perhaps both of these movements will eventually be front and center in calling upon the states to employ a never-before-used mechanism in Article V of the existing Constitution that's at their disposal: if two-thirds of the state legislatures give the go-ahead, they have the right to circumvent Congress and hold a new convention to introduce, without limit, amendments to the Constitution.

As it is, groups like MoveOn.org and the Tea Party have a good bit in common. Both are comprised of millions who had been political outsiders, they share a decided antiestablishment strain, and their members believe passionately in the right to self-government (though of course they differ on what that right amounts to in practice). But it's one thing to point out where common ground might exist between the two, and another altogether for the overwhelming majority in such movements to come together.

Yet against all odds, Jefferson forged common ground among colonists on both ends of the political spectrum, and everywhere in between, in the aftermath of the Boston Tea Party. He was convinced that they all were "constitutionally and conscientiously democrats," and managed to convert an event that had threatened to dash any hopes for achieving unity to one of common cause.

The Declaration of Independence that he was then charged to write was the work of a flawed man who in his words, and at times in his deeds, revealed an extraordinary empathy for the hopes and aspirations of people quite unlike him.

Jefferson's proposal to revise periodically our Constitution is also a declaration of independence of sorts. He believed we did our Founders and Framers a disservice if we looked at their works as iconic. As Joyce Oldham Appleby puts it, "The true Jeffersonian legacy is to be hostile to legacies." Jefferson had no doubt that coming generations could vastly improve on their accomplishments in ways that would better enable all Americans to realize their higher hopes for self-government.

In a letter to John Adams in 1823,[5] Jefferson composed these stirring, rabble-rousing words:[6]

> A first attempt to recover the right of self-government may fail, so may a second, a third, etc. But as a younger and more instructed race comes on, the sentiment becomes more and more intuitive, and . . . some subsequent one of the ever renewed attempts will ultimately succeed. For what inheritance so valuable, can man leave to posterity?

5. Jefferson and Adams died on the same day three years later, on Independence Day in 1826.

6. "He was a rebel to the very end," Joseph Ellis notes.

# ACKNOWLEDGMENTS

Special thanks go to Mike Li; Dennis Dienst; John Esterle; Stefanie Pfleger Byars; Mizgon Zahir; Hin Leung; Alex Moll; Laurel Sheridan; John Wren; Nathan Pollack; Evan Sinclair; Hallie Atkinson; Anas Shallal (owner of the incomparable Busboys & Poets); Jeff Anthony; Sierra Crocker; Sheldon Kelly (at a challenging crossroads, Uncle Sheldon reminded me what I can accomplish when I set my mind to it); Mark Padilla; Lelia Green; Giancarlo Ibarguen, rector of Universidad Francisco Marroquín; Bert Loan; Don and Donna Goertz; Wolfgang Somary; the Whitman Institute; Sam Sadler; Todd Carstenn; Ron Cooper; Beth Fogarty; Barry Kibrick; Gil Feinberg; Jack Ratcliffe; Bobbie DeLeon; Laura Norin; Clea Kore; Kathy Kremins; Sam Fairchild (who graciously opened his home to me and made available his comprehensive collection of books on Thomas Jefferson); Maddie Taterka; David Blacker; Steve Duncombe; Carole Brzozowski; Kate Gannon; Miriam Feuerle; Steve Hornsby; Mark Butler; Todd Carstenn; Ron Cooper; Zack Macdonald; Shirley Strum Kenny; and my agent Andrew Stuart. My longtime friend Larry Parker passed away just as I was putting the finishing touches on this book. When I first told Larry, a veteran of the sixties protests, of my project, he wrote back, "About time the younger generation did something radical and revolutionary!" Thanks also to my government professors of long ago at the College of William & Mary, in particular George Grayson, Alan Ward, John McGlennon, and Donald Baxter. I am indebted to my long-time editor, Alane Salierno Mason, as tough, caring, and conscientious as they come, and most grateful to kind-hearted and insightful assistant editor Denise Scarfi, as well as to copy editor Fred Wiemer. I am thankful for the love and support of my mom, Margaret Ann Phillips, and my dad, Alex Phillips. I also want to acknowledge my beloved father-in-law, Armando Chapa de Zambrano, who passed away just before this book went to press. My wife, Cecilia, and daughter, Caliope Alexis, make my dialogue projects sacred. Deepest thanks to all those who have taken part with me in Constitution Café exchanges.

# FURTHER READING

Richard Matthews's *The Radical Politics of Thomas Jefferson* (University Press of Kansas, 1984) presents a thoughtful and provocative exploration of Jefferson's ideas for evolving democracy over the long haul. Matthews makes clear his debt to Hannah Arendt, whose Jefferson scholarship, included in *On Revolution* (Penguin Classics, 2006) and *Crises of the Republic* (Mariner Books, 1972), remains underappreciated. Joseph Ellis's *American Sphinx: The Character of Jefferson* (Vintage, 1998) is acclaimed for its provocative analyses of Jefferson's character. Yet the author's penchant for dismissing out of hand Jefferson's more visionary political propositions diminishes some of his insights into Jefferson the human being. Some of the most erudite and insightful books that present a more admiring view of Jefferson include: Dumas Malone's classic series of works, *Jefferson and the Ordeal of Liberty, Jefferson and the Rights of Man, The Sage of Monticello Jefferson and His Time,* and *Jefferson the President, Volumes I and II* (all were reissued by the University of Virginia Press in 2006); Merrill Peterson's *Thomas Jefferson and the New Nation* (Galaxy Books, 1975), *The Jefferson Image in the American Mind* (University Press of Virginia, 1999), and *Thomas Jefferson: Writings,* a comprehensive 1,600-page compilation of Jefferson's public and private papers, addresses, letters, as well as his "Autobiography" and his only book, *Notes on the*

*State of Virginia*; Joyce Oldham Appleby's *Thomas Jefferson* (Times Books, 2003) and *Jefferson: Political Writings* (Cambridge University Press, 1999); Peter Onuf's *The Mind of Thomas Jefferson* (University Press of Virginia, 2006), *Jefferson's Empire* (University Press of Virginia, 2001), and *Jeffersonian America* (Wiley-Blackwell, 2001, coauthored with Leonard Sadosky); Fawn Brodie's *Thomas Jefferson: An Intimate History* (W. W. Norton, reprinted in 2010, with a new introduction by Annette Gordon-Reed); John Dewey's panegyric *The Living Thoughts of Thomas Jefferson* (Longmans, Green & Co., 1940) and *The Essential Jefferson* (Dover, reissued in 2008); Jean Yarbrough's *American Virtues: Thomas Jefferson on the Character of a Free People* (University Press of Kansas, reprinted 2009) and *The Essential Jefferson* (Hackett Publishing Co., 2006); R. B. Bernstein's *Thomas Jefferson* (Oxford University Press, 2005); David Mayer's *The Constitutional Thought of Thomas Jefferson* (University Press of Virginia, 1995); and Andrew Burstein's *The Inner Jefferson* (University Press of Virginia, 2006).

Insightful works that focus on particular aspects of Jefferson's life, works, or deeds, or that discuss Jefferson in the context of early American history, include: John Ferling's *Adams vs. Jefferson* (Oxford University Press, 2005); Pulitzer Prize–winning historian Edward J. Larson's *A Magnificent Catastrophe: The Tumultuous Election of 1800, America's First Presidential Campaign* (Free Press, 2007); Jeremy Bailey's *Thomas Jefferson and the Executive Power*; the Jefferson critic Leonard Levy's *Jefferson and Civil Liberties* (Ivan R. Dee, 1989); Annette Gordon-Reed's *Thomas Jefferson and Sally Hemings: An American Controversy* (University Press of Virginia, 1998) and her Pulitzer Prize–winning *The Hemingses of Monticello: An American Family* (W. W. Norton, 2008); Andrew Burstein's *Jefferson's Secrets* (Basic Books, 1996) and *Madison and Jefferson* (Random House, 2010); Charles B. Sanford's *The Religious Life of Thomas Jefferson* (University Press of Virginia, 1987).

Essential reading on the Framers and the Constitution they crafted includes Clinton Rossiter's *1787: The Grand Convention* (W. W. Norton, 1966), even if at times it resembles a pro-Federalist apologia; Philip Hamburger's *Law and Judicial Duty* (Harvard University Press, 2008); Charles Black's *A New Birth of Freedom* (Putnam, 1997); Bruce Ackerman's two-volume *We the People* (Belknap Press of Harvard University Press, 1993); John R. Vile's *A Companion to the United States Constitution and Its Amendments* (Praeger, 2010); Robert Dahl's *How Democratic Is the American Constitution?* (Yale University Press, 2003) and *On Democracy* (Yale University Press, 2000); and Larry Sabato's *A More Perfect Constitution* (Walker & Co., 2008).

Must-reads on the Revolutionary era and its movers and shakers include: Joseph Ellis's Pulitzer Prize–winning *Founding Brothers: The Revolutionary Generation* (Knopf, 2000); Gary B. Nash's *The Unknown American Revolution: The Unruly Birth of Democracy and the Struggle to Create America* (Penguin, 2006); Sean Wilentz's *The Rise of American Democracy: Jefferson to Lincoln* (W. W. Norton, 2006); Pauline Meier's *Resistance to Revolution: Colonial Radicals and the Development of American Opposition to Britain* (W. W. Norton, 1992); Rhys Isaac's Pulitzer Prize–winning *The Transformation of Virginia, 1740–1790* (University of North Carolina Press, 1999); Neil Stout's *The Perfect Crisis: The Beginning of the Revolutionary War* (New York University Press, 1976); the Pulitzer Prize–winning historian Gordon S. Wood's *The Making of the Constitution* (Baylor University Press, 1987), *Revolutionary Characters: What Made the Founders Different* (Penguin, 2007), *The Creation of the American Republic* (University of North Carolina Press, 1998), and *The Radicalism of the American Revolution* (Vintage, 1993).